Scope and Methods of Political Science

an introduction to the methodology of political inquiry

The Dorsey Series in Political Science

FOURTH EDITION 1985

Scope and Methods of Political Science

an introduction to the methodology of political inquiry

ALAN C. ISAAK
Professor of Political Science, Western Michigan University

 THE DORSEY PRESS Homewood, Illinois 60430

ISBN 0-256-03238-6
Library of Congress Catalog Card No. 84–73508

Printed in the United States of America

1 2 3 4 5 6 7 8 9 0 MP 2 1 0 9 8 7 6 5

To my Mother and Father and to Betty

preface

WHEN revising a book, one is faced with a number of difficult choices—what to change and what to leave untouched. This is the third revision of the book, and a new set of choices had to be made. As in the first two revisions, changes and additions have been made to most chapters. In addition, some rearranging of chapters has occurred, and several new sections have been included, mainly in the last part of the book.

The book has several objectives. Its first objective is to provide a description of what political scientists are doing today—what their main concerns are and what they are attempting to accomplish. Thus we will to some extent be characterizing the discipline called *political science*. A second objective is to provide a methodological foundation for reading, understanding, and criticizing the literature of political science. The book should also serve as a preparation for advanced work in the study of politics, including both graduate study and empirical research. It is my intention to serve several groups: first and primarily, middle- and upper-level undergraduates in political science who wish to gain a systematic understanding of the foundations of their discipline; and, in addition, the more advanced students of politics who are studying political phenomena in greater depth and therefore require an understanding of the principles around which such study should be organized.

This book is not an introduction to political science in the sense of providing a description of the fields of political science (comparative politics, international relations, and so on). Instead, it attempts to get at those elements which all political scientists should be interested in.

Let us, at this early stage, make clear the distinction between *methodology* and *research techniques*. We are primarily interested in the former, which refers to the basic principles and assumptions of political inquiry. Research techniques, on the other hand, are specific devices for gathering and analyzing data about political phenomena; examples are survey research, content analysis, and statistics. It must be pointed out, though, that a discussion of methodology must often mention such techniques, since what we have here are two levels of scientific activity.

In this regard, a basic assumption ought to be stated. In an age of rapid change, a discipline such as political science needs creative and innovative thinking as much as it needs technical expertise. While the two are not mutually exclusive, the latter is too often emphasized at the expense of the former. It is my contention that more emphasis should be placed on the development of new approaches to and models of politics—devices which stimulate our minds and suggest fresh orientations to the study of that timeless phenomenon, politics.

While this book deals with a complex subject matter, it nevertheless is, to a large extent, based on several fundamental principles that are often stated as distinctions. That is, much of the detailed analysis revolves around a small number of distinctions—facts versus values, discovery versus justification, and if one has these clearly in mind, then the analysis should be much easier to assimilate. Therefore, much time is spent on basics.

Each of the book's three sections attempts to answer several questions.

Part 1: What is the nature and scope of political science? What do political scientists study?
Part 2: What are the characteristics of political science as a science? What are the main elements of the logic of political inquiry?
Part 3: How do political scientists attempt to discover and organize political knowledge? What are the main approaches to the study of politics?

Much of the analysis of this book is based upon the work of philosophers of science. This is especially true of Part 2. Our main objective has been to make this significant body of work relevant for students of politics. The book also owes much to the writings of a number of political scientists. They are mentioned in the footnotes. In addition, I would like to thank Milton Hobbs for stimulating my interest in the philosophy of political science and for providing a framework for methodological analysis. I would also like to acknowledge the encouragement of my colleagues at Western Michigan University. Any errors in fact and interpretation are entirely my responsibility.

Finally, a special thanks to my wife Betty, who despite her own flourishing career has found time to give me constant encouragement; and to Eric, Greta, and Josh, whose continuing growth and maturity have been a source of inspiration for their father.

Alan C. Isaak

contents

Scope and Methods of Political Science

an introduction to the methodology of political inquiry

THE SCOPE OF POLITICAL SCIENCE

The scope of political science: Political philosophy and political science

PROBABLY the first question that a present-day student of politics ought to ask is, "What is political science?" Or putting it in more answerable form (that is, the way this book puts it), "What is the *scope* of political science?" This can be reduced to, "What kinds of activities interest those who call themselves 'political scientists'?" There are a number of ways to answer this question. Part 1 of this book examines several of these methods. This chapter takes a historical and comparative approach. That is, an answer, which at this point can only be stated in fairly general terms, is arrived at by describing the main concerns of traditional political thought and comparing them with modern political science. This also provides a foundation for the more analytic approach taken in Chapter 2, in which political science is characterized by analyzing its component parts, "politics" and "science."

TRADITIONAL POLITICAL PHILOSOPHY

Since the beginning of recorded history, people have observed, thought about, evaluated, and analyzed politics. Those who have analyzed politics on a fairly regular and systematic basis are called political philosophers; they include such well-known figures as Plato, Aristotle, Locke, and Rousseau. We can call the product of their analyses traditional political philosophy or theory. But there is a more precise and fruitful way of characterizing traditional political philosophy, which involves sorting out its main activities and indicating which of these activities political philosophers have spent most of their time on. Each activity is really a type of *analysis*.

Analysis is a word that has a variety of meanings; since it is so central to an understanding of political philosophy and political science, we must pause and consider some of them. To chemists, analysis means breaking things down into their constituent parts; to biologists, sorting things into categories; to mathematicians, deriving conclusions from premises; to social scientists, identifying the causes of various kinds of human behavior; to moral philosophers, showing which actions are good ones. What all of these activities have in common is the attempt to answer one kind of question or another: What is the nature of this substance? What species of animal do we have here? What is the solution to this problem? Why did she do what she did? Is what she did wrong? Thus, to analyze something means to ask a question, give an answer, and then give reasons for the answer. In looking at political philosophy, we discover that there are four activities, each a type of analysis, that political philosophers have engaged in: we have labeled them *scientific, normative, instrumental,* and *analytic* (also called *logical*).

Describing a political system, an aspect of it, or a general political phenomenon, and *explaining* or accounting for such facts are *scientific* activities. We will say much more about science and what it means to be scientific in later chapters. It is enough at this early stage if scientific is roughly equated with talking about and explaining the world of observation and experience, that is, to use a word that we will return to time and again, the *empirical* world. Traditional political philosophers have always been engaged in such scientific activities. For instance, Aristotle spent much time describing and comparing various kinds of constitutions, and in another section of the *Politics,* he attempts an explanation of political change and revolution.[1] Machiavelli is famous for his down-to-earth description of politics as it really is—namely, a struggle for power.[2]

---

[1] Ernest Barker, ed., trans., *The Politics of Aristotle* (New York: Oxford University Press, 1958), books 4 and 5.

[2] Machiavelli's most famous discussion of politics is found in *The Prince.*

However, it must be added that the political philosopher has rarely been a very good scientist, especially when it comes to explaining political phenomena. This is probably attributable to several factors. First, and largely beyond his control, was the lack of sophisticated scientific and methodological technology and hardware. The statistical and mathematical tools so essential to modern social scientists were not available to Plato and Aristotle, Locke and Marx. But second, and perhaps more crucial in the long run, is the fact that scientific activities have never been the main concern of the political philosopher.

The primary activities of political philosophers have probably been *normative*. These are activities which involve moral, ethical, or value judgments. While scientific activities deal with what *is,* value judgments express what a political philosopher believes *ought* to be. As we will see, the distinction between *is* and *ought* is fundamental to an understanding of current political science.

There are several varieties of normative activity. First, many political philosophers spend much time *prescribing* the best state or political system. Perhaps the first and most famous attempt is Plato's discussion of the ideally just state in which the absolute knowledge of the philosopher-kings is proposed as the standard for political and social decision making.[3] Political philosophers also engage in the normative activity of *recommending* the proper or true goals of politics. Thus Rousseau emphasizes the restoration of a sense of community and the fulfilling of man's moral and emotional needs as the legitimate ends of the political system,[4] and Jeremy Bentham argues that happiness should be the basis of all political actions.[5]

Instrumental or *applied* value judgments are often confused with normative statements. There is, however, a fundamental difference in that instrumental judgments recommend the best way of achieving a given end, but they do not attempt to justify the end itself. This is the significance of an alternate label, *means-ends analysis.* An instrumental judgment is therefore a scientific-empirical activity, for it is really an explanation of why certain conditions or actions lead to the desired end. But the confusion just referred

---

[3] Francis M. Cornford, ed., trans., *The Republic of Plato* (New York: Oxford University Press, 1945), part 3.

[4] Jean-Jacques Rousseau, *The Social Contract.*

[5] Jeremy Bentham, *Introduction to the Principles of Morals and Legislation.*

to is understandable when it is realized that political philosophers often combine normative and instrumental judgments. That is, an ultimate end or value is recommended and then the best means for achieving that end is described. Hobbes not only suggests that peace (the absence of civil discord) ought to be the end of the political system, but he then discusses the means to this end, namely, the absolute political sovereign, the Leviathan.[6] The first kind of analysis is, strictly speaking, normative; the second, scientific.

The last kind of activity we have labeled *analytic* or *logical*. This category includes both the analysis of political words and concepts and the examination of certain aspects of political arguments, for instance their logical consistency. Plato, using the dialetical method, analyzes and criticizes a number of definitions of *justice* in his attempt to arrive at its 'real' meaning.[7] Other political thinkers since Plato have engaged in such analytic activities—because the doing of any kind of philosophy is impossible without analysis of this sort. However, not until recent years has it become a distinctive kind of political philosophy.[8] But more about that later.

Some significant conclusions about traditional political philosophy can be stated at this point. First, in engaging in all four types of activity the traditional political thinker was in effect a complete political scientist, even though he was a poor scientist. The second conclusion, a qualification of the first, is that the emphasis in most political philosophies is on the "ought" questions, the normative ones. This leads to a current distinction between political *philosophy* and political *science,* a distinction which will be clarified in the next section. The emphasis of traditional political philosophy on normative questions has been explained in several ways. Alfred Cobban has presented one of the most reasonable arguments by pointing out that all of the great political philosophers considered their writings as part of the political process. In Cobban's words, "They all wrote with a practical purpose in mind. Their object was to influence actual political behavior. They wrote to condemn or support existing institutions, to justify a political system or

---

[6] Thomas Hobbes, *The Leviathan.*

[7] Cornford, *The Republic,* parts 1 and 2.

[8] See, for instance, T. D. Weldon, *The Vocabulary of Politics* (London: Penguin Books, Ltd., 1953). For a more recent example, this time an analysis of basic political concepts, see William E. Connolly, *The Terms of Political Discourse* (Lexington, Mass.: D. C. Heath, 1974).

persuade their fellow citizens to change it. . . ."[9] These activities are basically normative.

CONTEMPORARY POLITICAL SCIENCE

Political scientists, using the term at this point to include all those persons found in academic departments of political science, engage in the same kinds of activities as traditional political philosophers. Thus they describe and explain political phenomena and attempt to construct empirical theories so as to explain them more completely. They also recommend both the ends and the means to achieve those ends. Finally, they analyze the definitions of political concepts and the logical relationships between propositions and politics. However—and this is the significant fact toward which our analysis has been moving—it is becoming increasingly evident that there exists a distinction between normative and analytic activities on the one hand, and scientific activities on the other, with the former constituting political philosophy and the latter political science. Thus, those who do the former can be called political philosophers, those who do the latter, political scientists. It seems fair to conclude, then, that there has been a division of labor of sorts within the discipline of political science and that, therefore, "political science" has both a narrow and a broad connotation. It should be made clear, however, that while we can make the distinction between political science and political philosophy and use it meaningfully in our analysis, many of those within the discipline of political science (broad connotation) will be both political scientists and political philosophers, either simultaneously or alternately.

The nature of political philosophy can and should be made more explicit. What we have really said is that there are two kinds of political philosophy, the distinction between them following the basic difference between two conceptions of philosophy. The first conception claims that the philosopher seeks true knowledge of reality, goodness, or beauty, and therefore that successful philosophical reasoning produces knowledge different in kind but on a par with the results of scientific research. It is from this orientation that

---

[9] Alfred Cobban, "The Decline of Political Theory," *Political Science Quarterly,* vol. 68, no. 3 (1953), p. 330.

Plato proceeds in quest of the nature of absolute truth and the goodness of society. The other conception of philosophy rejects the notion that philosophical analysis produces any ultimate knowledge of reality or goodness. Instead, it argues that philosophy can only analyze language in order to straighten out linguistic muddles or clear away philosophical rubbish. Thus, the results of the analytic or linguistic philosopher's work are not ultimate truths but simply logical clarifications of philosophical discourse. It can be seen why one opponent of this interpretation has labeled it the *underlabour theory*.[10]

This chapter's discussion can be placed in a broader context by pointing out that throughout this book our attention will be focused upon those activities that can be placed within the boundaries of political science in the narrower sense. In short, normative questions become important mainly as they relate to the scientific study of politics; for instance: "Do values influence empirical research?" Value questions also emerge when certain ethical issues are raised during research: "Can a social scientist deceive a human subject in the name of science?" It will also become evident that we will be functioning as analytic philosophers when we examine the nature and logical foundations of political science.

Facts and values

The distinction between political science and political philosophy rests upon a more basic distinction between *facts* and *values,* or in terms we have already used, between the *is* and the *ought.* Let us now develop this distinction in a little more detail. Our analysis follows that of the 18th-century philosopher David Hume, who, to a large extent, provided the foundations for modern philosophy and science and who incidentally made many perceptive statements about politics.

Empirical or *is* statements are about and based upon evidence referring to the world of experience. They are therefore verifiable; that is, it can be determined if an empirical statement is true or false. A true empirical proposition states a *fact*. Truth, then, has some relation to jibing with the world of

---

[10] Peter Winch, *The Idea of a Social Science* (New York: Humanities Press, 1958). The term is originally John Locke's.

observation. However, empirical statements are not *necessarily* true. They simply state facts or relationships that we have observed or discovered through various methods such as experimentation or statistical control procedures. This is why we call empirical statements *contingent*.

Normative propositions state value judgments. They are neither true nor false, because no amount of empirical evidence can prove or disprove a value judgment. As Hume pointed out, an *is* never implies an *ought*. This is a statement of the fact-value distinction. Rather than being factual, a normative proposition is a statement of individual preference and perhaps, in addition, an attempt to change the values of others. The impact of this position on scientific thinking has been labeled *scientific value relativism,* that is, the realization that science is neutral in regard to normative values—it views them as relative to individuals and cultures, not as absolutes.

COGNITIVISTS AND NONCOGNITIVISTS

Many philosophers and political thinkers have held the view that the truth or falsity of normative statements can be demonstrated. The label *cognitivist* has been given to those who hold this position. That is, they claim that a normative statement can give us knowledge of the "good."[11] Since this is contrary to the noncognitive position we have just described, it is incumbent upon us to discuss some of these arguments and indicate how they differ from the views of noncognitivists.

Some thinkers have argued that the "good" (or the "good state") is discoverable through a *rational* process. The "good" is therefore objective in the sense that it is independent of human desires or needs. It might exist, as it did for Plato, in a "World of Forms" or it may be defined within a system of natural law. In any case, the assumption is that given the proper mental equipment, the nature of the good state can be discovered.

Another variant of this basic philosophical position is *institutionism*. It postulates a moral faculty or sense that tells man what is ethically or politically good. Intuition seems to differ from reason in that the former is not

---

[11] See Felix Oppenheim, *Moral Principles in Political Philosophy* (New York: Random House, 1968), for a discussion of this and many related points. For a complete survey of ethical positions, see William K. Frankena, "Ethical Theory," in Roderick M. Chisholm, ed., *Philosophy* (Englewood Cliffs, N.J.: Prentice-Hall, 1964).

describable or explainable, while the process of rational analysis is subject to analysis. When we reason, we follow a series of methodological steps (which vary from rationalist to rationalist), but when we know the good state through intuition, we simply know or intuit it. Thus, intuition is a much simpler and more direct source of moral knowledge.

This distinction should not be exaggerated, for in the end the claim of each variant can be reduced to the following: There is an objective good which is knowable by reasonable men; or, when a man is rational, the good will become obvious to him. To all of this the noncognitivist enthusiastically objects. The trouble is that two rational people may disagree over what the "good" is, and there is no way to resolve the disagreement. No outside criteria exists against which normative-rational claims can be measured. It does no good for one person to settle the argument with an appeal to reason—"I am rational, you are not"—because the second person can use the same strategy. The result is a return to the original unresolvable position. Noncognitivists are not questioning the importance of reason. Rather, they are rejecting the claim that rational analysis can lead to true or ultimate value judgments, for what is reasonable to one may not be reasonable to another.

Another method that some philosophers have used in their attempt to give normative propositions objective status is to equate "good" with a natural property such as "happiness." Thus, according to the 19th century Utilitarians, since happiness is desired by everyone, what makes people happy must be considered good. The attractiveness of this sort of naturalistic position is based in part on the ease one has in identifying with a psychological quality like happiness. Once one accepts the proposition that what gives pleasure is good, it is relatively simple to decide which actions, both individual and collective, are good. In the words of the great Utilitarian philosopher Jeremy Bentham, the only criteria is "the greatest happiness for the greatest number." Once again the noncognitivist objects: The Utilitarians have confused an "is" question with an "ought" question. The fact that everyone in a population wants or desires something is surely of great concern to the decision maker interested in maintaining a responsible political system. But the fact does not make the desired policy good in any ultimate sense.

There is another naturalistic philosophical tradition that views *existence* and *survival* as legitimate criteria for goodness. Such widely divergent thinkers as Thomas Hobbes, Friedrich Nietzsche, and Herbert Spencer have argued that what exists, survives, or triumphs is what ought to exist, survive, or triumph. Thus, in politics the system that lasts the longest is clearly the best.

It doesn't require extensive training in philosophy to see that *existence* and *survival* are actually values that have come in through the back door, so to speak. If one believes that they should be the ultimate values or objectives of a society, then he will naturally evaluate favorably those political systems that have achieved or at least try to achieve them. But to the noncognitivist this does not demonstrate their truth. How does one, arguing from this position, refute the contrary position which values freedom above existence? If to be free implies the breakdown of the political system, then breakdown it must be. Clearly, there is no solution, for what we have here is a conflict between ultimate values.

Aristotle developed the idea, usually called *teleology,* that everything, including men and political systems, has an end sown in it from the time of its origin. Thus, the acorn's end is to become an oak tree and man's end is to become, let us say, a good citizen. The significance of teleological thinking lies in the claim that every man and social institution has an objective end that is knowable and that this end can provide the basis for normative judgments. If a political system's end is to become a democracy, then it is morally right that it become a democracy; or those actions that tend to lead to democracy are morally commendable.

There are several criticisms that the noncognivitists would make of this position. First, how do we determine a person's or system's proper end? We know that acorns become oak trees, but would we want to conclude that they ought to? The teleological argument is really based on an empirical observation logically the same as the statement that "education leads to higher salries." But what about the ends of men? Can we say that every man has an end toward which he is moving? How do we discover them? Ability or skill might be equated with the end. But is a mediocre baseball pitcher who has great musical ability immoral in pursuing a baseball career? In the final analysis, the teleological grounding of value judgments is guilty of the common *is-ought* confusion. Even if ends are discoverable, and this possibility has been criticized, one need not agree that they are what ought to be realized. An opponent of this position might agree that most conflicts become wars, yet still bemoan the fact as being morally unjustified.

In recent years, an interesting turn has taken place in political philosophy. The value-free nature of moral relativism has been used to justify certain kinds of political systems, especially the liberal state. This type of political analysis is advanced by those who appear to be noncognitivists, but who still end up justifying a particular "best" political system.

The argument usually begins with the claim that since there is no such thing as knowledge of the ultimate good, one ought to be tolerant of others. Thus, tolerance becomes, in a kind of backhanded way, an ultimate good. The instrumental conclusion is drawn that the good political system is the "neutral state" where there is no ultimate good. The liberal state "must be neutral on . . . the question of the good life."[12]

But critics of this approach to moral justification suggest that several important questions remain. Why is neutrality desirable? Why should the political system be tolerant of each and every value? If there are no ultimate values, why isn't it equally justifiable to allow the play of power to determine, somewhat arbitrarily, what is considered "good" in each political system? This is essentially the position of such classic power theorists as Hobbes and Machiavelli. What seems to have happened here is that freedom is correctly seen as the central feature of the liberal state, but this leads to the unprovable position that moral relativism or neutrality logically implies a free society.

LOGICAL ANALYSIS

Now that we have discussed the distinction between empirical and normative statements, let us return to the analytic or logical statement. Unlike empirical statements, which can be contigently true, valid logical statements are necessarily true, that is for all time and for all possible worlds. But they have this quality because they are true within a specific logical system—they are true by definition, so to speak. Thus, for instance, the propositions of symbolic logic, the truths of arithmetic, or the theorems of geometry are necessarily true. But necessary truth comes at a price; an analytic statement says nothing new about the world: "$2 + 2 = 4$" does not give us the same kind of information as "U.S. businessmen tend to be Republican in poli-

---

[12] Ronald Dworkin, "Paternalism," in *Morality and the Law* ed. Richard Wasterstrom (Belmont, Calif.: Wadsworth, 1971), p. 127. Also see Bruce Ackerman, *Social Justice in the Liberal State* (New Haven, Conn.: Yale University Press, 1980) and the modern classic, John Rawls, *A Theory of Justice* (Cambridge, Mass.: Harvard University Press, 1971).

tics." Still, this is a clarification and not a criticism of analytic statements, for the powerful apparatuses of logic and mathematics are of immeasurable value to the political philosopher and political scientist.

CONCLUSION: TYPES OF KNOWLEDGE

The basic distinctions that we have been discussing should be obvious by now. There are three possible types of knowledge: empirical (based on observation of the world), analytic (based on logical derivations from premises), and normative (based on a host of different theories). To most modern noncognitivist political scientists, only the first two qualify as knowledge. The typical classical political philosopher accepts all three. There is, though, a common thread that connects the two traditions. From the very beginning, political analysts have had a practical bent even when coming across as philosophical and abstract. Just as Plato and Hobbes tried to formulate policies to save their disordered societies, modern political scientists, often calling themselves "policy scientists," attempt to apply their knowledge to real world social and political problems. The activity that all have in common is the analysis of instrumental questions: how to maintain order in ancient Athens and how to adjust to an energy-scarce world in modern times are logically similar. Each deals with a goal and the best ways to achieve that goal. Thus, despite the normative tilt of the philosopher and the empirical leaning of the scientist, the two meet at times on common ground.

Politics and science

W E have now described the general nature of contemporary political science by contrasting its interests with those of political philosophy. But the result, while basic to the arguments presented in this book, is nevertheless a skeleton in need of flesh. Some of the latter will be provided in this chapter, where a second, more analytical approach is taken to answer the question, "What is the scope of political science?"

We have already described the nature of analytic propositions and analytic political philosophy, so the use of the word *analytic* here should not generate any problems. We will *analyze* "political science"; that is, we will examine and explicate its component parts, "political" and "science." Another way of looking at this activity is to say that we are interested in two aspects of the discipline or field of political science; its content or *what* is studied, and its structure or *how* the content is studied. The first is politics or "the political", and the second is "science." In examining the meaning assigned to these concepts by political scientists, we will be describing the scope or boundaries of political science. "Science" refers to the *methods* of political science, the general topics of parts two and three. But the methodology that a political scientist adopts, the basic assumptions he makes, will to some extent influence his image of his discipline. Therefore, "scope" and

––

"method" cannot be completely divorced. Methodology can and should be studied in its own right (as it is in most of this book), but in addition, it ought to be considered as an important influence on the scope of political science, for the methodology adopted will, to some extent, determine what political science can and cannot do.

POLITICS

Most of us use the word *politics* without providing an explicit definition, yet we can understand others when politics is the subject being discussed. When a political issue is being discussed, the discussants seldom begin by working out an acceptable definition of "political." This probably indicates that there is a basic common-sense understanding of the term. At this point, however, some people, especially those interested in studying politics in a more rigorous fashion, point out that to really gain knowledge of politics one has to formulate a more explicit definition; that is, one can't simply rely on common sense.

In a later section, we will examine in detail the differences between scientific and common-sensical knowledge and see how the former, while to a large extent based on the latter, nevertheless goes beyond it in its ability to describe and explain the world. One might argue that perhaps the most important factor leading to the development of knowledge in a field of study is agreement among its members about the content of that field.[1] In other words, you can't expect knowledge of politics to develop and accumulate unless political scientists share a conception of what it is they are studying. In the context of our present discussion, this means a fairly clear-cut definition of politics.

One of the staunchest defenders of a clear definition of politics is E. E. Schattschneider. "There is something strange about the feeling of scholars that a definition is not necessary. Inevitably there is a lack of focus in the discipline because it is difficult to see things that are undefined. People who cannot define the object of their studies do not know what they are looking for, and if they do not know what they are looking for, how can they tell

––––––––––

[1] See David B. Truman, "Disillusion and Regeneration: The Quest for a Discipline," *American Political Science Review,* 59, no. 4 (December 1965), pp. 865–73.

when they have found it?[2] This leads Schattschneider to call political science "a mountain of data surrounding a vacuum."[3]

The next task, then, is to examine several definitions or types of definition of politics that have been given by political scientists. However, in doing so we should keep in mind an alternative position that answers Schattschneider by claiming that it is a waste of time to attempt an explicit definition of politics. It claims that it is more sensible to simply plunge in and study whatever the student of politics finds interesting and significant. This position holds that the definition of politics, or scope of political science, is contextually determined. The argument is that whatever political scientists say is politics, is politics, and one restricts the growth of political science if he prematurely advocates a definition. Thus, the outer limits of political science can be determined only by listing all the topics which interest political scientists at a given time.

This seems to be an important tradition within political science. In their analysis of the historical development of American political science, Albert Somit and Joseph Tannenhaus point out that the discipline has never had a clear conception of its content. This has often bewildered observers. For instance, the English historian Morse Stephens, after teching in the United States for two years, reported in 1896 that "he had not been able to find anyone who could tell him precisely what political science was."[4]

Despite this tradition of disinterest in the job of definition, many definitions of politics have been given by political philosophers and political scientists. As a matter of fact, their diversity is no doubt another reason for the bewilderment experienced by observers of political science. While there has been a wide range of definitions, most of them can be classified as one of two types. Some identify politics with government, legal government, or the state, while others revolve around the notions of power, authority, and/or conflict. After examining the advantages and disadvantages of each, we will consider a contemporary attempt to formulate a more useful definition that many people believe overcomes some of these disadvantages.

---

[2] E. E. Schattschneider, *Two Hundred Million Americans in Search of a Government* (New York: Holt, Rinehart & Winston, 1969), p. 8.

[3] Ibid.

[4] Quoted in Albert Somit and Joseph Tannenhaus, *The Development of American Political Science: From Burgess to Behavioralism* (Boston: Allyn & Bacon, 1967), p. 24.

Government

To the average citizen, politics and government are synonymous. It seems natural to identify politics with what occurs in Congress, the state legislature, or the mayor's office. Many political scientists take the same position but articulate it in a more sophisticated manner. Political scientist Alfred de Grazia says that politics, or the political, "includes the events that happen around the decision-making centers of government."[5] Charles Hyneman is more specific in claiming that most political scientists have assumed that *legal* government is the subject matter of their discipline. "The central point of attention in American political science . . . is that part of the affairs of the state which centers in government, and that kind or part of government which speaks through law."[6] There are two versions of this definition, a weaker and a stronger. The former speaks only about government; the latter adds the concept "legal." As we will see in a moment, they are the same. Thus, to most political scientists, legal government is internally redundant.

If a political scientist identifies politics with government or legal government, it is incumbent upon him to let us know what he means by government. Here we, as students of politics interested in the meaning of this widely used term, are faced with a problem that results in part from its wide usage. That is, because of the number of definitions, it is difficult to decide what is being referred to. However, if one is mainly interested, as we are, in discovering a basic or core meaning of government, it becomes clear that the problem is more apparent than real. After sorting through the definitions, one realizes that as it is used by most political scientists, government means something like "the legally based institutions of a society which make legally binding decisions." If this is an accurate statement, then Hyneman's definition is more specific than de Grazia's. Legal government is redundant because legality defines government; it is the characteristic that distinguishes government from other institutions in society. But whether we say government or legal government, the political scientist who adopts this type of definition is focusing his attention on formal institutions of a certain kind.

We conclude that the definition that equates politics with government has

---

[5] Alfred de Grazia, *Political Behavior* (New York: Free Press, 1965), p. 24.

[6] Charles Hyneman, *The Study of Politics* (Urbana: University of Illinois Press, 1956), p. 26.

a commonsensical basis. However, many political scientists would probably warn us to be wary of its commonsensical appeal, for they see in it
serious limitations. Perhaps the most significant is its limited applicability. In
emphasizing government, such critics argue, the political scientist must
overlook much that should and that often does interest him. In other words,
this definition is unrealistically restrictive. Take, for instance, a political
scientist interested in studying the politics of an African nation. He no doubt
spends much of this time examining tribal societies where no governmental
institutions or at best minimal governmental institutions exist. Yet he discovers that the tribal chief and elders are making basic decisions for the
community. Because the decisions are not made by identifiable legal institutions, such as a congress or a parliament, in other words by a government or
the state, are they to be classified as nonpolitical and therefore beyond the
scope of political scientists?

A large number of political scientiss would answer that it is a sign of
narrow-mindedness, a dangerous trait for a researcher, to use a type of
political institution as the basis for a definition of politics. Perhaps the heart
of the difficulty, as perceived by these critics, is a failure to look behind
governmental institutions for the element that makes them all political. The
emphasis should be placed, not on institutions, but, in David Easton's
words, on "a kind of activity that may express itself through a variety of
institutions."[7]

Power, authority, and conflict

Political scientists who make such criticisms of the "governmental" definition of politics and develop them beyond the negative stage usually end on
a positive note, formulating an alternative definition that equates politics
with power, authority, or conflict. Any of these could be the activity mentioned by Easton. Let us quote William Bluhm, a political scientist who
provides a rather elaborate definition: "Reduced to its universal elements,
then, politics is a social process characterized by activity involving rivalry
and cooperation in the exercise of power, and culminating in the making of

---

[7] David Easton, *The Political System* (New York: Alfred A. Knopf, 1960), p. 113.

decisions for a group.''[8] The appeal of this definition flows out of its apparent flexibility or wide scope. Politics is found wherever power relationships or conflict situations exist, which means that the political scientist can legitimately (i.e., as a political scientist) study the politics of a labor union, corporation, or African tribe, as well as what goes on in a legislature or administrative agency.

The emphasis is placed upon a type of activity or behavior rather than a particular kind of institution. Implicit in this definition is a refusal to prematurely answer the question, ''In what kinds of institutions is politics the most likely to occur?'' Or the more basic question, ''Does politics have to be institutionalized in the first place?''

Underlying our comparative analysis of definitions is the obvious fact that a definition of politics based on government is simply a version of one based on power in general. The political scientist who adopts the first type assumes that only one kind of power is political and therefore relevant to his discipline, namely, power exercised within and by governmental institutions. Thus, all definitions of politics are based upon notions of power and/or conflict. Consider, for instance, the definition of politics proposed by the German sociologist Max Weber. ''Hence, 'politics' for us means striving to share power or striving to influence the distribution of power, either among states or among groups within a state.'' Power is crucial but apparently only when it is exercised by or around the state or government. This realization does not, however, make our categorization of definitions less significant. The purpose of the present chapter is not to formulate the *real* definition of politics (as we will see later, there is no such thing as a real definition), but rather to discover how political scientists use the term. And, as a matter of fact, those who limit politics to governmental power concentrate on the governmental rather than the power definition. Thus, as the concepts are used in political science, there is a practical difference between a definition based on government and one based on power. As Chapter 3 will demonstrate, this difference can influence the research orientations of political scientists. Just as we assumed that it was the responsibility of those using the first definition to define ''government,'' it seems reasonable to expect that when the second is employed, the meaning of ''power'' will be specified.

---

[8] William Bluhm, *Theories of the Political System* (Englewood Cliffs, N.J.: Prentice-Hall, 1965), p. 5.

Once again the familiar problem of a diverse and ambiguous collection of definitions, seemingly defying analysis, faces us. Yet, once again, at the bottom of this agglomeration is a common-sense core that gives us a rough notion of what power means to those adopting this definition of politics. Running through all concepts of conflict and power is the idea of people or groups competing for scarce values, with some of them influencing the behavior of others and/or the outcomes of decisions. In the second and third parts of this book, power will be examined in much greater detail and it will be obvious that we have provided an oversimplified, but nevertheless accurate, definition of it.

Despite the growing appeal of this more liberal definition of politics, it has not gone without criticism. To some political scientists, especially those who feel the need for a discipline with clear-cut boundaries, it seems that the equating of politics and power destroys the possibility of specifying such boundaries. If the political scientist can legitimately study all forms of power and conflict (in the UAW, General Motors, or the local Kiwanis Club), then what is distinctive about political science? The sociologist does the same thing. Does this mean that there are no significant differences between sociology and political science? One answer is "yes"; another, "there is no reason to answer the question."

We will consider the nature and implications of these responses in a moment. But first, let us return to a consideration of the reply that claims that the content of political science is distinctive and that the discipline has boundaries that are more restrictive than those provided by "any power or conflict situation." As we have seen, one set of boundaries is equivalent to the institutions of legal government. However, some political scientists have formulated an alternative definition of politics, an in-between position that is neither as restrictive as the government type nor as broad as the power variety.

The authoritative allocation of values

Such in-between definitions are usually functional in nature. That is, they define politics in terms of the functions it supposedly performs for society. Over the centuries, political thinkers have identified numerous functions: maintaining order, resolving conflict, achieving justice, and providing the good life. In each case, politics is viewed as an activity; it probably involves the exercise of power, but more importantly it is an activity that serves a purpose (or purposes). Thus, to Thomas Hobbes, politics' only function is to maintain order among naturally egoistic and competitive human beings. If the function is not adequately performed, it is back to the State of Nature, where there is no morality, no law, and no politics.

Perhaps the most widely known and used alternative of this sort has been provided by David Easton. His identification of the political system with "the authoritative allocation of values for a society"[9] has provided many political scientists with a useful guideline for delimiting the content of political science. We have already quoted Easton's plea for an emphasis on political *activity* rather than *institutions*. The "authoritative allocation of values" is, Easton argues, the kind of activity we should be interested in. The first assumption is that in every society values are desired; that is, people have different interests or objectives and these must be allocated or distributed by someone or something. In a sense, this is a power and conflict situation. But saying that every society allocates values authoritatively does ot prejudge the question, "How is this done?" In the United States, we would expect legal governmental institutions to make such decisions, while in an African tribe, the activity would probably take place much more informally, without the elaborate institutions. Thus, every society has a political system, defined as that which authoritatively allocates values; but this system takes different forms.

The first conclusion we can draw is that the political scientist adopting Easton's definition is not limited to the study of legal government. This is significant for two reasons. First, it means that the U.S. political scientist is able to study other political systems or cultures objectively, without preconceived notions about political structures and behavior. Secondly, when studying his own political system, the political scientist is not limited to the formal institutions of government, such as Congress, but can include interest groups, political parties, and other less-obvious influences on authoritative decisions.

On the other hand, Easton's definition is not of the "anything goes" variety. He is not saying that the political system includes (is coextensive with) all power or decision-making situations. Only those decisions that are

---

[9] Easton, *The Political System,* pp. 129ff.

authoritative for the society are relevant to the political scientist. According to Easton, "A policy is authorative when the people to whom it is intended to apply or who are affected by it consider that they must or ought to obey it."[10] In other words, it is considered binding. However, not every authoritative decision is made within the political system. What, for instance, of those decisions that members of a Kiwanis Club accept as binding? How do they differ from acts of Congress? The answer is, of course, found in the qualifier, "for society." From the class of all authoritative decisions, the political scientist, following Easton's definition, selects only those definitions that apply to *all* members of society (although only a few might be affected).

If one thinks about it, there isn't a great deal of difference between Eaton's definition and the one based on power. Both assume a political world of scarce values and insatiable appetites. The basic question of politics then becomes, "How are values distributed?" or, in Harold Lasswell's classic phraseology, "Who Gets What, When, How?" The difference is mainly one of emphasis. Power theorists, such as Lasswell, emphasize the role of power in the distribution process, while Easton examines the relationship between what goes into a system (demands) and what comes out (decisions). Thus, Easton focuses his attention on the entire political system: Lasswell focuses on those who have the greatest impact on the distribution process, namely those with power, the elite. From different perspectives, each political scientist has come to a similar conception of what politics is all about.

The argument for an Eastonian-type definition of politics is based on the desirability of a compromise position that is neither too restrictive nor overly broad. Such a definition, based on the function supposedly performed by politics, it is claimed, is more useful for political scientists. However, this kind of definition does not go without criticism; in fact, to many political scientists, its advantages are only apparent. Instead of one word *(politics),* several words *(authoritative, allocation, values, and society)* have to be defined. Therefore, anything that may be gained from an explicit definition of politics is canceled out because of the addition of several complex concepts. For instance, what does it mean to make a decision for society, and how does this differ from one that is not made for society? To many political scientists, any elaborate attempt to answer this question is a waste of time.

---

[10] Ibid., p. 132.

Why define politics?

Earlier, an alternative approach was mentioned that questioned the usefulness of any attempt to define politics, on the grounds that since there is no final solution to a problem of definition (as we will see in Chapter 5), and since there are so many existing definitions of politics, the political scientist's time could be better spent in other activities. Although rarely articulated (by its very nature), this position has long been a significant one in U.S. political science. For instance, in 1904, a leading political scientist wrote that, "Such an attempt [to define politics] is not only dangerous but even if successfully made, it is not in my opinion sufficiently fruitful of practical results to justify the expenditure of thought and time necessary to secure the desired end."[11] Our point is that many, if not most, contemporary political scientists agree with this statement. Thus, rather than concern themselves with semantic questions, they "plunge in" and either do their research without worrying about the scope or boundaries of their discipline or allow the results of their work to set the boundaries.

There is another in-between approach to the problem of defining politics. It is based on the linguistic theories of philosopher Ludwig Wittgenstein.[12] The basic point is that it is perhaps a mistake to assume that words such as politics have a single definition. Instead, it is more useful to view politics as a *cluster* concept, a concept that is associated with many properties, with no one property essential to its definition.[13] This suggests that the particular definition that one selects will reflect one's values, beliefs, and perceptions.

Let us reiterate that the primary objective of this discussion is not to arrive at "the" or even "a" definition of politics. If the only conclusion drawn is that there is no such definition, then the discussion has been partially successful. But in addition, it is hoped that in becoming familiar with several of the more popular interpretations of politics or political science, the student will be able to better understand the literature of his discipline.

---

[11] Frank J. Goodnow, "The Work of the American Political Science Association," *Proceedings,* I (1904), p. 35; quoted in Somit and Tannenhaus, *Development of American Political Science,* p. 65.

[12] Ludwig Wittgenstein, *Philosophical Investigations* (New York: Macmillan, 1953).

[13] William Connolly, *The Terms of Political Discourse* (Lexington, Mass.: D. C. Heath, 1974).

Perhaps we can be more specific. Making it clear once again that no best definition of politics is being advocated, there nevertheless seems to be a recognizable common-sensical core meaning of the political scientist's subject matter. It is simply that politics has something to do with the use of power to reconcile conflicts over the distribution of goods and values. Typically, this is done through the institutions of government. Thus, the several definitions we have considered are not in opposition to each other. Rather, they emphasize different aspects of the same basic process, and so it follows that most political scientists are playing the same game. We have already seen that there are legitimate objections to any proposed definition of politics; someone will always be dissatisfied. In addition, as the next chapter will demonstrate, many political scientists reject as unrealistic and overly restrictive the notion of boundaries between the social sciences. If the political scientist and sociologist often seem to be studying the same thing, it is because of the nature of the work. Perhaps it would be wise to work out an efficient division of labor, but there is nothing sinister about the overlap. No discipline is being imperialistic. This attitude can result in the familiar conclusion that it is wrong to prematurely *define* the scope of political science. Political scientists common-sensically understand the label that has been assigned them. Unification of the discipline must come as a natural development from within, that is, through the discovery of facts that have relevance for all those who call themselves political scientists, rather than from the imposition of an elaborate definition that arbitrarily classifies some things as political and others as nonpolitical.

SCIENCE

What does the "science" in "political science" mean? A survey of the discipline's literature uncovers several answers. However, a close examination indicates that these answers are different in degree rather than in kind. Each interpretation is really a simplified version of a set of scientific principles that ultimately provides the basis for all scientific study. This is the model of science that will be the most closely analyzed here, for it is also the foundation that a science of politics must rest upon.

Preliminary considerations

The most primitive and least fruitful interpretation uses science in an honorific sense. Just as a nation in the contemporary world is judged good if it is democratic, a political scientist's status rises if he is scientific. Therefore, nations call themselves democratic, and political scientists call their work scientific, with public relations in mind. Science becomes a label to be used but not defined. If this were all that science involved, then there would be no point in continuing. However, there is more. We will survey in ascending order of sophistication several acceptable interpretations of the word *science* in the term *political science*.

The first of these interpretations simply equates science with *serious study*. Almost by definition, then, all those who study politics professionally become scientists, for at the very heart of their profession lies a commitment to study political phenomena more seriously than, for instance, the man on the street or even a journalist. While this is a step forward, it doesn't tell us what we really want to know: namely, "What distinguishes scientific from unscientific study?"

A familiar reply is that to be scientific is to be systematic or rigorous. Even when these adjectives are left undefined, as they often are, one at least senses what science is all about. Some rough operational guideline is provided to tell us in any given instance where the scientific ends and the unscientific begins. However, this kind of guideline is not going to take us far unless it is given more substance through explicit definitions of "rigorous" and "systematic." As we just noted, this is rarely done. When it is done, the result is usually an explication of "scientific," for as they are commonly used, rigorous and systematic are synonyms of our key word. Science has not been defined, it has simply been given a new name. Thus, while we know a little more now, we are still treading water rather than making headway. A political scientist who believes his discipline is scientific because it studies political phenomena systematically is right. But he hasn't said enough. What does it mean to be systematic or scientific? What are the distinguishing characteristics of a systematic or scientific discipline?

The answer most often given or assumed is that a scientific discipline is empirical. An empirical proposition, let us recall, is one that refers to and is based upon the world of experience and observation. Since the political scientist, as a scientist, is interested in one aspect of the world around him, he must make sure his descriptions of politics are empirical. Thus, according to this interpretation of science, the political scientist lives up to his appellation if he deals only with the *facts*. *Naive empiricism* is the appropriate label for this. We are all probably familiar with its consequences—the piling of fact upon fact, exhaustive descriptions of a single governmental institution, or detailed narratives of a particular political decision. The facts speak for themselves and usually there is only a limited attempt to organize and/or explain them. The naiveté of this position should not be exaggerated, however, for it seems clear, no matter how sophisticated one's conception of science, that science begins with empiricism. One must look at the world if he is to explain the world.

Let us summarize this section's main points. One significant interpretation equates the term *scientific* with systematic or rigorous. Another recognizes the empirical basis of science. These two positions are not mutually exclusive. In fact, the political scientist who adopts one probably assumes the other, so that the composite picture of science which emerges is a kind of ordered study that stays close to the facts (observation). Charles Hyneman has described political science in these terms: "the political scientist is pursuing scientific method if he makes a conscientious, careful, systematic effort to find out what actually exists and goes on."[14] We might characterize this orientation, which links systematic and empirical, as a liberal version of the set of scientific principles that have already been identified as fundamental to any science. A description of these principles provides a more sophisticated notion of science.

However, some political scientists accepting the more liberal interpretation would probably argue that they are principles of only the more highly developed physical sciences such as physics and chemistry and are not realistically applicable to political science or any social science. Therefore, the political scientist can be empirical and systematic only at a general level. This point of view raises a host of issues that will be handled at appropriate times throughout this book. In the present context, only one reply is necessary. If all notions of science are derived from this set of basic principles, there is no opposition between it and the liberal interpretation of science. Only a fool could fail to see the more highly developed nature of the natural sciences relative to the social sciences. However, this superiority is not

---

[14] Hyneman, *The Study of Politics*, p. 78.

derived from the acceptance of a different set of scientific principles. It has been achieved because of a clearer understanding of and more effective building upon these principles. The implications are that every science, natural or social, is based upon a common set of assumptions and this set is a more complete version of what has been called here the liberal interpretation of the "science" in "political science."

The assumptions of science

Let's run through these assumptions and principles, realizing that a more thorough discussion will have to wait until Part 2. At this point, we are mainly interested in a reasonably accurate sketch of an existing or potential science of politics based on the conception of science held by most practitioners and philosophers of science (this includes a growing number of political scientists).[15] There are two ways to approach science. On the one hand, it can be viewed as " a body of knowledge"; on the other, as "a method of obtaining it." According to the first approach, science or what is scientific includes the laws, facts, and so on of physics, biology, economics, and so forth. According to the second method, science is a particular set of principles that tells us to obtain these facts. We will take the second approach, for what interests us are the methodological foundations of political science.

Remember that science is being viewed as the second aspect of political science—*how* political scientists study political phenomena. Thus, a discipline can be judged scientific if it makes certain assumptions and follows certain principles, even though the knowledge it has produced is not impressive. It should be clear that there is no opposition between the two approaches. The adjective *scientific* can be applied both to the principles *(scientific method)* and the facts obtained *(scientific knowledge)*. We emphasize the first here because it is logically prior—scientific knowledge is obtained only by following scientific method.

A further distinction can be made between two ways of looking at scientific method. One is exemplified in the work of political theorist Arnold

---

[15] Among recent books on philosophy of science by political scientists are George Graham, *Methodological Foundations for Political Analysis* (Waltham, Mass.: Xerox College Publishing, 1971); and James L. Payne, *Foundations of Empirical Political Analysis* (Chicago: Markham Publishing Co., 1973).

Brecht. He lists 11 "scientific actions" or "steps of scientific procedure," beginning with observation, which together make up scientific method.[16] The other approach is to sort out the basic assumptions and principles, rather than operations or procedures, which scientists make and follow. This becomes a more fundamental analysis. But let us make it clear that these are simply two ways of looking at the same thing.

"Nothing in the universe just happens" is a simple way of stating the scientist's basic assumption. It is usually labeled "determinism" or the "principle of universal causation."[17] Most of us believe that there are reasons for everyday events or situations. This is the commonsensical basis of the scientist's assumption of determinism or causality. The scientist says, if we want knowledge of the world, we have to assume that the world is coherent, that there are certain recurring relationships which can be expressed in such propositions as "If *A* occurs, *B* occurs." This is a causal relationship, and it is what the scientist is searching for. If scientific knowledge is knowledge of such relationships, then the principle of determinism, or something like it, is a necessary starting point. However, it must be emphasized that the principle is not itself a scientific law that has been or can be substantiated but instead is an assumption which directs the scientist's work. As one philosopher has said, "It expresses a resolve, 'Let us find uniformities in the world.' "[18] This is why he calls it a "leading principle." It can be said then, that a science of politics begins with the assumption that no political phenomenon just happens. This enables the political scientist to carry out his main task, namely, to account for the phenomena which interest him—to show why they happen or exist.

The second characteristic of science is one we have already discussed. If the world is what we are interested in, then it is the world we must examine. Describing and explaining politics implies speaking about and basing our explanations on what has been observed (directly or indirectly) about politics. This means that every scientific statement is based upon an observation. The proposition, "There are 30 desks in this classroom," can be verified by counting the desks. Of course, matters are much more complicated in

---

[16] Arnold Brecht, *Political Theory: The Foundations of Twentieth-Century Political Thought* (Princeton, N.J.: Princeton University Press, 1959), pp. 28–29.

[17] For a clear discussion of the principle, see John Hospers, *An Introduction to Philosophical Analysis* (Englewood Cliffs, N.J.: Prentice-Hall, 1953), chapter 4.

[18] Ibid., p. 261.

scientific research, but the principle is the same. In studying voting behavior, for instance, we have to do much more than count a few votes. But observing voters' attitudes (responses to questions) and measuring social status (income and occupation), to name only some of the factors that might interest us, are empirical for the same reason that counting desks is.

It is often said that to be scientific is to be *objective,* as opposed to *subjective*. The scientist keeps separate his professional and personal judgments. In the latter he is subjective, which means that values or normative considerations often influence his decisions. But when he is scientific, such influences must be excluded; the scientist "tells it as it is." Perhaps *objective* is, in many ways, a synonym of *empirical*. To base your judgments on observation is to be empirical, and if your judgments are empirical in this sense, you are being objective. Another way of saying this is to call science "value-free." Recalling the discussion of the first chapter, science deals with *is,* not *ought* questions; with empirical, not normative questions. Thus, we see the relationship between *scientific* and *objective*.

Many students of scientific method, however, prefer an alternate term to *objective* when they describe science. *Intersubjective* seems more descriptive of how scientists actually operate, for it is not so demanding as *objective,* and it doesn't conjure up the images of ultimate reality and the completely unbiased scientist that *objective* seems to. Most scientists view perfect objectivity as unrealizable in the real world. Every scientist is human with all the human characteristics—emotions, biases, and value commitments. A professional scientist will be able to shake himself free from many, hopefully most, but probably not all, of these influences. Because he is a scientist, he is committed to being as objective as possible, but as a human being he will be human. The point of intersubjectivity is that no scientist has to be perfectly objective. Biases can be identified and weeded out.

As Arnold Brecht has pointed out, to be intersubjective, knowledge has to be transmissible. By this he means, "A type of knowledge that can be transmitted from any person who has such knowledge to any other person who does not have it but who can grasp the meaning of the symbols (words, signs) used in communication and perform the operations, if any, described in these communications."[19] Thus, if one scientist performs an experiment, a second scientist can repeat the experiment and compare the two sets of

---

[19] Brecht, *Political Theory,* p. 114.

findings. If the procedures are correct, then we would expect the results to be similar; although because of changing conditions and new factors, they might differ. This is scientifically acceptable. What is important is that one scientist can understand and evaluate the methods of others and can carry out similar observations to test the validity of scientific facts. This is the significance of intersubjectivity. The requirement is simply that all proposed scientific facts be open to inspection and the procedures used to arrive at these facts be clearly enough described so as to be repeatable. Thus, scientific knowledge is "transmissible" because science is a social activity in that it takes several scientists, analyzing and criticizing each other, to produce more reliable knowledge. When we contrast a scientific proposition such as, "Most businessmen vote Republican," with a metaphysical one, "Spirits motivate businessmen," the significance of the former's intersubjective nature is evident.

There is more to science than observation. We all look at the world and draw conclusions, yet this does not make us scientists. While science begins with common sense (everyone who looks sees the same chairs or analyzes the same attitude questionnaires), scientific knowledge is not the same as commonsensical knowledge. It is here that the systematic nature of science becomes relevant. The scientist takes his observations and attempts to classify and analyze them. His first objective is to formulate useful *empirical concepts* that organize the phenomena that interest him. Then, starting with the assumption of determinism, he attempts to find relationships between these concepts. If successful, he discovers a scientific *law* or *generalization.* Further systematization of empirical knowledge is achieved by the construction of *theories,* which are collections of logically related generalizations. Finally, the scientist uses his laws and theories to *explain* events and situations that have occurred or exist and to *predict* future happenings. It can thus be said that the scientist's attempts to systematize are all leading to this ultimate objective, to explain and predict—to show *why* things were, are, or will be. A glance at this book's table of contents will indicate that its second part has just been outlined. We have, in general terms, mentioned the basic elements of science and, therefore, of a science of politics—concepts, laws, theories, explanation, and prediction. How these elements are developed and used gives science its particular character. In organizing, in looking for relationships, in trying to explain and predict, the scientist moves beyond the commonsensical kind of knowledge that most of us accept as sound.

Finally, a characteristic that science does not have should be mentioned. We have already implied it several times. While science deals with the world of observation, it does not produce *necessary* truth. As stated in Chapter 1, only analytic propositions can be necessarily true. Empirical propositions are by their very nature contingent. This is why we said that many scientists shy away from the concept "truth"; it seems to imply necessity. It may seem strange and a bit disconcerting in this uncertain world to say that not even scientific laws are absolutely true. Once one stops and thinks about it, it should not seem strange for, to be considered scientific, a statement must be testable; if it is testable, it has to be potentially false. To be empirical, and therefore scientific, a proposition has to be disprovable. If there is no way to show that it is false, if no amount of observational evidence can put its claim to question, then it cannot be called scientific. Thus, if a scientific proposition is always open to disconfirmation, it cannot be necessarily true.

CONCLUSION: SCIENCE AND POLITICAL SCIENCE

This is an outline of science as it is viewed by scientists and philosophers. It is the set of principles that more and more political scientists are accepting as the basis of their own work. Our analysis, of course, assumes that the "science" in "political science" is based upon these principles. The other, more liberal, interpretations of science are acceptable, for they are simply less-complete versions.

However, it would not be fair to leave the impression that all political scientists accept this interpretation of political *science*. Some reject the notion that politics can ever be studied *scientifically*. Thus, while they probably accept the previously discussed model of science (or one of its derivatives), they deny that political science can ever meet its requirements. Instead, the political scientist must rely on nonscientific methods to study politics since no reliable knowledge of the sort found in physics will ever be produced in political science. The result is usually a political science more closely related to literature and philosophy than the social sciences. In Chapter 4, we will consider some of the specific arguments these political scientists present in their attempts to prove that political science can never be scientific. We will attempt to refute these arguments and indirectly demonstrate the possibility of a science of politics.

CHAPTER

Orientations in political science

IN Chapter 1, the broad interests of political scientists were described. Chapter 2 analyzed the meanings of "political" and "science." Now, in Chapter 3, the scope of political science will be viewed in a different light. We will deal with orientations, schools of thought in modern political science. Since there is a rough chronological order about them, it is possible to talk about the historical development of political science in the United States, an important topic in its own right. But more important to us is the fact that although different orientations have been dominant at different times, all of them linger on in contemporary political science.

This discussion will, it is hoped, serve two purposes. First, it will put into clearer perspective the conclusions of Chapters 1 and 2. It is interesting, for instance, to note the tendency of particular interpretations of "politics" and "science" to cluster together to form particular schools of thought. These schools represent definitions of *political science*. This was hinted at in the last chapter and will become more obvious as we continue. In providing such perspective, a foundation for the rest of this book is laid. But this foundation laying is accomplished more directly by examining what is probably the dominant orientation in contemporary political science, behavioralism, because most of the models and theories discussed in later chapters have developed within the behavioral tradition.

A general and well-known distinction today is drawn between the *traditional* and the *behavioral* approaches to the study of politics. Before we go any further, one point of clarification should be made. While we can with some justification distinguish one school from another for the purposes of analysis, in the real world the boundary lines are usually blurred. Few professional political scientists would allow themselves to be classified as out-and-out traditionalists or behavioralists. The reason, in addition to the natural academic aversion to self-pigeonholing, is that "pure" political scientists are rare. Most individuals' orientations are a mixture of old and new schools. This chapter is not a handbook for classifying professors of political science (although this is at times an enjoyable pastime). It is, instead, a characterization of the discipline of political science—an attempt to sort out and describe the major methodological tendencies in the discipline to gain a better understanding of the scope of political science.

TRADITIONAL POLITICAL SCIENCE

The so-called traditional approach includes several methods of analyzing politics which became popular among many American political scientists in the 19th and early 20th centuries, and that continue to be widely followed. It cannot be emphasized too strongly that traditionalism is a collection of approaches lumped together today mainly because of a common enemy, behavioralism. Perhaps the three most important approaches are the historical, legalistic, and institutional.

From its 19th-century beginnings, U.S. political science was looked upon by many of its practitioners as primarily an historical discipline. Little difference was recognized between history and political science; the latter was considered a branch or division of the former. According to Richard Jensen, the motto of this generation of political scientists was "History is past politics and politics present history."[1] Thus, political science was really political

---

[1] Richard Jensen, "History and the Political Scientist," in Seymour Martin Lipset, ed., *Politics and the Social Sciences* (New York: Oxford University Press, 1969), pp. 1–28. Jensen's article provides a useful survey of the historical relationship between the disciplines of history and political science.

history, and included such fields as the history of political parties, foreign relations, and great political ideas.

While the historical approach had its heyday in the last century, it is still evident today. One hears arguments, for instance, that historians and political scientists use the same methods. In 1938, U.S. political scientist Edward M. Sait wrote that, "The historical approach is indispensable. It affords the only means of appreciating the true nature of institutions and the peculiar way in which they have been fashioned."[2] And in how many colleges does a Department of History *and* Political Science still exist? A variation on the historical approach is used by those political scientists who might be labeled historians of the present. They give detailed descriptions of contemporary political events, in the narrative style of the historian. The results are often called "case studies." The well-done case study's realistic portrayal of politics is no doubt useful. However, Nelson Polsby, Robert Dentler, and Paul Smith have noted its shortcomings. "As more and more case studies are written, readers are overwhelmed by details. Case writers . . . often resist the codification of their findings in any but the most primitive ways, however."[3] Thus, while he gives us much information about a particular political event, the historian of the present usually refuses to generalize, to compare, and to find the common elements in his and other narratives. There are, of course, exceptions. One of the best is Graham Allison's analysis of the Cuban Missile Crisis.[4] It is an exception to the typical case study because it not only describes the missile crisis, but it attempts to explain it by critically examining several alternative models. In this type of study, extensive use is made of generalizations, for the case study is used primarily as a test case for the assumptions of the researcher. But, to repeat, Allison's book is an exception. A good example of the more typical straithforward narrative of the same event is Elie Abel's *The Missile Crisis*.[5]

It seems and has probably always seemed natural to link the study of politics to law or the legal system. This provides the basis for the *legalistic*

---

[2] Edward M. Sait, *Political Institutions: A Preface* (New York: Appleton-Century-Crofts, 1938), p. 529.

[3] Nelson Polsby, Robert Dentler, and Paul Smith, *Politics and Social Life* (Boston: Houghton Mifflin, 1963), p. 4.

[4] Graham Allison, *Essence of Decision: Explaining the Cuban Missile Crisis* (Boston: Little, Brown, 1971).

[5] Elie Abel, *The Missile Crisis* (Philadelphia: J. B. Lippincott, 1966).

approach in U.S. political science, an approach that views political science as primarily the study of constitutions and legal codes. In the previous chapter, we saw the importance of legality in many definitions of politics. At this point, the relationship between the definition and approach becomes clear. If politics, the subject matter of political science, is distinctive because of its legalistic nature, then it is only reasonable that the political scientist should concentrate on the specifically legal aspects of the political system. Some political scientists view the legalistic approach as an improvement over the historical approach because it makes a distinction between the realms of history and political science—the political scientist is now able to tell the historian what the two do *not* have in common. It should also be pointed out that in adopting a legalistic approach, the political scientist is not limited to the study of the legal system per se. Rather, the legal and constitutional aspects of any political institution can be examined. One of the most respected works of this kind is Edward S. Corwin's thorough analysis of the presidency as a *constitutional office*.[6] Thus, the primary data employed are court decisions which interpret the powers of and limitations on the President. However, other political scientists consider the legalistic approach as simply one kind of historical study. The political scientist who assumes the former will study the *history* of constitutions or court decisions. The political scientist then can take a legalistic and an historical approach simultaneously.

A number of factors can be cited to explain this inclination toward legalism in U.S. political science. We will mention two that seem especially important. In the 19th century, most U.S. political scientists received their graduate training in European (usually German) universities. Columbia University began the first successful graduate program of political science in the United States in 1880.[7] The political science professors were members of *law* faculties, which tells us something about their approach to the study of politics. In fact, German political science and political philosophy have always had a legalistic strain. Thus, the returning U.S. political scientists, with their new doctorates, tended to think along the same lines as their European teachers. And, more significantly for contemporary political science, this has remained a tradition in the discipline.

Perhaps an even more important and deep-rooted reason has to do with

---

[6] Edward S. Corwin, *The President: Office and Powers* (New York: New York University Press, 1957).

[7] Albert Somit and Joseph Tannenhaus, *The Development of American Political Science: From Burgess to Behavioralism* (Boston: Allyn & Bacon, 1967), chapter 1.

the U.S. political system and the picture most U.S. citizens seem to have of it. We have been taught that ours is a "government of laws, not of men." While most intelligent citizens realize that it takes men to make, implement, and enforce laws, the doctrine or folkway of the rule of law has always influenced popular political ideology in the United States. And so it no doubt influences the study of politics. What methodological guideline follows more logically from such a political system (or image of a political system) than, "Study the legal system, not the structure of political institutions or the behavior of politicians"?

Consider the legalistic manner in which political crises like the Watergate scandals have been analyzed and discussed. From the time of its initial disclosure, this episode was viewed primarily as a series of legal questions: "What laws were broken?" "Who broke them?" "What legal remedies exist?" While the political implications of Watergate have been widely discussed, its final resolution is still viewed in legal terms. The perceptive French historian Alexis de Tocqueville noted more than a century ago that in the United States there is "hardly a political question which does not sooner or later turn into a judicial one." A convincing argument can be made that this tendency has become even stronger as more and more people take their problems to court and judges adopt the role of final resolver of basic social, economic, and political problems.

Reaction to the historical and legalistic approaches probably stimulated the third traditional school of thought, the *institutional*. As political scientists realized that there was more to politics than legal codes and constitutions, a shift in emphasis took place. There was talk about studying political *realities,* that is, what politics actually is, not just its history or legal manifestations. The most obvious reality of politics is the political institution; legislatures, executives, and courts receive the primary attention of the institutionalist. What we have called *naive empiricism* manifests itself, for the work done is mainly descriptive—detailed descriptions of political institutions, not explanations of the political system, are the goal of the institutionalist. So, for instance, the powers, roles, and functions of the President might be listed and described.[8] One need not look far to discover examples of institutional political science, for many textbooks are institutionally oriented.

---

[8] See, for instance, one of the classic studies of the U.S. presidency, Clinton Rossiter, *The American Presidency* (New York: Harcourt Brace Jovanovich, 1956).

At least one political scientist has questioned this characterization of the institutionalists. Martin Landau argues that labeling these early political scientists "hyperfactualists," that is, scholars who cared only for description and not explanation, is misleading, for they assumed a rudimentary model based on a biological-evolutionary perspective.[9] If this is true, it is of some significance, for such a model would anticipate some of the most important contemporary models of politics, including functionalism and systems theory. Be this as it may, let us not forget that the main interest of the institutionalists was description.

BEHAVIORALISM

The traditional approach gains most of its meaning *as a single orientation* when it is contrasted with the behavioral approach.[10] The latter seems to have begun after World War II as a sort of protest movement by some political scientists against traditional political science. The general claims of the new behavioralist were first, that earlier political science did not measure up as a producer of reliable political knowledge, and many political scientists working in important wartime decision-making positions made this discovery when they had to draw upon existing knowledge of domestic and international politics. But, second, and on a positive note, more reliable knowledge of politics could be achieved through different approaches and methods. This turn in direction was not spontaneous, however. Beginning in the 1930s, there had been an influx of European social scientists in to the United States, and they were often skilled in the use of new research methods. They no doubt had some influence on their U.S. colleagues. At least the Europeans exposed their U.S. colleagues to new ways of analyzing social and political phenomena. Despite the significant contributions of European polit-

---

[9] Martin Landau, "The Myth of Hyperfactualism in the Study of American Politics," *Political Science Quarterly,* 83 (September 1968), p. 378–99.

[10] This section is based upon the following discussions of behavioralism: Robert A. Dahl, "The Behavioral Approach," *American Political Science Review,* 55 (1961), pp. 763–72; David Easton, *A Framework for Political Analysis* (Englewood Cliffs, N.J.: Prentice-Hall, 1965), chapter 1, and "The Current Meaning of 'Behavioralism'," in James C. Charlesworth, ed., *Contemporary Political Analysis* (New York: Free Press, 1967), pp. 11–31; and Somit and Tannenhaus, *Development of American Political Science,* chapter 12.

ical scientists, we must not overlook the solid foundation for the behavioral or new movement in political science, which had been laid by several political scientists in the 1920s. Perhaps the most deserving of credit is Charles Merriam, who, at the University of Chicago, anticipated many post-World War II developments in political science and educated and stimulated some of the most famous contemporary behavioralists.[11] So there is reason to say that many ideas articulated by the behavioralists were not original.

Before proceeding any further, perhaps we ought to say a few words about the label *behavioralism*. Most importantly, its relationship to *psychological behaviorism* should be made clear, for the two are often mistakenly identified. Behaviorism refers to a type of psychology that uses as data only overt stimuli and responses, mainly actions or behavior.[12] Thus, only observable physical phenomena such as pieces of cheese, electric shocks, and behavior like the running of rats can be included in the behaviorists' scientific language. Concepts such as attitudes, opinions, and personality traits, which are mental in nature and not observable actions (leg-kicks or eye-blinks), are rejected as meaningless. To the behavioralist, this approach seems much too restrictive. He does make extensive use of attitudes and similar concepts, attributing them to people based on observed behavior. Attitudes do not, therefore, take on some mysterious existential quality, for they are still tied to experience, and they are still linked to empirical referents. For instance, if a person scores high on a particular attitude scale, we say he is a pacifist (he has a pacific attitude). To the behavioralist, this means that any individual who gives a particular set of responses to a particular set of questions has by definition a particular attitude. The behavioralist shares the behaviorist's desire to keep his work empirical (and the latter has no doubt influenced the former in this regard). However, the behavioralist interprets this characteristic of science more liberally to allow for the use of attitudes and other dispositional concepts.

Up to this point, we have attempted to catch the general mood of behavioralism. Probing for a more precise meaning leads to two interpretations,

---

[11] See Charles E. Merriam, *New Aspects of Politics* (Chicago: University of Chicago Press, 1924).

[12] For a short presentation of behaviorism, see the relevant articles in T. W. Wann, *Behaviorism and Phenomenology* (Chicago: University of Chicago Press, 1964). For the definitive word by behaviorism's most famous modern proponent, see B. F. Skinner, *About Behaviorism* (New York: Vintage Books, 1976).

each based on a characteristic that supposedly improves upon traditional political science. One interpretation emphasizes subject matter or content. According to this view, behavioralism is characterized by its concentration on the *behavior* of political actors, and is to a large extent a rejection of the institutional approach. Let us recall David Easton's plea, asking political scientists to study activity, not institutions. This is a statement of the first interpretation of behavioralism. The behavioralist argues that, although an important aspect of politics, the institution as a thing in itself is not the real stuff of politics. It is the activity within and the behavior around the political institution that should be the main concern of the political scientist. The major portion of the behavioralist's energy is not, for instance, spent in describing the *structure* of the Senate or the *legal duties* of senators but rather in describing and explaining senators' *behavior* and explaining how the Senate as an institution operates—*why* it passes a tax bill but not a civil rights bill. The behavioralist does not completely reject the traditional approaches. He still uses historical data when necessary, he still studies the legal aspects of political systems, he still realizes the importance of institutions. But he always returns to behavior. History consists of human behavior; people make, follow, and break laws; and finally and most importantly, institutions are nothing more than combinations of behavior patterns.

In the broadest sense, both individuals and groups ("group" includes all organizations from the local city commission to the United Automobile Workers to the United States) behave—they act and react, they are stimulated and respond. However, there are two points of view about the respective significance of each level of behavior, and this disagreement is of some importance for behavioralism and political science. First, there are those, and it seems that most behavioralists are of this opinion, who argue that groups are nothing more than their individual members. This position is labeled *individualism*.[13] To say that an interest group is opposed to a particular legislative proposal means that a majority of its members is opposed. The behavior of the Supreme Court is really the individual behaviors of a small number of men. There are no properties of groups that are not reducible to individual properties. Thus, while the individualist does not deny that groups exist, he does deny that they have any independent status, that they are more than the sum of their parts.

---

[13] For a thorough analysis of the individualism-holism controversy, see May Brodbeck, "Methodological Individualism: Definition and Reduction," *Philosophy of Science,* 25 (1958).

Other political scientists argue that there are *emergent* group properties that are not reducible. Thus, groups are more than the sum of their parts. This position, usually labeled *holism,* represents an important tradition in historical and sociological thinking, and has no doubt influenced many political scientists. A holistic political scientist might argue, for instance, that an interest group has certain characteristics, such as cohesion, which none of its members has and that cannot be reduced to or defined in terms of individualistic characteristics. To this the individualist would reply: of course no individual is cohesive in the way that a group is. But the group's cohesiveness can, in principle, be defined or explained by referring to characteristics of and relationships between its members. For instance, cohesion might be defined in terms of the number of other groups a group member belongs to— a group is cohesive when a majority of its members belong to no other interest group.

Most behavioralists take the individualistic position. They stress the significance of individual behavior as the basic building block of political science. This is a turning point in political science. The institutionalist studies structures, powers, and responsibilities; the behavioralist studies attitudes, personalities, and physical activity (voting, lobbying). Behavioralism and individualism go hand in hand. If the characteristic feature of behavioralism is its emphasis on behavior, then the kind of behavior that should be emphasized is that of the individual. We will assume that there is a fairly strong correlation between behavioralism and individualism. But, note that this does not preclude the behavioralist from studying groups or nation-states. Groups and nation-states exist, this no one can deny. It is accounting for the group that leads to the controversy, and the political scientist's own resolution of the controversy will have much to say about how he studies politics.

There is another interpretation of behavioralism which, while closely related to the first, is nevertheless important enough to deserve separate consideration. According to it, behavioralism is equated with the scientific study of politics. This suggests several more specific elements. First is an explicit advocacy of scientific method, which can range from the weak or liberal notion of science (anything systematic and empirical) to the full set of scientific assumptions and principles. In any case, the behavioralist appears to make a distinction between scientific-behavioral and unscientific-traditional political science. Recently, the individualist-holism controversy within political science has become less important as a *philosophical* issue. Interest has shifted from the question, "Can we reduce the group to the individual?" to the development of models that postulate linkages between the micro (individualistic) and the macro (group) levels of politics. In short, political scientists now spend their time on the empirical question, rather than the philosophical issue. We will return to the question of linkages in Chapters 13 and 14, where we examine role theory and group theory. According to this distinction, behavioralism becomes the label applied to the scientific movement in political science. Its objectives are the development of empirical generalizations and systematic theory, and the use of these in the explanation of political phenomena.

There are variations on this interpretation. For instance, to some, many of them nonbehavioralists, behavioralism means counting heads (or votes), using numbers, quantifying. Often used for purposes of derogation (quantification dehumanizes political science; we can quantify only the more trivial feature of politics), this proposed essential characteristic is only one important technique of science. Quantification of data is a significant goal of every science, and no science will develop beyond a fairly primitive level unless it employs quantitative techniques of various sorts. But as we have seen, there are other characteristics of science that are more basic. To the outsider, behavioralism may be defined in terms of quantification, and this is all right as far as it goes; but the behavioralist realizes the more fundamental foundations of his approach.

Finally, there is an assumption about the relationship between political science and the other social sciences that seems to go along with a behavioral state of mind. It expresses the hope that some day the walls which separate the social sciences will crumble. The time spent by political scientists defending their discipline against the onslaughts of outsiders (sociologist are perhaps the most viable) could be more fruitfully spent in doing research, for the battle is a bogus one. While indicating a pragmatic division of labor, the boundaries do not reflect a logically necessary division.[14]

---

[14] For a good analysis of the interrelation between political science and the other social sciences, see the articles in Lipset, *Politics and the Social Sciences* (New York: Oxford University Press, 1969). Lipset's introduction presents a succinct defense of the "unity of social science" position. And for a readable survey of how much political science has borrowed from the other social sciences, see Monte Palmer et al., *The Interdisciplinary Study of Politics* (New York: Harper & Row, 1974).

There is a methodological basis for this position, which is usually labeled "the unity of the social sciences." It states that all social scientists are studying the same thing, the behavior of individuals (or groups of individuals). Political scientists study what is defined as *political* behavior; economists study what is defined as *economic* behavior. It is on this basis that the disciplinary boundaries are drawn. But the data, the basic observations of any social science, are of the same *type*. Thus, the social sciences are, according to the behavioralist, unified because of their common interest in behavior.

Another argument has focused on the policy orientation of social sciences, especially political science. According to this point of view, the social sciences have a common interest in processes through which real-world social, economic, and political problems are solved, that is, the ways in which policies are formulated and carried out.[15]

For the political scientist, this unity of data and method has important consequences. Practically speaking, it means that he can legitimately move from sociological to economic to psychological data in attempting to describe and explain political phenomena. To the antibehavioralist, this lack of disciplinary patriotism is an indication of the dangers of behavioralism. Most serious is a lost appreciation among political scientists for what is truly political.[16] As the boundaries between the social sciences become more blurred, the distinctiveness of political science will become less evident. The title of a book critical of behavioralism tells it all: *Apolitical Politics*.[17] "Archaic" or even "reactionary" would probably be the behavioralists' characterization of this criticism.

Let us now try to bring some order to our discussion of behavioralism. A general conclusion which immediately comes to mind is the lack of a single interpretation of behavioralism. The ambiguity is more apparent than real, however, for the two basic interpretations of behavioralism are complementary. If one interprets behavioralism as the "scientific study of politics,"

---

[15] The first and most thorough study of the social sciences as policy sciences is the collection edited by Daniel Lerner and Harold D. Lasswell, *The Policy Sciences* (Stanford, Calif.: Stanford University Press, 1951).

[16] The most effective recent defense of political science as a distinct field is by Bernard Crick, *In Defense of Politics* (Chicago: University of Chicago Press, 1962).

[17] Charles McCoy and John Playford, eds., *Apolitical Politics* (New York: Thomas Y. Crowell Co., 1967).

then chances are the basic unit of analysis will be individual behavior. More specifically, to advocate the use of scientific method in political science is to assume the existence of, or the possibility of developing, an intersubjective observation language of politics. Recall that intersubjectivity is a basic characteristic of science. If one scientist performs an experiment or proposes a generalization, his findings must be open to the probing of other scientists. This is possible only if there is a basic language referring to observational units that enables all scientists to observe the same events. In political science, behavior seems to be the proper framework for such a language.

So what appears as two interpetations of behavioralism are in fact two aspects of the same approach. The political scientist who advocates the scientific approach to politics (and is therefore a behavioralist in the second sense) will invariably formulate his scientific propositions in a language of behavior. Thus, the behavioral approach comes full circle.

POST-BEHAVIORALISM

Behavioralism has by no means been universally accepted by political scientists. In the mid-1960s, many of the criticisms directed against behavioralism came together to form the basis of a continuing movement to reform political science. Led by a group of predominantly young political scientists it nevertheless received its label, "The Post-Behavioral Revolution" from one of the most highly respected veteran political scientists, David Easton.[18] The revolution's basic premise is that in becoming more scientific, political science has become less relevant. That is, in emphasizing the need to be empirical, to base all statements on observation, and in most cases quantification, the behavioral political scientist has too often focused his attention on trivial questions. The really important topics (such as the causes of war) have received scant attention, while the more easily studied ones (such as voting bchavior) arc overanalyzed.

Post-behavioralists do not advocate an end to the scientific study of politics. In fact, most of them are highly competent in statistics and computer analysis, two of the most visible signs of methodological sophistication.

---

[18] See George Graham and George Carey, eds., *The Post-Behavioral Era* (New York: David McKay, 1972) for a series of articles analyzing this movement.

Instead, they argue for the application of their skills to the solution of crucial social and political problems—in short, to take the policy orientation seriously.

Many of them take it one step further by refusing to accept the fact-value distinction, or at least some of its implications. The upshot is a demand that political scientists make value judgments about government and politics and that the political science profession take public stands on policy issues; for instance, that they go on record as being against such events as the war in Vietnam.[19] After all, who knows more about politics than those who study it professionally? It follows that if anyone makes public recommendations about the basic direction public policies ought to take, it should be the political scientist. It must be noted that we are not referring to instrumental recommendations, that is, suggestions about how to achieve social and economic goals (a more efficient Department of Energy), but the goals (private versus public control of oil, supporting human rights, deciding between more order or more freedom).

This continuing interest in the goals of political systems is linked to the uneasiness with which many contemporary political scientists approach the dominant value relativism of their discipline. Although their minds tell them that noncognitivism is intellectually sound, their hearts keep them searching for a way to justify certain ultimate values—they would like to demonstrate the superiority of the liberal state and the inferiority of authoritarian regimes. This explains the efforts, briefly noted in Chapter 1, to use noncognitivism to justify the tolerant, neutral political system. Dissatisfaction with the moral relativism of behavioralism has led, according to some of the best-known behavioralists, to a revival of normative political philosophy.[20] The best indicator of this is the reaction to the 1971 publication of John Rawls's *A Theory of Justice*.

These efforts at reorientation have always been rejected by a majority of political scientists, suggesting that most still accept the basic assumptions and distinctions discussed in previous chapters. The fact that a significant

---

[19] For a particularly passionate statement of this position, see Lewis Lipsitz, "Vulture, Mantis and Seal: Proposals for Political Scientists," in Graham and Carey, *The Post-Behavioral Era*, pp. 171–91.

[20] Robert Dahl, *Modern Political Analysis*, (Englewood Cliffs, N.J.: Prentice-Hall, 1984), chapter 9. It is interesting to note that Dahl added the chapter on "Political Evaluation" to the 1983 edition of his highly influential book.

minority has asked for a fundamental redefinition of the role of the political scientist, however, is a significant development that must not be forgotten as we continue our discussion of scientific political science. The arguments of the post-behavioralists touch several of the more sensitive nerve endings of political science. Most of them are linked to the question of the role of values in political research and a host of related issues usually subsumed under the heading, "The Ethics of Political Research." They will be attended to in the next chapter. One more point should be made in this chapter. While most political scientists have not arrived at the position of the more radical post-behavioralists, the latter have nevertheless helped push political science along the road to becoming a policy science. As early as 1951, Harold Lasswell was suggesting that political scientists concentrate on questions of policy, "the most important choices made either in organized or in private life."[21] Through the years, the study of policymaking has become an ever more important activity within political science; it could even be argued that today, policy analysis has taken the discipline by storm. The link between post-behavioralism and policy analysis is clear. The student of policy is examining how policies are made within the political system and why certain policies have been pursued. He has clearly developed the concern for real social, political, and economic issues that the post-behavioralist has advocated.

Even more recently, a new criticism of political science has been made. In his 1978 presidential address to the American Political Association, John Wahlke argues that the discipline is still in a prebehavioral stage. That is, despite the behavioral cover, the book of political science is still dominated by nonbehavioral research. Wahlke also suggests that in order to become truly behavioral, "political scientists must apply the basic knowledge about human behavior provided by the behavioral sciences."[22] And beyond this, political scientists must begin to plumb the significant research of the sociobiologists, those who assume that social and political behavior is biologically determined.

In other words, contrary to the perceptions of the post-behavioralists, political science is not in danger of getting bogged down in too much science.

---

[21] Lerner and Lasswell, *The Policy Sciences,* p. 5. A modern treatment of policymaking is James E. Anderson, *Public Policy-Making* (New York: Praeger Publishers, 1975).

[22] John C. Wahlke, "Pre-Behavioralism in Political Science," *American Political Science Review,* 73 (1979), p. 25.

Instead, it must draw more upon the store of knowledge being developed by social scientists in all disciplines.

CONCLUSION

What conclusions can we draw from this survey of the development of political science? It should be clear that the modern discipline of political science has gone through a series of historical stages, each with different orientations and assumptions about how best to study politics. Actually, the different schools of thought that emerged at each stage produced alternate conceptions of what politics is all about.

During the last 30 years, political science has been dominated by behavioralism. In addition to its emphasis on behavior rather than institutions, this orientation has held out the promise of allowing political science to become more scientific. While supported by most contemporary political scientists, behavioralism has had its share of criticism. Some critics claim that it has not produced as much scientific knowledge as promised. Others argue that in its attempt to be scientific, behavioral political science has not always studied the important political questions, and has ignored fundamental normative issues.

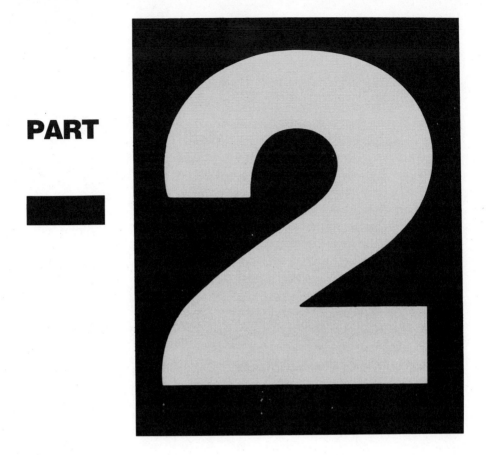

THE SCIENTIFIC STUDY OF POLITICS

Is political science a science?

I N Chapter 2, a short description of science was given. The chapters of Part 2 will develop the main points made earlier. Each of the primary building blocks of science—concept, law, theory, explanation, and prediction—will be analyzed with the special needs of the political scientist in mind. Before beginning this task, however, there is another task that must be attended to. The discussion in Chapter 2 assumed that scientific method is applicable to the study of politics. It was noted, however, in conclusion, that some political scientists question this applicability. Let us critically examine the assumption by analyzing several of the arguments made by those who are skeptical of or in opposition to it.[1] An attempt will be made to point out the shortcomings of each argument, and to provide a sound foundation for the detailed analysis of the science of politics in Chapters 5 through 8. However, before we go any further, the point should be made that some of these arguments have practical significance. That is, while they may not demonstrate that it is impossible to study politics scientifically, they suggest that the road to empirical political knowledge is a rough one; there are

---

[1] For a bitter refutation of the scientific study of politics, see Herbert J. Storing, ed., *Essays on the Scientific Study of Politics* (New York: Holt, Rinehart & Winston, 1962).

obstacles that every political scientist must be aware of. It is with this in mind that we begin our analysis of the antiscience arguments.

ARGUMENTS AGAINST THE POSSIBILITY OF A SCIENCE OF POLITICS

Science or scientific method is characterized by a number of assumptions and principles. They have already been discussed, but let us reacquaint ourselves with them. First, scientists assume some form of determinism or "law of universal causation." Again, this means that the political scientist who accepts scientific method plunges into his work assuming that nothing in politics just happens. The second major characteristic of science is its empirical basis. This implies a number of features, including an observational foundation, intersubjectivity, and the value-free nature of science. The objectives of science are summarized in the third characteristic, its systematic nature. They are to formulate and verify empirical generalizations, develop systematic theory, and finally explain and predict. The arguments against the possibility of a science of politics invariably attempt to demonstrate that political science does not and/or cannot have one or more of these characteristics. This strategy correctly assumes that if political science must have these characteristics to be legitimately labeled "scientific," then such a demonstration, if successful, would illustrate the quicksand upon which the scientific study of politics rests. At that point, the behaviorally or scientifically oriented political scientist would be well-advised to put the brakes on, admit the futility of his activities, and return to more traditional ways of doing things.

The complexity of political phenomena

One argument against the possibility of a science of politics claims that no regularities can be discovered because political phenomena are too complex. Because of a variety of usages, the meaning of "complex" is not clear. However, the basic point seems to be that in politics there are too many variables and possible relationships between them to find any order. In contradistinction, physicists and chemists are able to discover relationships and construct theories because the phenomena that interest them are less complex. This directly attacks the third characteristic of science. If political phenomena are so complex that they cannot be organized into generalizations—that is, if relationships are not discoverable—then there can be no science of politics; that is, there can be no scientific explanations and predictions of political phenomena. Let us turn to the writings of the well-known contemporary political scientist Hans Morgenthau for a statement of this position. After noting the complexity of social phenomena and difficulty involved in isolating causal factors, he concludes: "The social sciences can, at best, do what is their regular task; that is, present a series of hypothetical possibilities, each of which may occur under certain conditions—and which of them will actually occur is anybody's guess."[2]

A reply to this argument should first point out that the degree of complexity of political phenomena is an empirical, not a logical, question. That is, it is debatable whether the social sciences are more complex than the natural sciences, and the debate can only be resolved by systematically examining each science. But it is not even necessary for our purposes to resolve the controversy, since there are no logical grounds for this criticism of scientific political science. From the fact that it is difficult to sort out political factors and measure relationships (research-oriented political scientists need not be reminded of this), one cannot logically conclude that the discovery of generalizations is impossible. Note that the critic is not denying that relationships exist, only that the political scientist can discover them.

This is the logical-methodological answer. But, in addition, several empirical points can be offered to strengthen our case. Philosopher of science Adolf Grunbaum has wondered what someone living before Galileo and holding to the complexity thesis would have thought about the possibility of a science of motion. This observation is perhaps especially relevant in today's rapidly changing world, in which the word *impossible* is used with greater and greater discretion. (Thirty years ago, what would the betting odds be on the landing of men on the moon?) The point is that it is foolish to state on empirical grounds (even assuming that the evidence is sound) that something is logically impossible. In Grunbaum's words, "This argument rests its case on what is not known, and therefore, like all such arguments, it

---

[2] Hans J. Morgenthau, *Scientific Man versus Power Politics* (Chicago: University of Chicago Press, 1946), p. 130.

has no case."[3] Furthermore, we can refer the skeptic to the relationships that have been discovered in the fields of psychology, sociology, economics, and even political science; the discovery of a single law logically refutes the impossibility argument, and, on a positive note, the social sciences are more highly developed than many of their critics care to admit or seem to realize. The neater and apparently less-complex nature of the natural sciences is probably more the result of the laboratory conditions under which most physicists and chemists work, conditions that allow them to control the factors they study, than it is on any inherent lack of explanatory factors.

This argument boils down to the mistaken translation of a practical problem into a logically insurmountable barrier. As we have already implied, every political scientist knows how difficult it is to find order in the world of politics—but this does not prevent him from attempting to discover generalizations. Sometimes he even succeeds. Contrary to the image of science held by many laymen, scientists, whether natural or social, realize that no complete description or explanation of any empirical phenomenon is possible. Something is always left out. Thus, to chastise political science for something that is true even of physics is perhaps unfair. If political scientists are sobered by the practical wisdom implied by the complexity argument, if their rose-colored glasses are shattered, then it has been useful—utopian optimism is out of place in science. But if the reaction is to give up the scientific enterprise, then political science has been dealt a destructive blow.

Human indeterminancy

So much for the complexity thesis. Another argument against the possibility of a science of politics is based upon the so-called indeterminancy of human behavior. Russell Kirk, one of the most vigorous opponents of the scientific study of politics, has put it this way: "Human beings are the least controllable, verifiable, law-obeying and predictable of subjects."[4] Up to a point, this is a version of the complexity argument—one of the reasons for

---

[3] Adolf Grunbaum, "Causality and the Science of Human Behavior," in Herbert Feigl and May Brodbeck, eds., *Readings in the Philosophy of Science* (New York: Appleton-Century-Crofts, 1953), p. 770.

[4] Russell Kirk, "Is Social Science Scientific?" in Nelson W. Polsby, Robert A. Dentler, and Paul A. Smith, eds., *Politics and Social Life* (Boston: Houghton Mifflin, 1963), p. 63.

the complexity of political phenomena is the unpredictable behavior of political actors. The reply is the same. But there is an additional feature that makes the argument a new and probably more uncompromising one. This feature is a belief in freedom of the will. Because humans are free to choose their course of action at any given point in the political process, their actions cannot be classified, and so generalizations describing their behavior cannot be formulated. This argument is more uncompromising than the previous one, because the claim is not that it is extremely difficult to isolate causal factors, but that there are no causal factors in the first place.

As many philosophers have shown, this is a bogus argument. The ability to formulate laws of human behavior and freedom of the will are not incompatible. Those who opt for freedom of the will are usually saying that people are able to act without external restraints. "But would they also claim that what they do is not determined even by the sort of people they are, considered as a whole, individuals possessing a certain disposition, a certain character, certain motives, and so on?"[5] In other words, a free choice need not be uncaused. It is, rather, largely the result of the particular characteristics of the chooser. These characteristics, in turn, are subject to descrption; that is, inclusion in general laws that relate them to other factors. John Hospers neatly summarizes this whole reply when he points out that, "Freedom . . . is the opposite of compulsion, not of causality."[6] The distinction is important, for it allows us to accept scientific determinism while retaining a notion of legal and social responsibility. We are subject to punishment if we "freely" rob a bank; that is, if we are not forced by someone else to do so. It also allows us to exempt some, children for instance, from the laws of responsibility, for in their state of immaturity they are not always aware of the implications of actions. Martin Landau has suggested that the doctrine of free will has such great staying power because it has become a basic moral principle. "It has been sustained and sanctioned to such an extent that in some quarters it is a sin to hold otherwise."[7]

Some critics would now reject the defense just presented with a statement

---

[5] Quentin Gibson, *The Logic of Social Enquiry* (London: Routledge & Kegan Paul, 1960), p. 22.

[6] John Hospers, *An Introduction to Philosophical Analysis* (Englewood Cliffs, N.J.: Prentice-Hall, 1954), p. 271.

[7] Martin Landau, *Political Theory and Political Science* (New York: Macmillan, 1972), p. 27.

of indeterminism—"Not every fact has a cause." Unfortunately for social scientists, most of the uncaused ones are found in the social, economic, and political realms. This position strikes directly at the first assumption of our model of science. Now let us recall that determinism should not be considered an empirical statement about the universe; there is no point in trying to disprove it, for the failure to discover determining conditions does not prove that there are none. This is why it is not empirical—it fails to meet the testability and verifiability criteria. Instead, the thesis of determinism should be "construed as a regulative principle that formulates in a comprehensive way one of the major objectives of positive science, namely, the discovery of the determinants for the occurrence of events."[8] In other words, without some sort of assumption that events have causes, the whole attempt to describe and explain the world of politics might as well be given up. This suggestion is no doubt appealing to some. But why end science at this point? And I say "end" because progress has been made in the social sciences, including political science. For one engaged in the enterprise of understanding political phenomena, the assumption of determinism seems unavoidable. Why, when starting out to gain knowledge should one want to limit himself before he begins? Perhaps political science will never produce the kind of knowledge that characterizes physics and chemistry, but it is worth the try, and something is better than nothing. We can't tell what we can't do until we try to do it.

The reaction problem

It is often argued that even if people are not completely indeterminate, they have another characteristic that makes it impossible to systematically analyze and predict their political behavior. Much research in political science is based on the reactions of those being studied. What readily comes to mind is the survey research technique in which human subjects are questioned to elicit responses that will describe their opinions, attitudes, or general states of mind. This kind of research depends upon the reactions of the subjects. It appears to be an effective way to find out certain things about

---

[8] Ernest Nagel, *The Structure of Science* (New York: Harcourt Brace Jovanovich, 1961), p. 605.

people. But some critics of scientific political science point out that since the subjects are aware of the fact that they are being studied, their responses cannot be taken as valid indicators of their opinions. How many attempt to please the interviewer with their answers? How many try to offend? How many try to see through the questions to figure out what the interviewer is after? The point in each case is that the political scientist cannot be sure that he is obtaining accurate measures of the factors he is studying. As long as people know they are being studied, there is a good chance that they will adjust their behavior.

The problem of human reaction is not limited to survey research. There are research methods that place the political scientist in real-world political situations so that he can observe political behavior up close. Typical studies of this sort have been conducted in government bureaucracies, labor unions, and political conventions. For decades, anthropologists have known about and employed this technique and have given it a name: *participant observation*. Many readers have become familiar with this technique through the books of anthropologists like Margaret Mead and Ruth Benedict, who spent considerable time living in other cultures as participating members. The objective of participant observation is not only to observe behavior first-hand but to get a feel for the culture by actually being part of it. The problem is that in being aware of their role as objects of research, those being studied may change their behavior.[9]

Thus, the issue of human reaction boils down to the introduction of another factor, the researcher into the research situation. That the reaction of subjects is a real problem was clearly demonstrated in a study of worker motivation carried out in the Hawthorne, Illinois Western Electric plant during the late 1920s. Asked to discover ways to increase worker productivity, the team of psychologists discovered accidentally that not only did an increase in lighting increase productivity, but a decrease in lighting had the same effect. The conclusion was that the workers were not responding to the level of lighting or other changes in working conditions so much as to the fact that they were being studied, that someone was paying attention to

---

[9] Participant observation should not be confused with the memoirs of decision makers who have left office. Such writings are legion, and while an important source of data for historians and political scientists, they must be placed in the category of personal recollections rather than systematic research.

them. Thus was born the "Hawthorne Effect."[10] In the light of claims that this is a problem peculiar to the study of human behavior, it is instructive to note comments made by the great animal psychologist, Pavlov. In discussing the actions of researchers, Pavlov once wrote, "His slightest movements— blinking of the eyelids or movement of the eyes, posture, respiration, and so on—all acted as stimuli which, falling upon the dog, were sufficient to vitiate the experiments by making exact interpretations of the results extremely difficult."[11]

What we have here is a practical research problem, not an insurmountable methodological barrier. When the subjects of research are aware that they are being observed, they sometimes behave out of character. However, within certain limits, the extent to which this is occurring can be determined. When conducting survey research, the same attitudes can be measured by using several slightly different questions scattered throughout the question- naire. Each can be used as a cross-check aginst the others. The lesson is that one should always attempt to find several sources of data to test a hypothe- sis. The greater the correspondence among the different types of evidence, the more confidence the political scientist can place in his conclusions.

The same basic rule applies to participant observation. No matter how extensive, such observations are at best suggestive—not conclusive. In con- junction with other methods, they can prove useful. There are many types of research that do not depend upon human reaction. The examination of docu- ments and other historical records falls into this category. This type of research, which constitutes a significant portion of all political research, is not subject to the kinds of problems we have been considering.

The influence of values

Another argument against the possibility of a science of politics questions its presumed value-free nature. Here is the main difference between the natural and social sciences; practitioners of the former do not have to deal

---

[10] F. J. Roethlisberger and W. J. Dickson, *Management and the Worker* (Cambridge, Mass.: Harvard University Press, 1939).

[11] Ivan Petrovich Pavlov, in Michael Kaplan, ed., *Essential Works of Pavlov* (New York: Bantam Books, 1966), p. 108–9.

with values—protons and molecules are neither good nor bad—but social scientists do, because people are moral beings and thus social scientists are irretrievably immersed in value questions. This is especially true of political science, for several reasons. First, political science is a policy science. Politics is mainly concerned with goals and the means to achieve them—policies. Politics involves policies and policies involve values.

A second reason is the importance of value concepts—attitudes, opinions, and ideologies—to political science. No political scientist denies that values hold a significant place in his discipline. Much of politics involves the value commitments of political actors, and so political scientists must study values. The first claim of the antiscientist is, however, that because political scientists study values, they must be influenced by them. It would seem that no lengthy argument is required to demonstrate the weakness of this claim. There is a logical difference between having one's own values and studying attitudes and opinions. The latter can be treated in the same manner as any other political phenomena. They are just as susceptible to scientific treatment (for instance the tremendous progress that has been made in the analysis of opinions and attitudes). To admit this, the political scientist does not have to deny that he has values—this is patently foolish.

Looking at the other value aspect of political science, its link to policy-making, to say that we are interested in policies is not to claim that we are formulating basic values or goals for a society. The political scientist may do this, but not legitimately as a political scientist. While playing his professional role, he can only give instrumental value judgments, answers to means-not ends of questions. This is what a policy science is all about. Given the objective of preventing urban riots, the political scientist's task is to demonstrate how the goal can be achieved. This becomes an empirical question—the normative aspect (urban riots should be prevented) is no longer the concern (as an ultimate value) of the political scientist (although it may deeply concern the man).

However, the antiscientist might accept this analysis and then point out that because the political scientist is also a value-holding person, he cannot prevent his own values from influencing his professional research. Thus, every study and approach in political science is value-influenced. This is the heart of the matter. To quote Russell Kirk again, "Although the complete behaviorist may deny the existence of 'value-judgments' and normative understandings, nevertheless he does not escape, in his researches, the influence of his own value-judgments."[12]

What we are faced with here is a half-truth. That values influence research is undeniably true; but this influence is not inevitable.[13] Furthermore, there are ways to tell when values are distorting supposedly objective work. After all, when someone like Kirk argues that values exert an influence he must believe that there is a way to uncover this influence. Otherwise, how else could he make the claim? Every social scientist knows how difficult it is to prevent his values from intruding. But he does not have to throw up his hands; scientific method enables us to sort out what is *fact* and what is *value*. If the principle of intersubjectivity is followed by observant and critical scientists, then few biased propositions in political science will indefinitely exist.

A common rebuttal is that even if one admits the possibility of purging the content of political research of its value-biasedness, the fact remains that the political scientist must make other kinds of value judgments that inevitably affect his objectivity. First of all, when he decides to use scientific method, he is making a value judgment—he could just as well choose not to use it. There are several replies to this confusing position. One will be discussed in a moment because it is significant in its own right. We need say here only that one does not select a way of studying politics the way he does a new automobile—either one is as good as another or it is all a matter of personal taste and cost. Scientific method is a label applied to a set of assumptions and principles that those studying the world have formulated, developed, and accepted as the best foundation for their work. Scientists do not arbitrarily impose science upon a society. Thus, while a political scientist might "choose" the scientific approach, it is really not the same kind of choice as, "Democracy is the best form of government."

A second kind of value judgment that occurs before the research is done has to do with the selection of research topics. No one denies that political scientists choose to study the causes of urban riots, for instance, because the

---

[12] Kirk, "Is Social Science Scientific?" p. 63.

[13] For a discussion of ways of sorting out one's values, see William E. Connolly, "Theoretical Self-Conscious," in William E. Connolly and Glen Gordon, eds., *Social Structure and Political Theory* (Lexington, Mass.: D. C. Heath, 1974), p. 40–66.

problem interests them or because they think that the black ghetto is dys-functional or evil. But the results of their work need not be biased by their values. Once they plunge into their research, the original value choice is methodologically irrelevant. The claim that ghetto living conditions lead to urban riots can be tested intersubjectively. Until it is, it should be considered an hypothesis—a guess, educated or otherwise, about a relationship be-tween two factors. It is difficult to understand why the selection of a re-search topic *has* to bias the results of research. Political scientists might, because of their value commitments, ignore certain factors or data so that their conclusions and values agree. But here again we see the significance of scientific method; this kind of biased research will not survive the criticism of colleagues. This argument really ties in with the one we just considered, which emphasizes political science's interest in policy questions. Whether beginning with a society's government's, or individual political scientist's attempt to solve a particular social or political problem, there is no doubt that much political science research begins with a normative commitment. This refers both to the President, who wants to decrease the incidence of urban disturbances because they threaten the existing political system,[14] and to the political scientist, who studies racism because he believes it is morally wrong.

We can conclude from this sampling of arguments that there are no valid arguments demonstrating the impossibility of a science of politics, and that many of them are useful if they make manifest to the political scientist some of the difficulties of his discipline. For instance, while the complexity of political phenomena is no *logical* barrier, it creates serious problems. The same can be said of values and free will. In criticizing arguments against the possibility of a science of politics, we are not taking a complacent attitude toward the many problems facing political science. There is no full-blown science of politics just around the corner. As we have already said, utopian optimism is out of place in any science. The crucial point is that a science of politics is possible, and any attempt to end the pursuit of political knowledge at this point is premature and unreasonable.

---

[14] Two studies resulting from such motivations are *The Report of the National Advisory Commission on Civil Disorders* (New York: E. P. Dutton & Co., 1968); and *The Walker Report to the National Commission on the Causes and Prevention of Violence* (New York: New American Library, 1968).

ETHICS AND SCIENTIFIC POLITICAL RESEARCH

There are a number of commentators who while accepting the possibility of studying politics scientifically, nevertheless argue for ethical reasons against its advisability. It should be clear from the discussion in Chapter 1 that most political scientists would reject the notion that it is possible to formulate a set of ultimate ethical principles. However, each profession establishes modes of acceptable conduct for its members, either overtly through formal guidelines or unintentionally as a result of typical patterns of behavior.[15] The main point is that these standards are logically independent of those used to evaluate scientific rigor. In other words, it is perfectly possible that a particular technique considered methodologically sound will not measure up ethically. Is it proper for a political scientist studying decision making in the White House to find and cultivate an inside informer? Is it ethical for a political scientist to infiltrate a radical political organization, participate as a regular member and unbeknownst to its members keep a systematic record of their activities?[16] What about a student of public attitudes who deceives his subjects to elicit completely open responses from them?

While apparently scientifically appropriate, each case raises the question: Should the subjects of political resrach always be made aware that they are being studied? We have already dealt with the problem of human reaction. If the subjects of research are unaware of their status as subjects, perhaps the methodological problem is solved. But are the human rights of the subjects violated in the process?

Lest someone think that our examples are hypothetical, it should be pointed out that similar real-world cases are not unusual. One of the most famous and far-reaching cases in its political implications involved the placement of tape recorders in a jury room, without the knowledge of the jurors,

---

[15] See the discussion of codes for political scientists in "Ethical Problems of Academic Political Scientists," *P.S.,* (Summer 1968) pp. 3–28. For a thorough discussion of a number of ethical issues pertaining to political science, see Amy Gutmann and Dennis Thompson eds., *Ethics and Politics* (Chicago: Nelson-Hall, 1984).

[16] For the use of such a technique, see Scott McNall, "The Career of the Radical Rightest," in Scott McNall, ed., *The Sociological Perspective* (Boston: Little, Brown, 1974), pp. 392–406.

as a part of a large-scale study of the American jury system.[17] The researchers and consulting lawyers wanted to test a number of hypotheses about how jurors behave and what factors affect their decisions. They concluded that interviewing the jurors would lead to the aforementioned reaction problem. Thus, a method for obtaining data which does not involve this limitation was developed and approved by a federal district court judge; it included the use of tape recorders. After a year of data collection without incident, reports of the project began to filter into the public domain, and there was a great hue and cry against it. Congressional hearings and investigations were held during which it was charged that the study was actually another example of the Communist strategy of infiltration and subversion. The result of all this was an act of Congress making it a federal crime to record federal jury deliberations.

Whether political scientists like it or not, political research is often evaluated not only methodologically but also ethically and politically. Scientifically legitimate research may be impossible if it violates cultural norms of the society. While there is, as one might expect, a great deal of controversy over what is and what is not acceptable, there seem to be several criteria that all accept. The most obvious and important universal principle is that research should be neither physically nor psychologically harmful to human subjects. Government agencies and unviersities have established guidelines that those engaged in resarch are expected to follow. Even though this area is the least controversial, there is still no universally accepted set of boundaries that indicate how far a researcher can go in obtaining data necessary for resarch.

There are ethical concerns that involve stages of the research process other than the collection of data. These deal with such questions as, "Who is sponsoring the research?" and "What, if any, are the social and political objectives of the sponsor?" For the political scientist, the first question gets at the special relationship between government and political science, a relationship that takes on real significance since so much political research is funded by government agencies. Can political scientists be scientific when their research is being supported by political decision makers who might be

---

[17] Ted Vaughn, "Governmental Intervention in Social Research: Political and Ethical Dimensions in the Wichita Jury Recordings," Gideon Sjoberg, eds., *Ethics, Politics and Social Research* (Cambridge, Mass.: Schenkman, 1967), pp. 50–77.

affected by the findings of the research or who might wish to use the research for political purposes?

The most famous case in point is Project Camelot, a massive endeavor initiated in 1964 by the United States Department of Defense to discover the causes of social and poltical turmoil in developing nations.[18] On the surface, it appeared to be a legitimate, perhaps even highly significant research project and many social scientists joined the team. However, after several months of preliminary work, many of them reached the conclusion that the ultimate purpose of the project was to provide the Department of Defense with the basic information needed to develop successful counterinsurgency strategies in such hot spots as Chile. In short, the feeling grew that the scientific community was being used by the government. This resulted in great opposition from the community and an attempt by the State Department, then engaged in a power struggle with the Department of Defense, to abort the whole project. With the affair proving more and more embarrassing, President Johnson ended Project Camelot only seven months after its inception. Most involved probably uttered a sigh of relief, but not before a new type of criticism was made. Ironically, the same social scientific community, which several months before had questioned the motives of the government in developing the research, now condemned Washington for summarily ending it. The charge was censorship. The termination had occurred not because the resarch was methodologically unsound or ethically questionable, but because it was embarrassing the United States in the international political arena. Let us quote a leading critic of Project Camelot, the sociologist Irving L. Horowitz.

> In conclusion, two important points must be clearly kept in mind and clearly apart. First, Project Camelot was intellectually, and from my own perspective, ideologically unsound. However, and more significantly, Camelot was not cancelled because of its faulty intellectual approaches. Instead, its cancellation came as an act of government censorship, and an expression of contempt for social science so prevalent among those who need it most. Thus it was political expedience, rather than its lack of scientific merit, that led to the demise of Camelot because it threatened to rock State Department relations with Latin America.[19]

---

[18] The best description of the whole affair is Irving Louis Horowitz, "The Life and Death of Project Camelot," in Norman K. Denzin, ed., *The Values of Social Science* (Chicago: Transaction Books, 1970), pp. 159–84.

[19] Ibid., p. 183.

Project Camelot demonstrates that ethical and political problems often come together. The political scientist is faced not only with the great ethical questions common to all social sciences, but a whole host of political problems resulting from the special subject matter of political science as well. Political science and government interface, that is, they have many points of contact. In light of this relationship, what should be the role of the political scientist? Should it be only to study politics or to use one's special knowlege to work for or against political change? It now becomes obvious that we are back to the basic point raised by the post-behavioralists. It is not merely an academic point, for not only do political scientists receive resrach support from government, but they also serve as advisers to decision makers and they become decision makers themselves.

ALTERNATIVE ROUTES TO POLITICAL KNOWLEDGE

Not all political scientists who reject the viability of *scientific* political knowledge reject the possibility of political knowledge. Some claim that scientific method provides one route to knowledge, but there are other routes, such as metaphysics, theology, and intuition. The scientist is usually characterized as a sort of scholarly bigot, applying the seal of approval only to facts ground out of his own rigid set of rules, which he labels *scientific* method. This, however, is an unfair criticism and it fails to understand what science is all about.

The scientist does not deny that theological, metaphysical, or intuitive knowledge exists. He only claims that none of these is knowledge *about the world*. There is no way to verify a theological or intuitive explanation of an empirical event. Thus, the scientist does not have to be arrogant about the knowledge he produces or might produce. All he has to say is, "If man can ever know the world, it must be through the application of scientific method." He might then argue that science is not a conspiracy to impose a particular approach or methodology on the study of politics (or anything else). Scientific method develops as scientists do scientific work. It is the basic set of principles that have been formulated and refined to describe and explain the world of observation and experience. The logic or foundation of this activity is the concern of philosophers of science (including us). But neither the scientist nor the philosopher of science arbitrarily creates this foundation. Given the objectives of accurately describing and soundly explaining the world (of politics for instance), certain principles seem to follow—they are necessary to do the job. It is interesting to note that even he who advocates a nonempirical approach, such as theology, to analyze the world, usually begins making observations about the world and using them as evidence. At this point, whether he realizes it or not, he is using the same methods as the scientist. The point is that science is not imposed upon society by scientists. Rather, it is a more sophisticated version of the methods we all use to cope with the world in our day-to-day lives.

But why bother with the difficult and often frustrating enterprise of science if it is really nothing more than common sense with luxuries added? Is the scientist perpetrating a fraud, going through the motions and accepting credit that he doesn't deserve? Another kind of attack on a science of politics questions the superiority of scientific over commonsensical knowledge and claims that pursuing scientific method is a waste of time. How many of us have heard someone comment after reading a report of political research, "We knew this already"? Philosopher of science Ernest Nagel has given us a number of answers to this significant charge.[20] We will here only summarize and reinterpret them so as to make them relevant to students of politics. We will examine several reasons why scientific knowledge is superior to commonsensical knowledge and why, therefore, an attempt to create a science of politics is a worthwhile undertaking.

An initial shortcoming of common sense is its tendency to accept presumed facts without question, as a matter of faith. Propositions such as, "All politicians are corrupt," become part of the folk wisdom of American politics and are either never explained or explained improperly. If we accept a fact simply because it is obvious, reasonable, or self-evident, we may never be aware of the underlying conditions that account for it. The same can be said of the superficial explanations that often pass as scientific. For instance, several commonsensical propositions, which are accepted by many as sound historical explanations, claim that economic depressions are caused by Republican administrations and a Democratic administration will always be followed by war. First, their truth can be questioned. But assuming that there is a correlation between political parties and economics of war,

---

[20] Nagel, *The Structure of Science,* chapter 1. Also see Karl W. Deutsch, "The Limits of Common Sense," in Polsby, Dentler, and Smith, *Politics and Social Life,* pp. 51–58.

accepting such a commonsensical fact as an explanation of a historical or societal trend might be incorrect. The point is, commonsensically, we will never know—scientifically, we might find out. Perhaps the correlation is spurious, to speak statistically. It might be purely coincidental that the election of a Democratic President usually precedes a war; or the relationships may be deeper and more complex. Scientific method, with its stress on empiricism, intersubjectivity, and systematic generalizations, can probably be employed to sort out some of the more basic factors that common sense does not perceive. Once again it must be emphasized that scientific method is not a philosopher's stone, capable of providing ready answers to every question. Nor is common sense being rejected out of hand. In our day-to-day lives, there is usually no other basis for decisions. We are, instead, taking a more modest position which claims that the application of scientific method to problems of political analysis uncovers many of the mistakes and inconsistencies of commonsense knowledge and therefore leads to a more reliable brand of knowledge than its more primitive ancestor.

These shortcomings of commonsensical knowledge lead to several practical problems for those attempting to use it for purposes of explanation and prediction. First, although commonsensical knowledge may be true to a point, because it isn't explained its limits are seldom realized. A user of scientific method, on the other hand, knows approximately how far he can go in applying the knowledge he discovers, because in sorting out explanatory factors, he has become aware of its limits. Suppose we explain the relatively low rate of voting turnout in the United States on the basis of a widespread apathy, which is interpreted as an expression of basic satisfaction with the political system. This makes sense, so we accept it as commonsensically true. But suppose that as a matter of fact it is applicable only to certain segments of the population, the white middle class for instance. Other segments—blacks, the poor, and the isolated—don't vote because they feel alienated from society. Their behavior has nothing to do with satisfaction; on the contrary, much dissatisfaction goes along with alienation. The scientific study of voting behavior would be more likely to discover these facts than common sense. Therefore, the scientist would be less likely to overapply his explanation. He would know the basic difference between middle-class and lower-class nonvoting, a difference that the advocate of common sense would be more likely to miss. The relevance of this analysis for practical policymaking is clear.

Another serious problem that commonsense knowledge must face is its deficiency in accounting for political change. If explanatory factors are unknown, then if conditions change, especially the less obvious ones (which usually means the more important ones), a realization of inadequacy possibly leading to disillusionment might be the result for an advocate of commonsense knowledge. But if a sound scientific explanation has been given, and if we are aware of the implications of changing conditions, we will have a much better chance of anticipating the change. For instance, taking another oversimplified hypothetical case, let us assume that it is a commonsensical truth that urban disturbances occur primarily because of an increasing disrespect for law and order. However, if the primary conditions for such disturbances are urban living conditions (the ghetto, unemployment, and so forth), then if such conditions become worse, the commonsense explanation will not be able to explain and predict the increase in riots and demonstrations and thus to point out what steps ought to be taken to prevent them. Once again, common sense, in most cases, is not so much wrong as incomplete and superficial.

But isn't common sense sometimes correct—is a common reply? Correct, perhaps; substantiated, no. This is the gist of these last few pages. Knowledge is not knowledge until it has been substantiated, using the procedures that have been labeled *scientific method*. While we might say, ''I knew that all the time,'' we didn't know it—we sensed it, we intuited, we believed it.

On the other hand, common sense is useful as a source of hypotheses— relationships to be tested. No productive scientist can ignore the world of his own psychic experiences; it might not be a totally reliable world, but because he is human, it is his starting point. Several pages ago we referred to the acceptance of widespread political corruption in America as commonsensical folk wisdom. While not necessarily proof that such wisdom is generally true, the experiences of Watergate should provide an imaginative political scientist with some potentially fruitful leads. It is often said that a poet experiences and sees the same things as the average man except that he sees them differently. The same could be said of the scientist. The great scientist is great not because he knows more about scientific method; all competent ones have that knowledge. He is great because of imagination, insight, and the ability to draw implications from what he observes. But every imaginative insight must be subjected to the test of intersubjectivity. It is at this point that scientific method becomes relevant. This is what distinguishes the insights of the scientist from those of the poet.

In conclusion, let us make several points. First, while science begins with commonsense *observation,* scientific knowledge is not equivalent to commonsensical knowledge. Second, while the accumulated wisdom of common sense is sometimes duplicated by scientific procedures, it does not follow that science is a waste of time. Nothing is obvious until it has been empirically and systematically substantiated. This is not to deny that at times political science devotes its resources to the more easily studied at the expense of the perhaps more significant and harder to find phenomena. But, finally, let us note that political science discovers things that are unknown by and even in violation of common sense.

CONCLUSION: THE SCIENTIFIC STATUS OF POLITICAL SCIENCE

This chapter has attempted to show that the best route to solid knowledge of politics is through the use of scientific method. There are a number of obstacles that make the journey a difficult one, but none are insurmountable. At the same time, we should recognize that although useful in the accumulation of knowledge, alternate routes such as common sense are not substitutes for scientific analysis.

We are now ready for the systematic examination of the basic tools of scientific analysis—concepts, generalizations, and theories—and the way they are used to carry out the basic functions of science—description, explanation, and prediction.

Scientific concept formation in political science

ASSUMING that the study of politics can to some extent follow the basic principles of scientific method and that this is desirable (the last chapter attempted to demonstrate the validity of both assumptions), the question becomes, "How do we construct a science of politics?" Chapter 5 begins a detailed discussion of the building blocks of scientific political inquiry. They will be analyzed as stages in the scientific process, beginning with the formation of *concepts,* then the formulation of *generalizations* (relationships between concepts), the construction of *theories* (interrelated sets of generalizations), and finally the primary objective of science, the use of laws and theories to *explain* and *predict* political phenomena.

We will adopt a straightforward, step-by-step approach. This is not to say that the nature and logic of scientific political inquiry is an easy subject; only that the discussion of science can be organized around a compact set of notions. There are other notions that are significant, and many of these will be discussed as they become relevant, for they are in every case directly related to one of the basic notions—for instance, the relationship between generalizations and causality. Uppermost in our mind, though, is the clearness, coherence, and overall usefulness of the next four chapters. This is not a complete survey of the philosophy of science—such an attempt would be a perfect example of social scientific overkill—but it is an analysis of scientific method for students of politics. Some topics in the more general field of philosophy of science can be deemphasized. The objective here is to provide a foundation for further work and reading in *political science*.

Science begins by forming concepts to describe the world. While we have referred several times to the importance of explanation, it should be realized that whatever is explained must first be described—*what* questions are logically prior to *why* questions, and the former are answered within a framework of concepts that characterize, classify, order, compare, and quantify worldly phenomena. It is the concept that serves as science's empirical base. Although it is usually the elaborate and awe-inspiring scientific theory that attracts the attention and stimulates the interest of the layman, it is the unsung concept that supports the whole scientific enterprise. A science will never progress if it does not move beyond the concept-formation stage, yet no science can begin without such activity.

CONCEPTS AND LANGUAGE

Description requires language, a language that includes descriptive words. Let us continue our discussion by placing the concept in the context of language. There are several kinds of words and a number of ways to classify them. Perhaps the simplest and most useful method classifies all words as either *logical* or *descriptive*.[1] A logical or *structure* word, as it is sometimes called, such as *and,* does not refer to anything. There is nothing in the world that serves as the empirical referent of *and.* Rather, logical words act as connectives between descriptive words; thus the alternate label "structure"—the scientific language is structured, shaped, given its outline by its logical words. Examples, besides *and,* are *all, some, none,* and *or.* We might also want to include the terms of mathematics, although they can be derived from the basic set of words just mentioned. But the purpose is not to memorize a list of words labeled logical—any competent logic text provides such a list—but to understand what a logical word is.

But more than this, we want to know something about descriptive words.

---

[1] Gustav Bergmann, *Philosophy of Science* (Madison: University of Wisconsin Press, 1957), pp. 12–24.

Unlike logical words, they refer to or name something. *Chair, hard,* and *power* are descriptive words because they refer directly or indirectly to observables. This is why they are descriptive. To say that something is a chair is in a sense to describe it. A simple concept such as chair presents fewer problems than a more complex one such as power—a chair is an assemblage of a small number of directly observable parts, while power is only indirectly observable. Yet, in both cases something about the world of observation comes to mind when they are mentioned. We see a chair, or we see power being exercised. We call some things chairs and we label some politicians powerful. But we don't see "and" or "all."

There is another kind of descriptive word. It does not refer to a class of observable things such as chair or man, but instead to a particular example of something: "the brown chair in my office," or "George Washington." This kind of descriptive word is called, in the first case, a definite description; in the second, a proper name. In either case, something is being described, but the something is specific and uniquely identifiable. The picture that enters our mind when "man" is mentioned is not the same as the one that is produced by "George Washington" (unless the latter is our ideal of manhood).

There are two kinds of descriptive words, one referring to classes of things—all things having certain characteristics; the other to particular things—one man out of the class of all men. The first kind of descriptive word might be called a *universal;* the second, a *particular*. It should be clear by now that we are interested in the first, the universal descriptive word or *concept*. This is not to say that particular descriptive words are unimportant. The most common method of testing an hypothesis is to examine a number of particular instances or examples. In studying the modern presidency, we would have to examine the behavior of Presidents Kennedy, Johnson, Nixon, Ford, Carter, and Reagan. In trying to describe the attitude of the U.S. public toward the Supreme Court, we would question a number of *specific* U.S. citizens. Thus, the raw data, which is the source of all empirical propositions and theories, is made up of large numbers of individual cases or instances. However, a collection of particulars by itself tells us nothing. We need something that enables us to sort out the particulars, to classify them. At that point, the significance of concepts becomes evident.

Concepts, or character words, are the stuff of science. While the set of logical words structures a science—and their importance cannot be exaggerated—concepts manifest its content. Furthermore, while logical words are given to the scientist, so to speak, concepts have to be formulated. The scientist has to struggle with the task of developing a set of concepts that can describe the range of phenomena that interest him. This is why so much emphasis is placed upon concept formation. The political scientist ought to be especially aware of this. Nothing holds up the development of a newly developing science so much as an outmoded, inapplicable, and ambiguous set of concepts.

THE INTRODUCTION OF CONCEPTS

It is one thing to demonstrate the importance of concepts. It is another to describe how they are introduced into a scientific language. How they are introduced determines to a large extent their usefulness. There is a rather obvious answer to the question: concepts are defined, they are given meanings, and in this way they enter our scientific language. This is generally true. However, for several reasons, it is not enough to say that concepts are defined. First, there are two interpretations of definition and only one is acceptable within the framework of scientific method. Second, given this scientifically acceptable notion of definition, there are still several ways to define concepts. Let us examine each of these points in greater detail.

The question, "But what does it *really* mean?" is a fairly common one in everyday conversation.[2] It assumes that every descriptive word has an essential meaning that will become evident if we only dig deeply enough. Everyday conversation, however, is not the only context in which we find evidence of this interpretation. There is a strong and articulate philosophical tradition that argues in favor of *real* definitions. As early as Plato's *Republic* we find attempts to discover the essential characteristics of a particular concept, in Plato's case, "justice." A concept's meaning is not assigned; rather its essential nature is discovered. When applied to science, this interpretation of definition creates a problem. Time is spent searching for the true essences of concepts rather than empirical relationships between concepts.

---

[2] The discussion of this section is based primarily on Carl G. Hempel, *Fundamentals of Concept Formation in Empirical Science* (Chicago: University of Chicago Press, 1952). Also see Dickenson, McGaw, and George Watson, *Political and Social Inquiry* (New York: John Wiley & Sons, 1976), chapters 5 and 6.

The scientist does not have to face this problem when he adopts the other interpretation of definition, usually called the *nominal*. According to it, in defining power we say that from now on, when phenomena *X, Y,* and *Z* occur, power exists—we are naming that particular set of phenomena power. The same analysis holds true in regard to the definition of the concept *chair*. "Chair" is simply the word or linguistic expression we assign to a physical object with certain specified characteristics. There is a difference between the concept *chair* and the label or name "chair" we assign to it. A nominal definition is neither true nor false. You may have your own definition of "power," and I cannot reject it on the grounds that "it is not what 'power' really means," because "power" has no real meaning. The set of characteristics which have been so labeled can be clearly described and, it would be hoped, related to other concepts, but political science will never discover its true essence. I might, however, point out that my definition is sounder or more useful than yours for reasons that we will discuss later in this chapter. In other words, all concepts are not of equal scientific value, although none are more real than others. The point is that in science we deal only with nominal definitions. Science has no place for *real* meanings and *essential* characteristics. Concepts are used to describe the world as we observe it, and so the very notion of essentiality is foreign to science. A nominal definition then takes the form: "power" (the name of the concept) = characteristics *X, Y,* and *Z*. In effect, real and nominal definitions start from different directions. The former begins with a word and tries to reveal its essential nature. In the case of a nominal definition, on the other hand, a configuration of empirical characteristics is observed and described, or postulated and assigned a label.

Having discussed the general nature of definition, let us now analyze the several methods available for defining concepts—that is, the several ways of introducing concepts into our specific political language. To begin with, we are directly acquainted with some concepts. It is easy for us to define "chair" because its characteristics are directly observable. Putting it another way, the concept that we have labeled "chair" is directly tied to physical objects having a particular set of properties with which we are all familiar. It is probably fair to say that we are directly acquainted with many of the concepts used in everyday conversation. However, as we move beyond common usage and into scientific discourse, the concepts with which we are directly acquainted become less common.

Operational definition

As our science develops, it becomes necessary to think about other methods of definition. If we want to describe and explain the wide range of phenomena that are relevant to political science, then we cannot rely simply upon those concepts with which we are directly acquainted. Some political concepts, such as "Australian ballot" and "single-minded district," are related directly to observables and so can be defined according to the first method. But what of the concepts that give politics so much of its scope and depth, concepts like "conservative," "group cohesion," and "power"? Do we ever observe them directly? The answer is no. We define power by means of observable phenomena or behavior, but the concept does not correspond to a directly observable entity. Such concepts are said to be *operationally* or *dispositionally* defined.

There is a substantial body of philosophical literature on the nature and problems of operational and dispositional defintions, but there is no need for us to become deeply immersed in it. All we want to do is gain a basic understanding of what is involved in defining a concept operationally. The notion of operational definition was controversial at one time, and there are still scientists and philosophers who resent the slogan, "We must operationalize." But today, the controversy seems at an end. The operational definition is an accepted, indispensable piece of scientific hardware. This is due in part to the more realistic analyses of operational and dispositional concepts produced in recent years.[3] Instead of being a panacea for all problems of scientific concept formation, operationalism is now viewed as one basic method for introducing concepts into a scientific language. More generally, it refers to the attempt by all scientists to link their concepts to observational properties. To a large extent, operationalism is nothing more than a more flexible approach to empiricism. Everything still comes back to what is observable, but now we can indirectly *infer* concepts from directly observable properties. We are not directly acquainted with power or conservatism, but it makes sense to say that someone has power or is conservative. Let us see what this means by giving several examples.

---

[3] See, for instance, the articles contained in Chapter 2 of Phillip G. Frank, *The Validation of Scientific Theories* (New York: Collier Books, 1961). For a briefer and perhaps more readable example, see Walter Wallace, *The Logic of Science in Sociology* (Chicago: Aldine-Atherton, 1971), chapter 3.

A classic case of operational definition from the natural sciences is the definition of solubility. The chemist might say that a substance such as salt is water soluble if, when placed in water, it dissolves. The structure of this kind of definition is straightforward enough. If we perform an operation *(O)* on something, and a particular result *(R)* takes place, we say it has a particular characteristic *(D)*, which is our operational concept, in this case water solubility. Let us see if we can apply the same kind of reasoning to concepts in political science.

Take the concept *power.* For most people, power means influencing the behavior of others, controlling them, getting them to do something they don't want to do. These definitions suffice in everyday situations, but they cannot be called operational. Instead, each is *intuitive,* that is, a definition based on the feel we have for a particular phenomenon. We observe certain situations in which one person seems to be able to affect or even control the behavior of others. We might also notice that other observors have reported similar phenomena and have called them "power." Power is the label we assign to an inferred concept that seems to describe a class of situations. This kind of definition is intuitive because, for one thing, it is not formal—we haven't worked out a clear-cut set of conditions that would indicate the existence of power, nor have we formulated a definition that allows us to measure amounts or degrees of power. These come only with operational definitions. Why then mention intuitive definitions? Child psychologists like Jean Piaget give us one kind of answer.[4] They argue that all children begin organizing the world with intuitive definitions, that is, meanings that they use in everyday contexts. But in Piaget's words, such a conceptualization is "unreflective"; the children are not aware of the reasons for their meanings nor their concepts' various usages. Most of us continue to use such an intuitive language throughout our adult lives. So, being human, the scientist probably begins his research with an intuitive grasp of his subject matter. Perhaps the first political scientist noticed that it is not unusual for people to try to control each other's behavior. After observing a number of such interactions he said to himself, "This is something to look into. But first I must specify the phenomenon's boundaries and then label it—I will call it 'power'." While an oversimplified portrayal of reality, this brief scenario

---

[4] For a readable introduction to Piaget's ideas of concept formation, see Howard Gardiner, *The Quest for Mind* (New York: Vintage Books, 1974), pp. 51–110.

shows that operational definitions do not spring fully developed from the minds of scientists. Instead, they begin with an observation, or an act of intuition sparked by a touch of creative imagination. However, as he begins to examine the phenomenon more systematically, the political scientist must move beyond this intuitive grasp. So we return to the operational definition.

Take our familiar friend *power*. Imagine a bargaining situation—negotiations between two diplomats trying to settle a boundary dispute. When in such a situation diplomat A can get diplomat B to accept A's definition of the boundary, even though B went into the meeting publicly declaring that he would never agree to such a line, A has power over B. We have just given an oversimplified but nevertheless valid operational definition of power; it boils down to this: Whenever A can get B to do something B would not otherwise have done, A has power over B.

One thing must be made clear, however. In political science, we cannot usually *perform* the operations that give the operational definition its label. The political scientist cannot manipulate people the way the chemist manipulates chemical elements. In this strict sense, the definition of "power" is not operational. However, the *structure* of the definition is the same, and that is what matters. If in a given situation—the placing of salt in water, or the negotiations of diplomats—a particular result occurs—the dissolving of the salt, or the acceptance against his will by one diplomat of the proposals of the other—then we attribute a particular characteristic to the entity: solubility to the salt, power to the second diplomat. The meaning of "operational" for the political scientist is not the performing of operations so much as the more general requirement of observing reactions to given situations and defining concepts in terms of these reactions (or behaviors). It would no doubt be less confusing if this method of definition had another name without the connotation of manipulation—perhaps "dispositional" is such a word. But as long as we know what "operational" means *in political science,* we can continue using the label. Or, if one still anticipates confusion, "dispositional" can be adopted.

Sometimes we have an intuitive grasp of a concept, yet find it difficult to operationalize in a general way. Power is probably such a concept. This has led some political scientists to argue that the only way to operationalize power is to define it *in a specific context*. That is, one can operationally define "senatorial power," "international power" and "Presidential power" but not "power." All examples of power are probably traceable to the same basic intuitive notion, but in each specific context, a different operational definition is required. The idea of such *contextual* definitions is closely related to the notion of the cluster concept mentioned in Chapter 2. Remember, the point is that there may be some concepts that cannot be defined with a single operational definition.

Another kind of dispositional concept is examplified by attitudes or opinions. We might say that an individual is a pacifist if he answers a set of questions in a certain way; if he answers questions *X, Y,* and *Z* yes, he has a pacific attitude. Some political scientists argue that there is something in a person's mind that the questions reflect or measure. Others reject this kind of analysis, saying that the attitude is nothing more than a set of answers to a set of questions. It makes no sense to talk about entities that no one can see—to act as if our questionnaire is an imperfect reflection of the real attitude. There is a more moderate way of stating the second position. Perhaps this is also the most sensible position to take. It says that since we can't see inside people's heads, the whole controversy is a waste of time. We can use attitudes and other kinds of dispositional concepts to summarize sets of observables; this holds true for attitudes, opinions, ideologies, and personality traits. What really interests us is behavior, and relationships between types of behavior. We broaden the scope of political science immensely by using such concepts, and their use does not force us to talk about mysterious invisible entities.

Many scientists prefer to use the terms *variable* and *measure* when describing how they operationalize their concepts.[5] Variables, like "liberal" and "democracy," are characteristics that things have in varying degrees. The use of a variable allows one to say more than "she is a liberal"; now it is possible to indicate who is more liberal than whom and perhaps how liberal each is. Just as it can be said that concepts must be operationalized to become part of our scientific repertoire, so it is that variables, which are best thought of as abstract or intuitive, must be translated into something that is observable. Measures serve this function. If political instability is our variable, then its measure might be the number of riots in a country during the year. Political instability is an abstract variable or intuitive concept, but riots

---

[5] See for instance, Ted R. Gurr, *Polimetrics* (Englewood Cliffs, NJ: Prentice-Hall, 1972), chapter 3; and McGaw and Watson, *Political and Social Inquiry,* chapter 6. For a more advanced discussion, see David C. Leege and Wayne Francis, *Political Research* (New York: Basic Books, 1974), chapter 2.

can be observed, classified, even counted.[6] Thus, the use of a measure is equivalent to operationalizing a concept. An attitude questionnaire is a measure of the variable "liberal" just as the reading on a thermometer is a measure of the variable "temperature."

Often a variable is such that political scientists are not satisfied with a single measure. So they use several indicators or partial measures. Instead of basing the definition of political instability on one measure, number of riots, they might use several more indicators such as number of strikes, regularity of political resignations, and occurances of declarations of martial law. A combination of these four indicators would become a new measure, apparently more complete and satisfying than a single-factor measure.

Let us, however, reiterate that from the standpoint of the political scientist constructing such a definition, there is no *real* meaning of political instability. Instead, there is an intuitive definition in his head that hopefully catches an idea other political scientists are also thinking about, and a set of observable indicators that enable political scientists to study the phenomenon of political instability.

Theoretical concepts

A third way to introduce concepts into a scientific language is through their placement in theories. While a full understanding of theoretical concepts must await the analysis of theories in Chapter 8, we can say enough now to make them understandable. In simplest terms, a theoretical concept is defined within a theoretical system. Think of a theory as a set of interrelated concepts, some that are defined directly or operationally, and some that are not. The latter are theoretical concepts. They gain their meaning from the theory—take them out of context and they become meaningless. However, if the first two kinds of concepts are removed from a theory that employs them, they retain their meaning.

A theoretical system familiar to everyone is Euclidean geometry; it is formal-mathematical rather than empirical-scientific (the distinction will be explicated in Chapter 8), yet because at this point we are interested only in

---

[6] For an example of such counting, see Rudolph J. Rummel, "Dimensions of Conflict Behavior within Nations 1946–1959," *Journal of Conflict Resolution,* 10 (March 1966), pp. 65–73.

the structure of theories and their relationship to theoretical concepts, geometry is a useful example. "Line," "point," and other Euclidean concepts gain their meaning from their placement within the system, from their relationships to other concepts. Remove a Euclidean "point" from its natural habitat and you have not only a lonely concept but a meaningless one.

Now, as we have just hinted, there is a vast difference between a scientific theory and a mathematical system, even though their structures are similar. The difference is that the former is somehow linked to the world of observation—it describes the world; while mathematics, geometry for instance, has no link to the empirical. Such a system is merely a logically related set of symbols; *X,* 1, or *A* would do just as well as the Euclidean "point" because the structure, the logical relationships, are what count. Structure is also important in an empirical theory; this is, as we have said, what makes the theoretical concept distinctive. But, in addition, the empirical theory has empirical content—structure is not everything—and the content is achieved by making sure that some of its concepts are tied to the world; in other words, they are directly or operationally defined. If, in addition, the theory is logically sound (put together correctly), those concepts not defined according to the first two methods will be theoretically defined. Thus, they will not be without empirical meaning as are the concepts of Euclidean geometry, but neither will they have meaning outside their theory, a trait they share with "line" and "point."

An obvious and legitimate question which comes to mind at this point is, Why does science need theoretical concepts?[7] There are two points that must be clarified to answer the question and demonstrate the significance of theoretical concepts. First, the distinction between operational and theoretical concepts might not be entirely clear. What, for instance, is the logical difference between a concept in atomic theory, let us say "meson," and the concept "power" in political science? It would seem that power is no more visible to political scientists than mesons are to physicists—we are directly acquainted with neither. Yet there is a difference. "Power" is independently defined; there is a set of empirical circumstances that we call "power." Therefore, it is misleading to say that power cannot be seen. The nature of

---

[7] Carl G. Hempel attempts to answer this question in "The Theoretician's Dilemma," in Herbert Feigl, Michael Scriven, and Grover Maxwell, eds., *Minnesota Studies in the Philosophy of Science* (Minneapolis: University of Minnesota Press, 1958), pp. 37–98.

an operational definition is that a concept is defined in terms of directly observable properties. "Meson" cannot be analyzed in the same manner. A theoretical concept is not defined independently, but within a theory. This is the key point. Its meaning depends upon the other concepts in the theory and their interrelationship. That mesons are not visible is obvious. But neither are they invisible. A theoretical concept has no separate set of observables that define it.

Granted that theoretical and operational concepts are logically distinct, that the former are not directly tied to observable properties. The question remains, Why does the scientist use them? This question cannot be completely answered at this point because it really asks for a justification of theory. All we can say now is that theories expand our ability to explain. A theory is wider in scope than any set of purely empirical generalizations (generalizations using directly acquaintable or operational concepts), and this widening of scope is due in large part to those theoretical concepts that act as connective links between the other two kinds of concepts.

We have now made some general points about the third method of introducing concepts; as students of the methodology of political science, we need say little more about theoretical concepts, because, strictly speaking, there are few in political science at the present time. Theoretical concepts are found only in sound empirical theories, and developed theories are rare in political science. However, the last few pages were not written in vain; for as we will see in later chapters, there are primitive and potential theories—political scientists are presently trying to formulate theories that might account for wider segments of political phenomenon. Thus, even though for the time being we will be working primarily with directly acquaintable and operational concepts, it is hoped there is a place for theoretical concepts in political science. We can make the point even more strongly: Until political science begins constructing sound scientific theories, it will be considered an immature discipline. For the building of scientific theories and the formulation of theoretical concepts takes a large dose of creative imagination, something that is often overlooked in discussions of the nuts and bolts of scientific methodology. We are not overlooking it; as a matter of fact, much of what is said in Part 3 is based on the contention that political science will develop only if its practitioners display this creative impulse in abundant quantities.

THE FUNCTION OF SCIENTIFIC CONCEPTS IN POLITICAL SCIENCE

Concepts are used to describe political phenomena—at least this much is clear from the foregoing analysis. When we identify a set of observable characteristics as "power," we have defined a concept and designated a class of observable phenomena. More can be said about the descriptive qualities of concepts than that they are used to identify political phenomena. In other words, there is more to description than identification. If we are serious about developing a science of politics, we would also like to use concepts to classify, compare, and measure. As a matter of fact, there are several kinds of concepts, each with its own particular function, each with its own usefulness. More specifically, there are classificatory, comparative, and quantitative concepts.[8] Let us spend the next few pages describing the nature of each and determining its applicability to political phenomena.

Classification

Some concepts provide the basis for classification—the placing of political actions, systems, or institutions into classes or categories. As is true of science generally, classificatory concepts have a commonsensical basis. A substantial portion of our everyday thinking is spent classifying, arranging, and sorting out the phenomena that confront us. This is a primary method for making sense out of the world. Similarly, it is the way the scientist begins his scientific analysis.

The scientist sharpens the classificatory apparatus of common usage. Instead of characterizing all nations as Communist or pro-American, as the man in the street is inclined to do, the political scientist might formulate a concept of democracy and then classify all political systems as either democratic or nondemocratic. This is an example of *dichotomous* classification, the simplest variety. It involves defining a concept, *democratic,* according to the scientific procedures already outlined, linking it to observables, such as "number of political parties and their rate of turnover," or "ratio between total adult population and eligible voters," and then treating it as a charac-

---

[8] Hempel, *Fundamentals of Concept Formation in Empirical Science,* part III.

teristic of political systems, placing all systems that have the characteristic in one slot or category, and all those that don't in another. A dichotomy is thus created; there are only two categories according to this classificatory concept. If the concept has been soundly defined and is applicable to the population being considered, then the classification will be exhaustive (all members of the population will be classified) and exclusive (no member will be placed in both categories).

Some variables seem to be naturally dichotomous. We assume that people are either right-handed or left-handed and, therefore, it should be easy to formulate a dichotomous concept that describes this characteristic. Likewise, it makes sense to assume that in American politics everyone is either a Democrat or a non-Democrat. While this line of thinking is commonsensically true, it overlooks the possibility that what appear to be either-or concepts are actually situations that allow for gradations and additional categories; we know that there are ambidextrous people. This is why, for instance, in most studies of political-party identification and voting behavior the population is broken down into the categories of Weak Democrat, Strong Democrat, Independent, and so forth. There is nothing wrong with a dichotomous classification—it is often the most efficient way of describing a group of items; it is only that more is said descriptively when the categories begin to multiply.

Thus, it is that science also employs multiple classificatory concepts, that is, concepts that enable us to place the members of a population into more than two categories. Once again, the same procedure is used in nonscientific activities, such as when we list the positions of a football team. Quarterback, halfback, fullback, end, tackle, guard, and center are the classes of a multiple classification. In political science, the ancient but useful monarchy-oligarchy-democracy classification can be cited as a fairly straightforward example of a multiple classification scheme. Whether we are classifying football players or political systems, the principles of exhaustiveness and exclusiveness still apply. If, after classifying the members of the Cleveland Browns according to the above scheme, we still have a player left over, we can conclude that our scheme is incomplete. The same criticism applies if we find a nation that does not fit our three-fold classification. Or suppose a player or nation fits in several categories. Again, our classification scheme is less than perfect. It should be pointed out that perfection is usually impossible when classifying large numbers of items. But here the well-known dictum, "Do the best you can," applies. There are always several easy ways to handle an unclassifiable item—create a new category or establish a miscellaneous category. While the latter gambit can get one out of a tight situation, it can also hide a weak classification concept; if a high percentage of the items being classified end up in such a catchall category, the real sorting out process is not being done. The creation of new categories can also be a useful expedient in the face of obstinate data. But if more often than not a new item is given its own category, the purpose of classification is undercut. Ending up with 100 items classified into 50 categories accomplishes little.

Comparison

Classification is important. Every science begins by sorting out the phenomena that seem relevant to it. As we have already said, this is the first method of making the world coherent and comprehensible. However, how far can a science go with concepts that only classify? The answer, it would appear, is, not far. We would probably like to know more than which political systems are democratic and which are not; perhaps, for instance, which in the first category are the most democratic. A logical step of progression from classificatory concepts is to comparative or ordering concepts.

A comparative concept is, in the last analysis, a more complex and useful type of classificatory concept. The members of a population are sorted out and placed in categories; but in addition, because the categories represent a particular property, the members are ranked according to how much of the property they each have. For instance, we might want to compare those nations that are very democratic, those nations that are moderately so, and those nations that are much less democratic. This would be done by categorizing the empirical referents of democracy. Those political systems that fall in the upper one third of a list of ratios of total eligible voters to total population would be classified as very democratic, for instance. So we could say that a nation placed in the first category is *more* democratic than one placed in the second or third categories.

Usually, however, a comparative concept will allow a more refined analysis than this, for the categories will probably be more than three in number. In fact, a sophisticated comparative concept (such as "hardness" in geology, or "power" in political science) will allow us to compare every member of our population (whether a collection of rocks or a group of politicians) with every other member; thus, practically speaking, the number of categories is theoretically infinite, practically limited only by the number of members of the population. The result of this analysis is a rank order of items, of *every* item—of more or less democratic nations, or more or less powerful senators, or of harder or softer rocks. In a study of the social conditions of democracy, Deane Neubauer has developed such a comparative concept that provides the basis for an "Index of Democratic Performance."[9] The empirical indicators used are *(a)* percent of the adult population eligible to vote, *(b)* equality of representation, *(c)* information equality, and *(d)* competition.

In every case, the advantage of the comparative over the classificatory concept is based upon the additional knowledge produced by the fine distinctions of the concept and the fact that the question is not either-or, but more or less. To know how 10 senators rank on a power index is to know more than that six have power and four don't, or that all 10 have power. Let us pursue the second possibility further. Suppose that according to our original dichotomous classification, all senators are placed either in the powerful or nonpowerful category. What does this tell us? A great deal depends on the concept of power that is used as the basis of classification. A choice might have to be made, for instance, between calling all senators who have 50 percent of their bills passed powerful, or those who have only 25 percent passed. The comparative concept does not present us with this problem of definition, for it is not a matter of either-or, of having power or of not having power. Rather, we are interested in how a number of senators are ranked in regard to the concept of "power"—how they measure up against one another. Thus, the claim that "Senator Smith is powerful" makes sense only if we expand it to read, "more powerful *than most other senators,*" which means the following: in a rank order of all senators on the concept "power," Smith comes out near the top of the list.

The advantages of comparative or ordering concepts over classificatory concepts should be manifest by now. The more refined and explicit descriptions make possible the development of more sophisticated generalizations about, and theories of, politics. In using classificatory concepts, we might

---

[9] Deane Neubauer, "Some Conditions of Democracy," *American Political Science Review,* 61, no. 4 (1967), pp. 1002–9.

discover, for instance, that *democratic* political systems tend to be unstable. Analyzing the same phenomena with comparative concepts could produce the following generalization: the more democratic a nation is, the more unstable it is. We may hope that political science will develop a greater number of comparative concepts. At this point, we can say *optimistically* that such concepts are being formulated and applied by political scientists— examples are conservative-liberal attitude scales, and indexes of political power; but *realistically,* the kinds of concepts most evident in a science roughly reflect the maturity of the science. At this point, political science is relatively immature (on a rank order of all natural and social sciences), and so political scientists are still concerned primarily with classificatory concepts.

Quantification

Take a population that has been ordered by a comparative concept; then give the concept certain mathematical characteristics so as to allow one to say not just "Senator Smith is more powerful than Senator Jones," but "Smith is twice as powerful as Jones." A *quantitative* concept has been formulated. Our rank order of senatorial power tells us nothing about how much more powerful one senator is than another. This gets to the very nature of the comparative concept and is its basic limitation. More significant to the political scientist interested in more reliable knowledge of politics is the development of concepts that allow us not only to rank items on a particular characteristic, but also allow us to say something about how much of the characteristic each item has. And if "how much" is the question, we have to perform certain mathematical operations that are impossible when classificatory or comparative concepts are being used; thus, the use of the label "quantitative."[10]

There are really two levels of quantitative concepts. The first, and less rigorous, is usually introduced into our scientific language in the form of an

---

[10] We will not say much about the mathematical foundations of quantitative concepts. For discussions of mathematics and political science, see Hayward R. Alker, Jr., *Mathematics and Politics* (New York: Macmillan, 1965); Gurr, *Polimetrics;* and the more general but advanced John G. Kemeny, L. J. Snell, and G. L. Thompson, *Introduction to Finite Mathematics* (Englewood Cliffs, N.J.: Prentice-Hall, 1956).

interval scale.[11] For this discussion, we can think of a scale as a device for ordering items. An interval scale has the additional feature of equal intervals between its categories. A good example of an interval scale we are all familiar with is the thermometer. Thus, temperature is a quantitative concept measurable on an interval scale. The distance between, let us say, 30° and 40° Fahrenheit is equal to the distance between 40° and 50° and so on. But notice that it is not the case that 60° is twice as warm as 30°. The significant fact about an interval scale is that we can quantitatively compare (carry out certain kinds of mathematical operations on) the intervals between items on the scale, but not the items themselves. This is attributable, speaking as nontechnically as possible, to the interval scale's lack of an absolute zero, or point of origin.

Take temperature again. The zero point on the thermometer does not represent the absence of temperature. A leisurely walk outside on a −15° winter day will convince anyone of this. As long as there are temperatures below zero, we cannot say that 30° is twice as cold as 60°. Thus, we can say that 0°F. is an arbitrary cutoff point, manifesting convenience and not truth. The concept "temperature" can be viewed as property having an indeterminable beginning and end. We can measure heat or cold by means of our everyday thermometer, which marks off equal amounts of the property and limits itself to the normal ranges of temperature. There is no difference in kind between above- and below-zero temperatures, despite the almost mystical characteristics often attributed to the zero point.

There are some quantitative concepts in the social sciences that allow for the construction of interval scales. For instance, a refined concept of intelligence defined as the score made on a test might be so characterized. While it makes sense to say that an IQ of 100 is exactly halfway between 90 and 110, it doesn't make sense to say that a man with an IQ of 200 is twice as smart as one with an IQ of 100. As far as political science goes, quantitative interval concepts are few and far between. Some political attitude scales might be so classified, and there are no doubt others; but, by and large, the knowledge of politics which has been accumulated is based upon classificatory and comparative concepts. This is not to say that the development of quantitative concepts will not become more common. On the contrary, the future of

---

[11] The following discussion of scales is based on S. S. Stevens, "On the Theory of Scales of Measurement," *Science,* 103 (1946), pp. 677–80.

political science no doubt depends largely upon the extent to which political scientists can develop quantitative concepts.

If it is true that quantitative interval concepts are rare in political science, then we would expect the second variety of quantitative concepts to be even more rare. For it forms the basis of the most highly developed quantitative scale, usually called the *ratio* scale. Like the interval type, it begins with a rank order, adds equal intervals, but then grounds the intervals with an absolute zero point. While this allows many technical refinements, the only one that concerns us here is the newfound ability to say, by means of a ratio scale, "*X* is twice as big as *Y*." In other words, no longer are our mathematical operations limited to the intervals between points on the scale. Now the points can be measured and compared. The reason is the zero point, the fact that there is an end to the scale. There is a point at which an item no longer has the characteristic.

The ratio scale most familiar to most of us is the system of cardinal numbers—the scale that is employed when we count. Obviously, eight chairs are twice as many as four chairs, because we start from a nonarbitrary zero point; it is impossible to have fewer than zero chairs. Few of the more useful concepts employed by political scientists are based on the ratio scale. Those that are based on the ratio scale involve simple counting—counting the number of votes is an example; if candidate *A* receives 50,000 votes, he has received twice as many as candidate *B*, who received only 25,000. But once we move beyond such straightforward, easily counted phenomena, the requirements of ratio scaling are more difficult to meet.

EVALUATING CONCEPTS IN POLITICAL SCIENCE

Running through our discussion of concept formation has been an implied requirement of all sound concepts. Perhaps best labeled "empirical import," it is a straightforward requirement and, given the basic arguments of this book, not a surprising one.[12] "Empirical import" suggests that since concepts are the basic building blocks of empirical science, they must be linked to the world of observation. As the political scientist formulates concepts, he must make sure that they have empirical import. Recall the three ways this is

---

[12] Hempel, *Fundamentals of Concept Formation in Empirical Science,* pp. 39–45.

achieved. Some concepts are directly linked to corresponding observables, and we are directly acquainted with them. Could anyone doubt, for instance, that "Australian ballot" has empirical import? Another type has no observable characteristics that it directly corresponds to, yet is defined in terms of observables. Such an operational or dispositional concept as power also has empirical import. The third type of concept we analyzed is the theoretical. We hope that the last few paragraphs made clear that although it is neither directly linked to observables nor operationally defined, a theoretical concept nevertheless has empirical import. A scientific theory is empirical—some of its concepts are directly or operationally related to observables. Therefore, those that are not defined according to these methods also have empirical import because of their logical relationship to the other concepts. Thus, there is a world of difference between the term *ghost* and the concept *meson,* even though neither is directly tied to observables, and so far as we know, neither ghosts nor mesons exist the way chairs do.

There is another characteristic that scientists would like their concepts to have. Labeled *systematic import,* it has to do with the relationship between concepts.[13] Stated as a criterion of usefulness, it asks that they not be constructed in isolation. This is significant because a concept is of little use if it cannot be related to other concepts. Consider the following example—it is extremely absurd, but absurdities often make important points better than perfectly reasonable examples. Suppose a political scientist doing research on the personal characteristics of politicians constructs a concept labeled *shame,* which is defined as a product of more than 150 resulting from the multiplication of the number of letters in the last name and shoe size. In other words, a politician who wears a size 13 shoe and has 12 letters in his last name has the characteristic of shame. Clearly, the concept has empirical import; it is rather easy to discover a shoe size, count the letters of a name, and multiply the two. However, can shame be related to any other characteristics of politicians or the political system? At this point, we would probably have to say no, unless there is some less than obvious relationship between politics, large feet, and long names. So we would conclude that for political science, shame has no systematic import, and thus is currently not a useful concept, even though it is an empirically sound one.

Notice that this is not the same kind of requirement as empirical import.

---

[13] Ibid., pp. 45–49.

The latter is a necessary characteristic of concepts. We might even say it is the characteristic that defines a concept. Systematic import or usefulness, on the other hand, is less clear-cut. In the more advanced sciences, such as physics and chemistry, concepts will have both characteristics. In political science, we *demand* that a concept have empirical import and *hope* that it has systematic import. To make the latter a necessity would be to prejudice the usefulness of concepts. When we formulate a concept, even an absurd one like shame, we don't know that it won't some day be useful, that there doesn't exist a relationship between it and other political concepts that simply awaits discovery. Or, turning things around, we can't determine the systematic import of sound concept, such as power, until we have discovered that it is related to other concepts. A case in point is the concept of alienation. Developed and refined by Marxian theorists, it went out of favor and was rejected as a useful empirical concept (a concept with systematic import that could be related to other concepts). Recently, it has been rejuvenated as social scientists speculate about the test possible relationships between it and other phenomena; for instance, alienation leads to urban disturbances.[14] The usefulness of a concept is relative to the accumulated knowledge of the particular field in which it is found. However, as a practical matter, the political scientist usually begins his work with those concepts— power, influence, policy, participation, law—that seem to have systematic import rather than concepts that have a less certain payoff. The political scientist's task is not an easy one. He must be aware of the immediate needs of political research, while anticipating its future development. He must simultaneously keep his feet on the ground and his mind in the air.

Whenever we operationalize a concept we must not only make sure that it has empirical import, but that, in addition, it actually measures what it is supposed to measure; if it does, the concept is called *valid*.[15] Most political scientists who develop measures of liberalism (or conservatism) hear the criticism, "That's not what liberalism really is." How is one to reply? That is, how can it be shown that the concept is valid? Usually, the researcher is

---

[14] For a summary of findings on alienation, see Robert Lane, *Political Ideology* (New York: Free Press, 1962). Also see Murray B. Levin, *The Alienated Voter* (New York: Holt, Rinehart & Winston, 1960).

[15] For a brief description of validity and reliability, see David Nachmias and Chava Nachmias, *Research Methods in the Social Sciences* (New York: St. Martin's Press, 1976), pp. 59–68, and Gurr, *Polimetrics,* chapter 3.

satisfied if he can establish the concept's *face validity*. Based on his knowledge and experience, do the operational indicators actually correspond to
the common understanding of the concept? Or, at a more rigorous level, a
sample of others may be asked to label the operational indicators. If their
consensus label corresponds to the researcher's, he will be more confident
that his concept is really measuring what he intends it to measure.

Often the researcher is satisfied if he can establish a concept's face validity. However, in more sophisticated types of political research there might
be a need for even more rigorous tests of validity. One of the more widely
used techniques, called *convergent validation,* measures validity in terms of
the extent that different indicators of the same concept or variable result in
the same findings. Let us return to the study of liberalism. Suppose the
researcher not only administers a liberalism questionnaire to a sample of
U.S. senators, but also keeps track of their voting records—many interest
groups, Americans for a Democratic Society, Americans for Constitutional
Action, to name a few, provide measures of liberalism and conservatism
based on senators' voting behavior in Congress—ideological batting averages, so to speak. If the results of the questionnaire correspond to the
recorded vote—liberals tend to vote in a liberal manner—it can be concluded that there is some validity in each measure. Each gains credibility
because it points in the same direction as the other.

It should be clear that there is no absolute test of validity. A judgment
must be made. There is no guarantee that our two measures of liberalism are
really measuring the same thing. But, as more tests of this sort point in the
same direction, we become more and more confident that we are observing
manifestations of the same phenomenon. That is all any scientist can expect.

Not only do we want our concepts to be valid, but in addition it is reasonable to require that they be *reliable,* that is, produce similar results in similar
situations. The chemist expects a combination of elements A and B to produce, under controlled conditions, the same result every time the experiment is performed. The psychologist assumes that a person who scores 120
on an IQ test will score about the same a week later. Likewise, the political
scientist must have confidence that the use of a particular variable will
produce results that are similar under similar conditions. Political scientists
can rarely be as rigorous as chemists. But they must make their concepts as
reliable as possible; otherwise their observations will not be taken seriously.
When a measure of liberalism produces different results within the same

group, it is reasonable to conclude that the concept of liberalism being used is unreliable. How can this happen? One possibility is that the concept has been ambiguously defined so that as different researchers using the concept make their observations, their interpretations are different; they are allowed too much latitude.

It is a mistake to confuse validity and reliability. Both are characteristics of sound concepts and variables, but they refer to different requirements. We can construct a completely unambiguous concept that is very reliable: a liberal person is one who has a last name containing more than 10 letters. Assuming the ability to count, observations will not vary between observers. But according to any notion of validity, the concept would have to be rejected as invalid; it is simply not getting at the characteristic we wanted to measure, liberalism.

THE ANATOMY OF A CONCEPT

Now that we have discussed the basic nature of concept formation in political science, it might be a good idea to select a single widely used political concept and examine its formulation and use. This analysis will give substance to the methodological points made earlier in the chapter, and it will illustrate the many twists and turns one must take in developing a useful scientific concept. We have selected a concept that has already been used as an example, mainly because it is so familiar to students of politics.

There is no doubt that power holds a significant place among the concepts of politics. As Harold and Margaret Sprout have put it, "Some concept of power underlies virtually every description of political interaction, domestic as well as international."[16] Many argue that power is especially significant in the field of international politics, where moral and consensual factors seem to be much less important than they are in domestic politics. Power has assumed such lofty status in international politics that some writers view it as the field's *central* concept.[17] There seems to be a true commonsense core

---

[16] Harold Sprout and Margaret Sprout, *Foundations of International Politics* (Princeton, N.J.: Van Nostrand Reinhold, 1962), p. 136.

[17] See the writings of Hans Morgenthau, for instance, "Power as a Political Concept," in Roland Young, ed., *Approaches to the Study of Politics* (Evanston, Ill.: Northwestern University Press, 1958), pp. 66–77.

in this position. Be this as it may, we should not allow it to overshadow the importance of power at other levels of politics.[18]

It is difficult to imagine an action between political actors at any level that does not manifest itself in some notion of power. But because there are so many notions, it might be misleading for the political scientist to talk about political power in general. What is clearly needed is a concept of power that is both rigorous and intuitively satisfying. If both conditions are realized, a concept will probably be scientifically useful. Let us recall the requirements of a sound concept: (1) It must have empirical import; that is, it must be directly or indirectly tied to the world of observation. This would mean that, given our definition of power, we could tell if power is present or not in a given situation. (2) A concept ought to have systematic import. If it is to be of immediate use, one must be able to relate it to other concepts to formulate generalizations.

This section will examine the concept of power and its role as a centralizing and organizing concept in the study of politics. Two general themes will be developed: (1) power is behavioral; (2) the relation between the elements of power and power behavior must be formulated to allow for empirical testing if the former are to be of any explanatory and predictive importance.

It is clear that as it is used by many political scientists, power is not just one concept among many. It is the common characteristic of all political situations; and so it, better than others, can order and direct the political scientist's research efforts. This is why we are using it as our sample concept.

Power is a relational concept. One nation has power *over* another; Senator Smith controls the Foreign Relations Committee (has power over its other members). However, many students of politics use power as if it were something that a nation or a senator might possess without using it. In the words of Harold and Margaret Sprout, "a quantifiable and commensurable mass, something like a pile of bricks or a stone wall perhaps."[19] This point of view is manifested in discussions of the elements of national power, includ-

---

[18] See Roderick Bell, David V. Edwards, and R. Harrison Wagner, eds., *Political Power: A Reader in Theory and Research* (New York: Free Press, 1969) for a collection of the leading articles in the field. Also see Marvin E. Olsen, ed., *Power in Societies* (New York: Macmillan, 1970). Also see Jack H. Nagel, *The Descriptive Analysis of Power* (New Haven: Yale University Press, 1975).

[19] Sprout and Sprout, *Foundations,* p. 136.

ing population, natural resources, and, above all, military strength.[20] It is not unusual to discover that military strength *is* power in international politics, or that wealth *is* power in domestic politics. Upon further analysis, however, it becomes clear that such discussions usually assume that the elements are significant because they allow a nation or a politician to control or influence others. Danger lies in concentrating upon the elements, for in doing so, the need to relate them to power behavior is often obscured. It cannot be over-emphasized that if power is to be a useful concept in political research, it must be viewed in relational and behavioral terms. That is, the research focus is on the behavior of one political actor insofar as it influences the behavior of others. If this is so, it makes no sense to speak of a nation's power if it has not affected the behavior of another nation. The elements are best considered as power bases. Power is not, therefore, military strength; nor is it wealth. The contention that a nation with great military strength is powerful, if true, is true because it has been discovered through empirical observation that influence and the ability to control are related to the posses-sion of arms and soldiers.

This analysis seems reasonable enough. However, students of political power have too often overlooked the need to relate power to power-based variables. The most general point of view taken in this section is that if the concept of power is to serve as a focal point for models and theories of politics, two tasks have to be undertaken: (1) the development of a sound concept of power; (2) the formulation of hypotheses using this concept that allow political scientists to test assumed relationships between power behav-iors, and between behavior and power bases. This ultimately means testing by observing the behavior of political actors.

There are two general reasons for adopting a behavioralistic approach to the study of political power. First, as we have argued, power involves con-trol or influence, and therefore it is an activity. The possession of armed forces by nation *A* does not necessarily imply that they will be used to control or influence nation *B*. Perhaps there are other features of the situa-tion that prevent such employment, or make it unlikely. For instance, what of the intentions or will of *A*? It seems that a number of factors are necessary

---

[20] A useful discussion of military strength that does not take this point of view is Klaus Knorr, *Military Power and Potential* (Lexington, Mass.: D. C. Heath, 1970). Knorr analyzes international power in relational terms.

if power is to exist. These include the proper bases of power and the ability to use them (the lack of restraint upon them), which together might be labeled *capability*. Secondly, the powerful actor must have the will or desire to control the actions of others, or so it would seem.

But let us consider another situation that might cause us to question the claim that power can only exist if it is exercised. Imagine two geographically adjacent nations, one with a large but inactive army, the other with no army at all. The very existence of nation *A*'s army may influence the behavior of nation *B*, even though it is never used. This is analogous to the influence that the presidential veto can have on Congress, even though it is not employed or even mentioned. The solution of this problem is based upon the realization that these are cases of behavioral power and not potential power. It might be said that the possession of military forces by a nation and the right of veto by an executive are acts of power. Possession in these instances is behavior. The political scientist Carl Friedrich has described this situation in his "rule of anticipated reactions." It proposes that often a political actor will adjust its behavior in light of what it thinks another might do.[21] This position does not imply that mere possession is always power behavior. For we can distinguish this type of situation from one where a nation has a substantial military force but demonstrates no desire or will to use it. We might say that its force is not *credible* and has no influence on the behavior of other nations. In this case, possession does not lead to power.

We can now conclude that both capability and will are necessary ingredients of power situations, except in those cases when possession alone leads to influence; and even in the latter case, credibility must be ascertainable.

A second reason for viewing power as a behavioral concept has to do with the basic scientific task of measurement. We will assume that the immediate objective of power theory is to use the concept to measure and compare power. If the "pile of bricks" definition is used, problems arise. The most significant problem is that the elements or bases of power provide no common unit of measurement. That is, how does one compare a man with a net worth of $10 million and one with a prestigious family background, if the question is which has more power in a particular community? Quincy Wright seems to refer to the problem in the following statement: "It is difficult to find any common measure by which one of these forms for exerting political

---

[21] Carl J. Friedrich, *Man and His Government* (New York: McGraw-Hill, 1963), pp. 199–215.

and social power can be equated with others as is true of the physical concept of power measured in horsepower or watts."[22] The solution is to use the activity of political actors as the basis of a common measure. Thus, in the example just cited, the behavioral consequences of wealth and prestige could be compared using, let us say, "*X* number of people controlled" as the unit of power. How else would one compare one nation's military forces with another's strategic position? No claim is being made that it is easy to measure or compare power. We will discuss some of the difficulties involved in these activities shortly. If we are to use power in any scientifically meaningful way, a concept based on behavior will have to be developed.

What is power in behavioralistic terms? The concept surely has a commonsense core, having something to do with control of or dominance over others. This is what we have called an intuitive definition. But, as we pointed out then, an intuitive definition is not enough. Robert Dahl attempts a more rigorous definition: "*A* has power over *B* to the extent that he can get *B* to do something that *B* would not otherwise do."[23] A similar definition has been given by Herbert Goldhamer and Edward A. Shils: "A person may be said to have power to the extent that he influences the behavior of others in accordance with his own intentions."[24] Dahl's definition seems to get to the heart of the matter. In form, it harks back to the old argument from moral philosophy that an act cannot be morally good unless it goes against our inclinations or appetites. The point is that if *B* does something that *A* wants it to do, but *B* does not feel the action is in opposition to its interests, then *A* does not have power over *B*. However, it might seem rather difficult to apply this test to political actors. It calls for a knowledge of their intentions and might lead one to overlook manipulation, propaganda, and forms of sublimated aggression as influences. A nation may claim that its actions, in accordance with the politics of another nation, are of its own free will, while they may really be the result of one of these less overt forms of power. With the complexity of political relations, the ferreting out of such influence is exceedingly difficult.

---

[22] Quincy Wright, *The Study of International Relations* (New York: Appleton-Century-Crofts, 1955), p. 140.

[23] Robert Dahl, "The Concept of Power," *Behavioral Science,* 2 (July 1957), pp. 201–15. Reprinted in S. Sidney Ulmer, ed., *Introductory Readings in Political Behavior* (Chicago; Rand McNally, 1962), p. 344.

[24] Herbert Goldhamer and Edward A. Shils, "Types of Power and Status," *American Journal of Sociology,* 45 (1939), pp. 171–82. Reprinted in Ulmer, *Introductory Readings,* p. 334.

This is why Goldhamer and Shils' definition might seem more attractive. In using the phrase "in accordance with his own intentions," they make it unnecessary to draw a distinction between acts in accordance with and in opposition to the influenced one's will. But if one ignores this distinction, he is faced with another problem: Does a nation have power every time its wishes are fulfilled?

For example, imagine a small, geographically remote nation that wants to exist in isolation, and because of the play of international forces is not bothered by uninterested nations preoccupied elsewhere. Can we say that this nation is powerful? This is a rough restatement of David Hume's analysis of the problem of causal connections, which will be discussed in the next chapter. Anticipating this discussion, it can be stated that a power relationship requires (1) that acts be performed by both the influencer and the influenced, and (2) that there be some contact or communication between them. Consequently, it might be found that there is a direct correlation between the power of a nation and its contact with other nations. In any case, it seems fair to say that any acts of other states in accordance with nation A's interests (as manifested in its words and deeds) that cannot be traced to an act of A cannot be called manifestations of A's power.

A behavioral definition of power refers to behavior where one political actor influences the behavior of others in accordance with its own intentions. However, in examining the acts of politicians or nations, another question arises. It is whether power is a symmetrical or asymmetrical relation. Long ago, Hume argued that all relations must be symmetrical; that is, all actions have reactions and thus, there can be no one-way causal connections. This is of crucial importance for the study of political power.[25] For it must be recognized that many power actions generate feedback. If nation A influences the behavior of nation B, there is a good chance that B will also influence A. The problem is, how do we measure this type of power relation? One could give up the idea that it is asymmetrical, or that there can be a one-way power flow. This could mean a return to Hume's position. But this would also make it impossible to compare power. As an alternative to this position, an asymmetrical relation operating in the opposite direction to the first may be postulated. Thus, we have two relations which, if there is a

---

[25] The asymmetrical nature of power relations is discussed in Herbert Simon, "Notes on the Observation and Measurement of Political Power," *Journal of Politics,* 15 (1953), pp. 500–16.

sufficient time lag, might be individually observed. The amount and direction of the power differential would indicate the party with the most power.

We have given a general intuitive definition of power. Attention is focused on action and reaction leading to adjusted behavior. But further refinements are needed. Several classification schemes have been proposed to accomplish this refinement. One suggests three main types of power: force, domination, and manipulation.[26] These categories should be fairly easy to distinguish from one another. Force is the only one that involves physical activity, *physical* signifying an employment of visible resources. Domination, perhaps an inexact term, occurs when an actor makes explicit to others what he wants them to do. It can be seen that force and domination will usually occur together, with the former being used to back up the latter. Manipulation is the attempt to influence behavior without making explicit what the desired behavior is. This calls for various actions that are much less easy to find and observe. Nevertheless, there might be methods of observing such forms of undercover influence.

A more recent classification scheme takes a different approach. Instead of identifying types of power, it makes power one type of political control along with *authority, manipulation,* and *influence.*[27] Power is distinguished from the others in that it is based on the threat of severe sanctions; sanctions include such things as force, economic boycotts, and support with or withdrawal of votes. While power often depends upon the threat of force, the two are not the same. When force is applied, power is no longer being exercised. A political leader has authority when others do his bidding because they accept his right to rule—he is considered legitimate and does not need to employ power. The definition of manipulation is similar to the one used in the first classification. One is manipulated when his behavior is controlled without his knowledge through such a technique as propaganda. Finally, influence identifies a situation where one person affects the behavior of another because the second respects the first; consider the case of a son whose respect for his father causes him to emulate his father.

Both classification schemes suggest sets of actions that might be expected of a nation or politician attempting to gain power over others. They are

---

[26] Goldhamer and Shils, "Types of Power," pp. 334ff.

[27] Peter Bachrach and Morton S. Baratz, *Power and Poverty* (New York: Oxford University Press, 1970), chapter 2.

actions that hopefully can be observed and related to other actions and power bases as hypotheses. But before this can be done, actions must be specified that are characteristic of those who are being influenced or controlled. These variables will probably be more difficult to pick out, since they could include a wide range of actions. Nevertheless, certain types of reactions might be discovered that are characteristic of political actors who are acting against their wills. Here we see the reason for making contact or communications between actors a necessary condition for a power relationship. The final step in this strategy would be the empirical linking of the two types of actions to show that those of the first class temporarily precede those of the second class. If, after an observable contact beween two nations, we observe at least one of each type of act, we may say that this is a power relationship. Suppose that the President has a private talk with a senator who has opposed one of his judicial appointments. When the Senate vote occurs, the senator votes for the appointment. We can conclude that, in this case, the President exercised power.

Comparing power

Having demonstrated empirically that these two types of action are related, a method still has to be found to compare power. Robert Dahl has pointed out that "the main problem is not to determine the existence of power but to make comparisons."[28] The question, "Who has power?" is in one sense meaningless, for if power is relational, it is relative. Thus, if X has power, it is always power over someone else. This immediately raises several problems. How is one to compare power found in different situations? For instance, suppose (1) nation X has caused nation Y to perform act Z; (2) nation A has caused nation Y to perform act B; (3) nation A has caused nation C to perform act D. Can these situations be compared to determine which contains the most power? Can nation X's power in situation (1) be compared with nation A's in situations (2) and (3)? Situations (1) and (2) are alike because nation Y is the influenced nation, while (2) and (3) both have A as the influencer.

It would appear that those sets of situations having common actors might be compared more profitably than those that do not. However, has this

---

[28] Dahl, "The Concept of Power," p. 349.

gained us anything? No common unit has been extracted. Perhaps Dahl has come up with the best test of power.[29] It can be stated by two probability statements: (1) the probability that nation Y will do act A if nation X does act B is N; (2) the probability that nation Y will do act A if nation X does not do act B is N^2. The difference between N and N^2 might be said to be a nation's power—the greater the difference, the more power nation X has. However, the question remains, can all acts or responses be considered equal?

That is, suppose we want to compare the power of Great Britain in removing Argentina from the Falklands, and the actions of the United States to convince the Soviet Union to remove its missiles from Cuba. Suppose that the $(N - N^2)$ regarding Great Britain is greater than the United States. Can we say that Great Britain has more power than the United States? Or are we limited to saying that Great Britain had more power in its situation than the United States had in its situation. The answer is that the situation must be comparable if the relativity of power is to be compared. In our example, some way must be found to compare the withdrawal of Argentinian troops from the Falklands and Russian missiles from Cuba. One possible method is to determine how many nations could be affected by the power relationships. That is, how many nations might have their behavior changed by either the action of the influencer or the reactions of the influenced? In the contemporary international situation, the action of the United States in blockading Cuba affected many nations besides the Soviet Union. The British-Argentinian confrontation involved fewer nations. What we are talking about here is what might be called the *scope* of power action: How wide are its repercussions in the international political system?[30]

Measuring power

Even after developing a method of comparing specific events, one still has the feeling that it is not enough. For a statement such as "The United States has more power than England" is not quite clear. Up to now, our comparisons have been of individual situations (actions and reactions). But the more general statement seems to go beyond single actions. It encompasses all the acts of a nation or politician. This is a way of determining an actor's total

---

[29] Ibid., pp. 347ff.

[30] The scope of power is discussed in Dahl, p. 347ff.

power. That is, the total amount of a nation's power may be measured by the ratio of its successful power acts (those with a certain high difference between N and N^2) to all of its attempted power acts.[31]

Now we might ask, can one say that the United States is powerful, or must one only say the United States is more powerful than England? Probably the most meaningful proposition is the latter. One can use the methods outlined above and then make a comparison by analyzing and totaling the acts of each nation. The result of this will be an ordering concept rather than a quantitative concept. We will be able to say that X has more power than Y, but not that X has twice as much power.

As it is often employed by political scientists, the concept of power is deceivingly simple. We can agree with Robert Dahl that "the concepts of influence and power are full of logical traps, and most people—including many people who write about politics—are not accustomed to talking logically about power and influence."[32] We have emphasized one of these traps, the equating of the elements of power bases with power. It was suggested that approaches using power as a central concept should concentrate on actions, for methodologically speaking, power does not exist unless it is used. The elements of power would have no significance if politicians and nations did not act. This calls for a behavioral concept of power that meets the requirements of scientific concept formation. It is only after the problems involved in this task are solved that one can undertake the more significant tasks of measuring and comparing power and using power in the explanation of other kinds of political phenomena.

CONCLUSION

We have now discussed the basic nature, requirements, and functions of scientifically defined concepts in political science. Our analysis of power has indicated how difficult it is to develop a concept that is simultaneously intuitively satisfying, empirically rigorous, and scientifically useful. We must strive to translate our intuitive notions into concepts that are linked to observable indicators, while retaining the sense that they are measuring the phenomenon that we developed them to measure.

---

[31] This kind of measure is developed in Dahl, pp. 356ff.

[32] Ibid.

Generalizations in
political science

A SCIENTIFIC generalization expresses a relationship between concepts. To identify those nations that have democratic political systems (according to a dichotomous classificatory concept) is significant. To discover that democratic nations tend to have a higher level of education and economic prosperity is probably more significant, for our knowledge is broadened; the world of politics makes more sense because we begin to see its patterns, that is, the relationships between apparently individual facts. It is at the point when concepts are connected and the connections tested and either confirmed or rejected that science begins to take off.

We might say that generalizations are important to political science first of all because they give us a more sophisticated and wide-ranging description of political phenomena. Knowing that a particular senator has more power than another senator is an interesting and often useful bit of information. But being able to say that in any competitive situation, the competitors who are the most highly motivated will dominate (have power over) their less highly motivated opponents, is clearly more impressive and in the long run probably more useful. This suggests a difference between the journalist or historian of the present, interested in the facts and detailed case studies, and the political scientist, whose goal is the development of a systematic knowledge of politics. Here, systematic means generalized.

The second reason for the importance of generalizations follows from the nature of scientific explanation and prediction. In the next chapter, the argument will be made that the primary functions of science are the explanation and prediction of empirical phenomena—the demonstration of why they are or will be. Furthermore, every sound explanation and prediction contains at least one generalization; without generalizations there could be no explanations or predictions. This scientific fact of life will be clarified in this chapter and fully analyzed in the next chapter. At this point, let us remember that the development of generalizations is essential if political science is not only to describe political phenomena, but also to explain and predict them.

THE NATURE OF GENERALIZATIONS

Let us first distinguish between two forms of generalization, *hypotheses* and *laws*. Both are generalizations because they share certain characteristics: they have the same form and must meet the same structural requirements. We cannot tell whether the sentence "Democratic political systems tend to be stable" is a law or an hypothesis if we are unaware of its context. The major difference can be traced to the claim that is made about each. An hypothesis is a guess about a relationship between concepts. After being tested against available evidence according to the principles of scientific method, it is accepted or rejected. If accepted, it is labeled a law. We might say that a law is a *true* hypothesis; or for those who prefer a weaker notion than truth, a well-confirmed hypothesis.[1] The latter formulation might be more desirable, for it implies that unnecessary or contingent nature of all scientific knowledge. The use of "truth," on the other hand, seems to many to imply that scientific laws express eternal and immutable relationships. For the scientist, however, the difference between "true" and "well-confirmed" is largely semantical, for he realizes the conditional nature of scientific knowledge, whichever label is used.

Since hypotheses and laws have the same form and differ only in regard to whether or not they have been empirically confirmed, we can, in a method-

---

[1] See Arnold Brecht, *Political Theory* (Princeton, N.J.: Princeton University Press, 1959), pp. 48–52, for a statement of this position.

ological analysis, talk about "generalization" without concerning ourselves with the distinction between its two main varieties. Later, when the basic principles of hypothesis confirmation are being analyzed, this distinction will move closer toward the center of our attention.

Conditional

A scientific generalization states an empirical relationship (confirmed or merely hypothesized) between concepts in the form of a generalized *conditional*. This rather technically phrased sentence compactly describes the nature of generalizations. But in order to make sense of it, it must be unpacked, as the philosopher might say which, in this case, means explicating empirical, generalized, and conditional.

Let us take the last characteristic first. Assuming that *B* and *R* are concepts, let us say "businessman" and "Republican," respectively, and *X* stands for any person, the general form of a generalization is: "For every *X*, *if X* is *B, then X* is *R*." In other words, every person who has the characteristic of being a businessman also has the characteristic of being a Republican. This could also read, "If *X* is *B*, then *X* is *R* 75 percent of the time." The distinction between statistical laws, which say that only a certain percentage of a population has a given characteristic, and universal laws, which, argue that all of them do, will be analyzed later in this chapter. At this point, we need not concern ourselves with it. An alternate statement of the generalization is, "All *B* are *R*," all businessmen are Republicans. The two statements are logically the same. The second is translatable into the conditional form of the first—to say that all businessmen are Republicans is simply shorthand for, "If a man is a businessman, then he is a Republican."

Structurally, generalizations are marked by the conditional "If . . . then . . . ," which expresses the basic relationship between their concepts.[2] If you find someone with characteristic *A*, then you can also expect him to have characteristic *B*. The generalization does not say you will ever find a person with *A*. It only tells you what to expect or what to be looking for if you do. Thus, "All unicorns have poor eyesight" is an acceptable general-

---

[2] See Ernest Nagel, *The Structure of Science* (New York: Harcourt Brace Jovanovich, 1961), chapter 4.

ization (based on what we know so far), even though no one has yet confronted "a horselike animal having a single horn growing from the center of its forehead." But if someone who takes this hypothesis seriously crosses paths with a unicorn, he will be confident of getting a close look. The *if* sorts out certain things (those with characteristic *A*), the *then* tells us to expect them to have another characteristic, *B*.

Empirical

All generalizations have, or are translatable into, conditional form. But not every conditional statement is a valid scientific generalization, for several other requirements must be satisfied. Given the nature of science, the one that probably comes most readily to mind is the need for scientific generalizations to be empirical—somehow grounded in observation and experience. Let us be more specific.

First of all, since generalizations are basically proposed or confirmed relationships between empirical concepts, we would expect the soundness of a generalization to be dependent to a large extent upon the soundness of its concepts. The expectation is justified. A generalization that contains concepts not meeting the criterion of empirical import cannot be empirical. The hypothesis, "All ghosts are liberal," would have to be classified as nonempirical because "ghost," as it is usually defined, has no empirical import. This initial fact is obvious. But in addition, a generalization must be gramatically correct if it is to be considered empirical. This means that the whole generalization must make sense. Thus, the combining of any two good concepts with the proper logical words does not ensure the empirical soundness of the resulting generalization. What this requirement comes down to is the need to make generalizations testable—susceptible to confirmation or negation. If it is logically impossible to negate a generalization, then it cannot be labeled empirical. A major reason for this impossibility is the failure to put concepts together meaningfully, to allow for testing.

An example should clarify this criteria of grammatical soundness. Consider the generalization, "All political power is blue," which is translatable into the standard "If . . . then . . ." form. Taken individually, each word or concept of the generalization is meaningful: the logical words "all" and "is" present no problems, and "power" and "blue" have or can be given empirical import. Yet, there is something strange about the generalization. When all of its component parts are assembled, the result is untestable because it makes no sense—incompatible concepts have been placed together. Given any reasonable definition of power, it is absurd (note, not just difficult) to imagine a situation in which it is blue. One way out of this absurdity is to use blue in a metaphorical sense analogous to the "black" in "Black Power." Metaphorically, "blue power" might refer to the activities of a police union. But "blue" is no longer an empirical concept, but a symbolic device, suggesting a number of ideas and images. Thus, we can conclude that when its concepts are taken in their usual sense, "all political power is blue" is nonempirical because it is absurd. But let us emphasize again the more important methodological reason, namely, that such absurd or meaningless sentences are not testable. Since empirical generalizations must be testable or potentially confirmable—this is the very nature of empirical—an absurd generalization is not empirical.

Thus, we have returned to the basic foundation of empirical science, the basing of knowledge upon experience and observation. If there is no way that observation can influence our acceptance or rejection of an hypothesis, then it cannot be counted as scientific, although, it might be part of another kind of intellectual system such as religion or metaphysics. Finally, notice that we have not been using true or confirmed as the test of a generalization, but confirmability. Thus, negated generalizations are still empirical in the sense that they have met the criteria of (1) containing concepts with empirical import, and (2) being formulated so that they are testable, so that they *can* be negated. According to this analysis, *absurdity* and *falsity* are not synonymous. False statements are not necessarily absurd.

So far, our examples have been absurd. But as we have said before, absurdity is often a useful device in making a methodological point (which is not the same as saying methodology is absurd). At this point, however, it must be pointed out that the empirically unsound generalization will not always be so absurd and easily rooted out. Every scientific discipline, especially a developing one such as political science, ought to be aware of the many more subtle ways that this scientifically undesirable end may be realized. A generalization so generated will usually appear as sound as any other and will be adjudged acceptable. The fact that it will often have a respected place in the discipline makes it especially important to be able to recognize such a proposition.

Like all nonempirical generalizations, these ultimately fail because they are not testable—there is no way to confirm or deny them. But unlike those already considered, this characteristic is not attributable to the juxtaposition of incompatible empirical concepts, but to how the concepts are defined and intepreted within the generalization.

Let us consider an example. Studies of community power often produce such generalizations as, "All important decisions in city X are made by a single elite group." Apparently this is a valid empirical generalization—the concepts have or can be given empirical import, and the sentence makes sense; it might even be accepted as a commonsensical truth (which is not important, but indicative of the generalization's sound grammar). Thus, it appears that it can be tested; it is possible to devise methods for confirming or denying it. Let's see what might happen when the generalization is employed by political scientists.

Suppose a researcher studying decision making in a city hypothesizes that, "All important decisions in community X are made by a power elite."[3] Let us say he begins examining a number of local issues—defeating a cross-district school busing plan, building a new civic center, creating a citizen's police review board—to see which persons within the community were the most influential in making each decision. His findings might indicate that on the first two issues the same small group of business and political leaders had the greatest influence, but not so with the third. Here, a second group carried the day. Now if the political scientist concludes that the third issue is not important (because it was not made by the power elite) and thus not the basis for a refutation of his hypothesis, he has defined away its empirical nature. Let us consider what has happened. The concept "important decision" has been defined in terms of a particular group of men who are called "the power elite." The "power elite," on the other hand, is defined as "the group that makes the important decisions." Thus, if we come across a decision not made by the elite, we can conclude that it is not important. The result is a hypothesis that is true *by definition*. It cannot be refuted by evidence; deci-

---

[3] All such statements are variations on the central thesis of C. Wright Mills in his classic, *The Power Elite* (New York: Oxford University Press, 1956). For an early test of this hypothesis, see Floyd Hunter, *Community Power Structure* (Chapel Hill: University of North Carolina Press, 1953). For an interesting survey of elites in the United States, see Kenneth Prewitt and Alan Stone, *The Ruling Elites* (New York: Harper & Row, 1973).

sions not made by the elite are summarily labeled unimportant. Therefore, since it is impossible to deny, it cannot be considered empirical and cannot be counted as a scientific generalization.[4]

This method of insuring the "truth" of generalizations, not uncommon in the literature of political science, is usually the result of methodological sloppiness rather than intentional trickery. Its roots go back to the problem of concept formation. As we have pointed out several times, a generalization expresses a relationship between concepts, and thus the soundness of the generalization depends largely upon its concepts. This implies the point we want to make. The concepts of the generalization must be *independently* defined—not defined in terms of one another. The hypothesized or confirmed relationship between them is *empirical,* a question of fact, not *analytical,* a question of defintion. Returning to the example, "important decision" and "power elite" must each be defined so that they are logically independent—it is logically possible for one to exist without the other one. This is just a backhanded way of stating our basic criterion. If it is logically impossible for one to occur without the other, then the hypothesis is not testable and not empirical because no amount of evidence could negate it. To make the hypothesis testable, the concept "important decision" would have to be defined in terms of empirical criteria (how many people the decision affects; how much political, social, and economic change it causes, and so forth). Political scientists could study those who influenced the decisions to see if a single group played the major role in most of them.

Scope

There is another requirement that generalizations must meet. It is designed to prevent sentences that refer to finite objects (President Carter) from being classified as generalizations. Consider the sentence, "President Carter always supports increased defense spending." That it is empirical no one can deny; there are ways to test the assertion. However, do we want to

---

[4] For a discussion of this kind of methodological shortcoming in the study of community power, see Nelson Polsby, *Community Power and Political Theory* (New Haven, Conn.: Yale University Press, 1963), chapter 4.

include it in the same category with, "All businessmen are conservative," or "Radical ideologies tend to become less radical as they become more successful"? An immediate response might be, "Yes, why not? They are all empirical, so why make a distinction?" Upon closer examination, it becomes clear that there is a meaningful distinction that can be made. It has to do with the scope of each sentence's concepts, and ultimately, the scope of the sentence.[5]

The second two sentences used such concepts as "businessman," "conservative," "radical," and "ideology." These are concepts that are operationally defined or with which we are directly acquainted. But so is "President Carter." The difference is that in regard to the first set of concepts, we identify a particular assemblage of characteristics and say any entity that has these characteristics (meets the definition of concept) is included within the scope of the generalization. The generalization tells us something about those entities possessing the first set of characteristics: that they possess another. So, all things that have the characteristics of being a businessman will also be expected to have the characteristic of being conservative. But how many President Carters are there? The answer, "Just one," provides the basis for our distinction between generalizations characterized by unlimited scope and particularistic factual assertions. A sentence that includes "President Carter" cannot be a generalization because its scope is limited to one man (and the importance of the man is methodologically irrelevant). The power of a generalization stems from the fact that it makes no reference to specific things or individuals. Let us recall from the last chapter the two kinds of empirical or descriptive words, particulars and universal concepts. This is the basis of the present distinction, and indicates that the requirement of unlimited scope is intimately related to the requirement of properly formed concepts. The fact is, "President Carter" is not a concept, but rather a particular—a proper name, to be specific. We can now draw a significant conclusion: a sentence that contains particulars (common names or definite descriptions) cannot be counted as a generalization. The label "generalization" means that something is being said about a *class* of entities, not just a single identifiable one.

---

[5] For a general discussion of the criteria of scope in generalizations, see Nagel, *The Structure of Science,* chapter 4.

However, a generalization can be made more or less restrictive through the use of qualifiers. Thus, instead of "All politicians are extroverts," we might hypothesize that "All *local* politicians are extroverts." But this does not call for a limiting of the generalization's scope. it still applies to an entire class; methodologically, it makes no difference whether it is the class of politicians, local politicians, or local politicians with long names and big feet. In fact, it might be possible to define our concept so closely that only one person is included in the class it designates. For instance, how many politicians have been a farmer, engineer, naval officer, governor and President? Suppose we hypothesized that politicians who have been all five tend to have strong egos. Is this a generalization? The answer is yes, even though its scope is *narrow;* but note it is not *limited,* for it is open to any politician who meets the requirements. Compare this situation with the one in which "President Carter" was used. In that case, the result was not an open class, because a particular word was used instead of a general concept. Thus, "unlimited versus limited" must be distinguished from "broad versus narrow" when evaluating a proposition. A statement that is limited cannot be a generalization, although an unlimited statement (generalization) can be either broad or narrow.

It is here that the political scientist is faced with a dilemma. He must make a difficult decision about the emphasis that his research is to take. Should he formulate narrow generalizations, which are subject to accurate testing because they refer to only a few items, or should the emphasis be placed on more inclusive generalizations, which have greater power but are more difficult to test? In short, the question before the political scientist is which is of more value, being able to place more confidence in his generalizations or having them extend to a wider range of cases? There is no final resolution of this dilemma, although most political scientists would probably be willing to give up a degree of confidence to increase the applicability of their generalizations. At the same time, one must be wary of achieving more general applicability through vagueness or ambiguity. If generalizations and their constituent concepts are vague or ambiguous, they can appear to have greater scope than they actually do. For instance, a definition of democracy might be so vague that a generalization containing it applies to every existing political system. Surely, on the face of it, we would have doubts about the usefulness of such a generalization.

UNIVERSAL AND STATISTICAL GENERALIZATIONS

Earlier in this chapter, reference was made to statistical generalizations. Let us pick up the discussion again, for the distinction between universal and statistical generalizations is crucial, especially for a discipline such as political science, which has few, if any, of the former.[6]

A universal generalization takes the form, "All *A* are *B*," or, "If *X* is an *A*, then *X* is *B*." The key word here is "all," for it tells us that something is being said about *every* member of a particular class—every man who is a politician is also an extrovert. One need not be a specialist in scientific method to realize that the universal generalization is the most powerful kind in the scientist's arsenal. But what if the scientist is not confident that every politician is an extrovert; that is, suppose his evidence is not sufficient to make a claim of universality. Must he give up the hope of developing meaningful generalizations of politics? The answer is no, and the reason is the statistical generalization.

Statistical generalizations take several forms. Weaker versions are, *"Some A are B," "Most A are B,"* or *"A tends to be B."* A stronger, and more useful version might say, "75 percent of *A* are *B*," or, "The probability that *A* is *B* is 0.75." The superiority of the latter is obvious. "Seventy-five percent" tells us a great deal more about a population than "most." Yet, the two are not logically dissimilar; both are statistical, because only a portion (it is hoped a substantial one) of a population is being referred to.

Philosopher of social science Quentin Gibson makes another distinction between two kinds of statistical generalizations. The first, labeled by Gibson the "statement of chance," is equivalent to all the varieties we have been talking about, from "75 percent of *A* are *B*" to "Most *A* are *B*."[7] The second is the "tendency statement."[8] According to Gibson, such statements attempt to get around the probabilistic (nonuniversal) nature of statistical laws by using phrases like "other things being equal." So, when used in the generalization "other things being equal, all politicians are extroverts," the

---

[6] For an easily assimilated account of universal and statistical generalizations, see Carl G. Hempel, *Philosophy of Natural Science* (Englewood Cliffs, N.J.: Prentice-Hall, 1966), pp. 54–67.

[7] Quentin Gibson, *The Logic of Social Enquiry* (London: Routledge & Kegan Paul, 1960), chapter 12.

[8] Ibid., chapter 13.

phrase is supposed to indicate to us that all politicians are not extroverts because of unknown factors; other things are not equal. The "other things being equal" phrase is a kind of disclaimer added to what appears to be a universal law in order to indicate that there are exceptions. One gives a statistical generalization the form of a universal generalization by saying "If no other factors were operating, then 'all *A* would be *B*,'" fully realizing that other factors are exerting an influence.

This tells us something else about the nature of statistical generalizations. Most social scientists assume that statistical knowledge is imperfect universal knowledge.[9] This implies that all imperfect statistical knowledge can eventually be made more perfect, for the basis of its inferior status is incomplete knowledge of influencing factors, not the inherent statistical nature of the universe. That is, the statistical notion "chance" is not a throwback to such ideas as Machiavelli's "Fortune": "I hold it to be true that Fortune is the arbiter of one half of our actions, but she still leaves us direct the other half or perhaps a little less."[10] The difference is that while "Fortune" and similar concepts from the pages of traditional philosophy and political science stand for or symbolize the segment of social life which is presumed to be fundamentally unpredictable and so unknowable, "chance," as used by most contemporary social scientists, stands for all the factors influencing a particular phenomenon that are unknown. This interpretation is reinforced by observing the development of knowledge in particular areas of political behavior. Take, for instance, the study of voting behavior—why people vote, and why they vote for one candidate rather than another. An examination of the four leading voting studies published during the last 40 years indicates that the amount of unexplained behavior, and therefore the significance of chance, has been steadily eroded as new variables and relationships are worked into the explanations.[11] The most obvious tendency has been a

---

[9] For a contrary view, see Nagel, *The Structure of Science,* p. 23.

[10] Niccolo Machiavelli, *The Prince,* chapter 25.

[11] The studies are, in order: Paul F. Lazarsfeld et al., *The People's Choice* (New York: Duell, Sloan & Pierce, 1944); Bernard Berelson et al., *Voting* (Chicago: University of Chicago Press, 1948); Angus Campbell et al., *The Voter Decides* (Evanston, Ill.: Row, Peterson, 1954); Angus Campbell et al., *The American Voter* (New York: John Wiley & Sons, 1960); Angus Campbell, Philip Converse, Warren Miller, and Donald Stokes, *Elections and the Political Order* (New York: John Wiley & Sons, 1966). For a discussion of some of the main issues of American voting research, see Richard G. Niemi and Herbert F. Weisberg, eds., *Controversies in American Voting Behavior* (San Francisco: W. H. Freeman, 1976).

movement away from gross sociological explanations toward more refined psychological accounts of voting behavior. The important point to remember is that progress has been made in the explanation of voting behavior, and in consequence, less variance is attributable to chance. In fact, the authors of *The American Voter* developed an attitudinal measure with which they were able to predict the vote of many individuals more accurately than the individuals could themselves.[12] Even the ''chance'' of the gambler is of this empirical kind. If we were able to scientifically analyze a roulette wheel and its ball in terms of weight, balance, and so forth, it would be possible to predict its behavior. The influence of chance would be decreased because of the identification of more influencing factors. Thus, it is *logically* possible that some day every existing statistical generalization in political science will take a universal form because of the discovery and incorporation of these new factors.

Statistical and universal generalizations are cut from the same cloth and differ only in regard to the claims that they make. Certainly it is more impressive and significant to say ''All *A* are *B*,'' than ''The probability that *A* is *B* is 0.75''; but notice that in both cases a percentage of probability is being referred to, 100 percent and 75 percent respectively. It is necessary to emphasize this point to make clear that a sound statistical generalization does not suffer from lack of scope. As in the case of the universal generalization, an entire class is being referred to. It is simply that in the one case, only 75 percent of its members have been found to have another characteristic, while in the other case, all its members can be so characterized.

One general conclusion that seems justified at this point is that political science rests upon a solid empirical foundation even though it employs statistical generalizations almost exclusively. While it would be desirable to have a body of scientific knowledge in the form of universal generalizations, and the development of such knowledge is surely the objective of any science, the statistical nature of existing political science generalizations should not act as a damper upon further attempts at discovery; disillusionment is not a constructive reaction to a statistically oriented discipline.

---

[12] Campbell et al., *The American Voter*, p. 74.

HYPOTHESES AND LAWS

At the outset of this chapter, we noted the distinction between hypotheses and laws, between those generalizations that have been formulated but not tested and those that have been tested and either confirmed or not rejected. But the distinction was ignored because of our initial interest in the structural or logical characteristics of generalizations. At this point, let us return to the content of generalizations and ask the question that has been dangling for some time now: namely, how do we go about confirming or rejecting hypotheses? In other words, what is the difference between a hypothesis and a law?

We will, in this section, discuss only the logical basis of hypothesis testing and not particular techniques for collecting and organizing evidence. That discussion will come in the next section. The basic process, usually called *induction,* which involves going from a particular body of concrete evidence to a generalization, is really quite commonsensical.[13] We test a hypothesis by seeing if it fits the world of observation. Suppose we want to test the hypothesis, "Businessmen tend to be conservative." A sample of businessmen would be questioned (it would be practically impossible to study all businessmen) to determine their ideological orientations. On the basis of this sample—and the confidence we place in our conclusion depends upon its size and randomness—we accept or reject the hypothesis.[14] If three out of four businessmen score high on a test of conservatism, our hypothesis would be confirmed. We would be making a claim about the class of all businessmen on the basis of what we have discovered about some of them. Wesley Salmon has given us a comparable example from the natural sciences: "According to Kepler's first law, the orbit of Mars is an ellipse. The observational evidence for this law consists of a number of isolated observations of the position of Mars. . . . Clearly, this law (conclusion) has far more content than the statements describing the observed positions of Mars (the premises)."[15]

---

[13] For a straightforward discussion of the logic of inductive reasoning, see Wesley C. Salmon, *Logic* (Englewood Cliffs, N.J.: Prentice-Hall, 1963), chapter 3. A more advanced analysis of the logic of the confirmation of hypotheses is Israel Scheffler, *The Anatomy of Inquiry* (New York: Alfred A. Knopf, 1963), part 3.

[14] For a readable introduction to sampling, see Charles H. Backstrom and Gerald D. Hursh, *Survey Research* (Evanston, Ill.: Northwestern University Press, 1981), chapter 2.

[15] Salmon, *Logic,* p. 15.

That scientists use induction to construct laws is indisputable. Every generalization, whether it claims that most or all *A* are *B,* is based on a number of concrete observations. This is why the scientist is said to take an *inductive leap* from his evidence to his generalization. Note that while it is most obvious in the case of generalizing from a sample to the entire class (How can we be sure that the members we didn't sample have the characteristic in the same proportion?), it is logically no less a leap when, in a rarer situation, we have sampled all the members. Even though we have more confidence in the conclusion, can we be sure that all members of the class have been sampled, or that future members (not yet sampled) will have the same characteristic? The single question that lies at the root of this is just because we have observed that something is the case, can we conclude that it is and will continue to be the case?

This question implies another, namely, how do we demonstrate the validity of induction?[16] If we are going to use inductive reasoning to confirm or reject hypotheses, we had better be certain of the logical validity of induction. Returning to our example, how do we justify the movement from, "Three out of every four businessmen whom I have talked to are conservative," to "0.75 of all businessmen are conservative?" In Edward Madden's words, "What reason justifies the belief that something will happen simply because it has happened?"[17]

The justification cannot be based upon deductive logic; the generalization is not a logical consequence of the evidence in the sense that it would be a contradiction to reject the truth of the former while accepting the latter. Nor can induction be justified inductively, that is, on the basis of empirical evidence; it is the use of such evidence in confirming general hypotheses that is being questioned. In the same sense, one cannot prove the validity of the Bible by quoting the Bible. So what have we left? Was David Hume right when he pessimistically concluded that scientific generalizations, that is, observed relationships between events or variables, are simply accepted as matters of faith?

---

[16] For various approaches to the justification of induction, see the articles reprinted in part 6 of Edward H. Madden, ed., *The Structure of Scientific Thoughts* (Boston: Houghton Mifflin, 1960); and Wesley C. Salmon, "Should We Attempt to Justify Induction?" *Philosophical Studies,* 8 (1957), pp. 33–48.

[17] Madden, *The Structure of Scientific Thoughts,* p. 287.

In response to this well-worked controversy, many contemporary philosophers of science have adopted a pragmatic approach to the problem of induction. This approach does not justify induction in any final or absolute sense—we have just demonstrated that this is impossible. It only moderates Hume's pessimism by pointing out that if there is any way to know the world, it must be through induction. That is, the only method available for the testing of generalizations is observation. Thus, if we want to explain and predict empirical phenomena, there is nothing else to do but take the inductive leap, move from concrete observations to universal or statistical generalizations. In the words of Hans Reichenbach, the philosopher who more than any other has developed the pragmatic justification of induction, "The justification of induction is very simple; it shows that induction is the best means to attain a certain aim. The aim is predicting the future. . . ."[18]

Remember that we begin this section with the observation that induction is quite commonsensical. The pragmatic justification of induction reaffirms this by showing that scientific knowledge, that is, knowledge about the world, can never go beyond our ability to observe. It would be satisfying to have a demonstration of the infallibility of our inductive methods of hypothesis testing (that is, moving from observation to generalization), but given the contingent nature of our existence, we must do the best we can without one. Although it cannot be demonstrated that this will lead to truth, it is reasonable to argue that if there is any way to test our assumptions about what is true or false, it must follow the inductive method.

TESTING HYPOTHESES

Induction deals with the philosophical basis of hypothesis testing. Let us consider the more practical side of the matter, how hypotheses are actually tested by political scientists. That is, what kinds of data are used to support or refute proposed relationships and what methods are used to generate or gather the information. Strictly speaking, this is a topic usually reserved for books on the techniques of empirical research, where it can be explored in

---

[18] Hans Reichenbach, *The Rise of Scientific Philosophy* (Berkeley: University of California Press, 1951), p. 246.

great detail.[19] However, our purpose is not to provide a detailed understanding of such techniques, but to indicate how they function in the process of empirical political analysis.

Once the hypothesis has been formulated, the political researcher must decide which of many testing methods is most appropriate. Each is designed to gather evidence the hypothesis can be compared against. The choice of methods will depend upon the nature of the hypothesis, the amount of existing knowledge, and the skills and resources of the resarcher.

Nonscientific methods

When we test assumptions about our everyday lives, we often rely upon common sense, intuition, and empathy. The complexity of the world and the need to make immediate decisions require such sources of evidence. But in science, they must be considered inadequate. Common sense, as we have pointed out in an earlier chapter, varies from person to person and is often unreliable. Intuition, which by definition is an unknowable mental process, provides no objective grounds for distinguishing between sound and unsound evidence. Empathy, putting oneself in someone else's place, while a potentially useful source of hypotheses, is inadequate as a source of evidence because, like intuition, it provides no outside criteria for evaluating its conclusions. We must turn to more reliable methods.

Reactive methods

Some hypotheses are best tested through the use of methods that require the reaction of political actors. That is, the political researcher systematically observes the reaction of people to certain stimuli. Perhaps the best-known reactive measure is the attitude survey, popularized by the Harris

---

[19] A good basic introduction in workbook form is Eduard A. Ziegenhagen and George Bowlby, *Techniques for Political Analysis* (Boston: Holbrook Press, 1971). A more advanced but readable book is Julian L. Simon, *Basic Research Methods in Social Science* (New York: Random House, 1969). Also see Barbara L. Smith et al., *Political Research Methods* (Boston: Houghton Mifflin, 1976), chapter 6. For a combination text and workbook, see Louise G. White and Robert P. Clark, *Political Analysis: Technique and Practice* (Monterey, Calif.: Brooks/Cole Publishing, 1983).

and Gallup polls.[20] Its objective is to describe the attitudes of a population by eliciting responses to questions. For instance, if a responder answers a set of questions in a certain way, he is considered a liberal.

The purpose of a survey is to describe and analyze a population, all citizens of the United States, all citizens of Michigan, Midwestern farmers, Southern Blacks, and so forth. In most cases, the population is too large to observe in its entirety. Thus, it is necessary to select a proportion of the population, a sample, to represent the population.[21] The trick is to select a manageable sample, which despite its relatively small size, allows one to describe the population accurately. To do this, the researcher must, to the best of his ability, *randomize* his sample; that is, ensure that every member of the population has an equal chance of being selected. If this is accomplished, and if the sample is large enough (several thousand people can adequately represent the American voting public), then the characteristics of the sample can be generalized to the population. In other words, if the proper sampling techniques have been employed, the researcher can, with great confidence, assume that what is true of the sample (80 percent of a random sample of American citizens agrees that the United States should occupy the Persian Gulf) is also true of the entire population (all American citizens).

A random sample is not easy to come by. If the population is small (all U.S. senators), a simple device can be used; put all the names in a hat and select an adequate number. But if a larger population is being studied, such simplicity is impossible. The student of national voting behavior could not find a large enough hat. Thus, the temptation arises to use haphazard sampling. If one is trying to describe the attitudes of Chicago citizens toward their mayor, why not simply stand on a street corner in downtown Chicago and ask the first 500 people who come by? This method is less than adequate because it is likely that certain types of people will be overrepresented or underrepresented as a result of where and when you conduct the survey; if it

---

[20] For a readable and thorough introduction to sampling, see Charles H. Backstrom and Gerald D. Hursh, *Survey Research* (New York: John Wiley & Sons, 1981), chapter 2. Also see Herbert Weisberg and Bruce Bowen, *An Introduction to Survey Research and Data Analysis* (San Francisco: W. H. Freeman, 1977).

[21] For a thorough discussion of sampling techniques, see Seymour Sudman, *Applied Sampling* (New York: Academic Press, 1976).

is noon in the banking district, the sample will no doubt include a higher proportion of bank employees than exists in the general population.

If the population is too large for a simple random sample, yet haphazard sampling is scientifically unacceptable, what is the researcher to do? He would probably use a modified system of random sampling, using the techniques of stratification and clustering. A stratified sample is one that first breaks the population down into basic categories such as sex, race, and occupation. Then, a random selection is conducted within each strata. If 55 percent of the population is female and 75 percent is white, then the sample, because it is designed to have the same proportions, is more likely to be truly representative. The cluster or area sample is also designed to overcome some of the physical limitations of the simple random sample. If a national sample of 2,000 is the goal, then the nation is divided into levels or clusters— regions, states, urban and rural areas, large cities, small cities, and so forth. Random sampling is used at each level. For example, after dividing the nation into regions such as Northeast and Northwest, several large cities are randomly selected to represent all large cities in that region. After Cleveland is selected as one of three large Northcentral cities, the random selection of smaller units continues—precinct to neighborhood to block to home. Thus, if you are the person who is finally interviewed in such a study, you can be sure that your selection has been the result of a rigorous, random procedure. When used together, as they usually are in larger and more sophisticated attitude and voting studies, stratification and clustering can achieve the basic objective, randomness, that would be physically impossible with the simple random sample.

Besides obtaining a representative sample, the political scientist who is using the survey technique to test an hypothesis must also be concerned with the questions to be asked. The primary objective is to make them as neutral as possible; that is, write the questions so that they do not reflect the biases of the researcher. Another consideration follows from the basic nature of reactive research. The fact that people are asked to answer questions means that an additional factor is thrown into the situation—the researcher. The subject is responding to the questions and to the questioner. It is now well known that some people tend to answer yes no matter what the question and some tend to answer no. The political scientist must keep this in mind when formulating his questions. In practical terms, it means getting at a particular opinion or attitude by asking the same question several times using different language.

Another type of reactive research is experimentation.[22] Experiments are so common in the natural sciences that many students of science equate scientific method with the experimental method. While this equation makes sense in physics and chemistry, it is misleading when applied to political science. Experimentation can be given a broad meaning or a narrow meaning. If the former is used, experimentation refers to any research where the researcher prods or stimulates the real world and most reactive research, including survey research, must be considered experimental. Most scientists use the narrow definition and define the experiment in terms of three basic requirements: (1) the ability to manipulate the factor (usually labeled the *independent variable*) that is assumed to be influencing the factor (usually labeled the *dependent variable*) that is being explained; (2) the ability to control, to hold constant other factors that might have some impact on the dependent variable; (3) the ability to measure the impact of the independent variable on the dependent variable. For instance, experimentally testing a hypothesis about the impact of certain kinds of campaign propaganda on voting behavior would require that we be able to remove the effect of all factors except the hypothesized independent variable. This is not easily done. Thus, if a narrow concept of experimentation is used, that is, if experimentation implies that the scientist is in control of and can manipulate all of the relevant conditions affecting the dependent variable, then it would seem that political scientists will use the experiment relatively infrequently; few political situations lend themselves to such control. The student of politics must usually attempt to test his hypotheses about political behavior not by manipulating the political actors he is studying, but instead by analyzing the information that flows from his systematic observations. In this sense, the survey is the social scientist's alternative to the natural scientist's laboratory experiment.

As political scientists become more interested in the formulation and evaluation of government policies, some of the methods of experimentation have been incorporated into what is known as policy analysis. The basic rationale is fairly obvious. Governments formulate and implement policies to achieve social and economic goals. To decide if the goals have been met,

---

[22] For a summary of experimental techniques that are available, see Donald T. Campbell and Julian C. Stanley, *Experimental and Quasi-Experimental Designs for Research* (Chicago: Rand McNally, 1966).

there must be ways to measure the results. A good example is the attempt by the state of Connecticut to determine if more police surveillance of the highways leads to fewer traffic fatalities. The use of experimental techniques by governments leads to the notion of *social experiment*—attempts by policymakers to bring about changes in the social, political, or economic systems in certain predictable ways, and then to evaluate the success or failure of their policies.[23]

Some political scientists have taken a different approach to the experiment in political science.[24] They recognize the limited use of the pure experiment in political research, but argue that there is an alternate strategy, which while not as pure, nevertheless can be useful. This is the technique of simulation. The real world is simulated in a classroom or laboratory and the behavior of the participants is observed. Returning to a previous example, a simulated election might be held in a political science class; the class could be divided into two groups. The composition and environment of each group would be made as similar as possible with one crucial exception; only one would be exposed to the propaganda. After a simulated election, any difference in voting between the two groups could be attributed to the independent variable. More often simulation is used to test hypotheses about decision making, such as the development of military strategy. While this method seems to meet the basic requirements of the classic experiment, the claim that it is truly an experiment, in the sense that the chemist's experiments are, is subject to a serious objection. The simulation is an attempt at recreating the real world of politics; it is not the real world. Students in a classroom acting as if they are voters in a presidential election or military strategists mapping out a nuclear war are neither voters nor strategists. Thus, the hypotheses are not really being tested. In Chapter 8, we will argue that while simulation should not be thought of as a method for testing hypotheses, it can be a major source of hypotheses.

---

[23] Donald T. Campbell, "Reforms as Experiments," in Frances Caro ed., *Readings in Evaluation Research* (New York: Russell Sage Foundation, 1971), pp. 233–61. For a more thorough discussion of policy evaluation and the use of experimental techniques, see a good policy analysis text such as Gary D. Brewer and Peter de Leon, *The Foundations of Policy Analysis* (Homewood, Ill.: Dorsey Press, 1983).

[24] See J. A. Laponce and Paul Smoker, eds., *Experimentation and Simulation in Political Science* (Toronto: University of Toronto Press, 1972).

Nonreactive research

Not all hypothesis testing in political science is based on reaction. Some hypotheses are better tested by using nonreactive methods, that is, observations not requiring the reaction of political actors.[25] Several types of nonreactive research can be identified. First is the systematic examination of governmental documents, historical records, newspaper files, voting statistics, and all other stored data. The most important characteristic of this material is that it already exists. The problem for the researcher is how to systematically examine it. One method in widespread use is content analysis.[26] This technique assumes that any body of written information can be used as an indicator of political attitudes, values, and intentions, if the information is examined systematically; that is, according to explicit criteria that indicate how words and messages are to be interpreted. Let us suppose that a political scientist interested in international conflict hypothesizes that anxiety about the military status of other nations will cause all nations to increase their military strength and that the resulting arms race will often lead to war. The testing of this hypothesis might involve the systematic examination of newspapers and official government communications for key words and phrases, "missile gap" for instance, assumed to indicate national anxiety. The words and messages could be counted, and conclusions could be reached about typical verbal behavior during prewar periods. By itself, the content analysis might not be conclusive, but along with other sources of data, it could be useful.

Besides the analysis of secondary data, the political scientist often makes first-hand observations that do not require the reaction of political actors. The political scientist might place himself in the midst of a political situation, make observations and take notes, all without the knowledge of those being observed. Taking it one step further, the political scientist might join a group, a labor union for instance, with the intent of observing its members in action. Despite its usefulness in many situations, this kind of undercover research has serious moral implications.

---

[25] A useful and creative introduction to this type of research is Eugene Webb et al., *Unobtrusive Measures: Nonreactive Research in the Social Sciences* (Chicago: Rand McNally, 1966).

[26] For the best introduction to content analysis, see Ole R. Holsti, *Content Analysis for the Social Sciences and Humanities* (Reading, Mass.: Addison-Wesley Publishing, 1969).

GENERALIZATIONS AND CAUSALITY

One interpretation of "If *A*, then *B*" is "*A causes B*"—being a business-man causes one to become conservative. That there is a relationship between the notions of generalization and cause is obvious. However, the assumption underlying the above-mentioned interpretation, namely, that generalizations are reducible to causal relationships, is not the only one that can be made. We will argue that it is the other way around: a causal relationship is a type of lawful relationship. This fact has led some students of scientific method to view the notion of cause as expendable, that is, unnecessary in any description of the fundamental elements of science. This section's objective is the clarification of these views about causality.

Modern conceptions of causality have their origins in David Hume's analysis, which replaces the necessary connection of events with a mere constant conjunction. As we have seen, empirical relationships are contingent and not necessarily true. Hume's position was that all we can conclude from our observations is that one event or situation always or usually follows another. In his commonsensical style, he wrote: "Having found, in many instances, that any two kinds of objects—flame and heat, snow and cold—have always been conjoined together; if flame or snow be presented anew to the senses, the mind is carried by custom to expect heat or cold. . . ."[27] There is no way to demonstrate that the relationship is necessary, that the events or variables must be invariably linked. Thus, we are justified in noting the constant (or nearly constant) conjunction of events (this is what we do in every generalization); but it is going beyond the limits of our knowledge to view this conjunction as a *necessary* connection. The latter interpretation makes the relationship analytic—it is a logical contradiction to say *B* occurred but *A* didn't; assuming that the relationship is intended to be empirical, and recalling that analytical propositions are nonempirical, it follows that causal statements do not express necessary connections.

The relationship between cause and generalization can now be briefly explicated. If saying that "*A causes B*" is tantamount to "*B* always follows *A*," then they are both reducible to the generalization, "If *A*, then *B*."[28] In

---

[27] David Hume, *The Treatise of Human Nature*, book 1, part 3, section 3.

[28] Herbert Feigl, "Notes on Causality," in Herbert Feigl and May Brodbeck, eds., *Readings in the Philosophy of Science* (New York: Appleton-Century-Crofts, 1953), p. 410.

other words, we can express what is traditionally known as a causal relationship without using the term *cause*. Suppose a political scientist who wants to explain the outbreak of war hits upon "If economic rivalry, then war," which is simply the generalized form of the observation that "economic rivalry between nations tends to be followed by military conflict." The notion "cause" adds nothing to the analysis just given, or so it would seem. Most natural scientists would take this argument one step further by claiming that the notion of cause can be reduced to that of "quantitative relationship." If factor *A* (the amount of money spent in an electoral campaign) and factor *B* (the number of votes received in an election) always change together—for every \$1 million another 50,000 votes—what more has to be said? A quantitative relationship has been discovered that allows one to predict the results of elections.

However, even while accepting this analysis, which demonstrates the logical expendability of cause, it is not inconsistent to admit that there is a practical reason for distinguishing between causal and noncausal generalizations and for continuing to use the concept cause. What of a generalization that describes a relationship between two variables at a given moment? This kind of *cross-sectional* generalization is clearly noncausal in that one variable or event is not known to occur before another. In Gustav Bergmann's words: "Such laws state functional connections obtaining among the values which several variables have at the same time."[29] If we discover, for instance, that two political attitudes are usually associated—a person who has one tends to have the other—we will probably not be able to say that one causes the other, because we don't know which one comes first. Thus, Herbert McClosky has examined the relationship between conservatism and personality.[30] He discovers that high scores on a conservatism scale and high scores on a number of clinical-personality variables (hostility, rigidity) hang together so that an individual with the former tends also to have the latter. While the relationship is clear, McClosky refrains from drawing the commonsensical conclusion that personality causes conservatism. "The association between conservatism and the traits outlined exists in the form of correlations, which only tell us that the two go together. How they go together,

---

[29] Gustav Bergmann, *Philosophy of Science* (Madison: University of Wisconsin Press, 1957), p. 102.

[30] Herbert McClosky, "Conservatism and Personality," *American Political Science Review*, 52 (1958), pp. 27–45.

and which is antecedent to which is a more difficult and more elusive problem.''[31] In other words, because no temporal sequence has been identified, the relationship must be considered *cross-sectional* and not *causal*.

There is another kind of observed relationship that appears to be causal but is not. This is that constant foe of statisticians, the *spurious association*. We might observe that two phenomena always occur together—they are statistically correlated. For instance, let us assume that it is discovered that whenever traffic congestion increases, it soon follows that the literacy rate begins to rise. This relationship crops up in study after study in a variety of countries. Our common sense tells us that it is probably a mistake to claim that traffic congestion causes an increase in literacy; yet the statistical correlation is always there. A solution is found when it is discovered that both phenomena are the result of a third factor, industrialization. Thus, when a country becomes more industrialized, its streets become filled with cars, and people are more likely to learn how to read and write. The relationship between congestion and literacy is spurious, because while statistical tests indicate the relationship exists, there is no causal relationship.

The question that emerges from this analysis of types of observed relationships is how do we distinguish between causal and noncausal relationships? What criteria can we use to sort them out? The major difference between cross-sectional and causal generalizations is one of sequence or time. Carl Hempel's terminology makes this point very well.[32] He calls the former laws of coexistence (*A* and *B* occur together), and the latter, laws of succession (*A* is followed by *B*). In more down to earth terms, it seems reasonable that an event that happened today cannot be a cause of one that happened last Friday. Likewise, if one's personality is formed before the age of six, and one's political values are formed no earlier than adolescence, then if a statistical relationship is discovered, it cannot be that values are causing personality; if there is a causal relationship, it must be the other way around. This analysis, by itself, does not establish a causal pattern. But it does allow us to eliminate some possibilities. Until we examine the temporal sequence, a statistical relationship must be considered cross-sectional, or in Hempel's terms, a law of coexistence.

---

[31] Ibid., p. 44.

[32] Carl Hempel, "Deductive Nomological vs. Statistical Explanation," in Herbert Feigl and Grover Maxwell, eds., *Minnesota Studies in the Philosophy of Science*, 3 (Minneapolis: University of Minnesota Press, 1962), p. 108.

What about spurious correlations? Is there any way to identify and sort them out? There are no fool-proof methods. The important question to ask is, "What else do we know about the apparent relationship?" In some cases, our reason and empirical knowledge suggest that the two phenomena or events are in no way connected. What could be the connection between traffic congestion and literacy? There seems to be no evident contact between them; if there is, it is extremely obscure. Thus, we search on. In some cases, we may conclude that the relationship is coincidental, and predict that it will not occur again. If it does, then perhaps there is a third variable that comes into contact with each of the other factors. It violates neither our sense of logic nor our empirical observations to speculate that industrialization is causing both congestion and increased literacy. The process of weeding out the spurious relationship has begun.

Thus, a causal generalization is distinctive because it refers to a temporal sequence. Our conclusion is that while cause is logically expendable, there are still times when a political scientist might want to refer to causal laws to distinguish them from the cross-sectional variety; but this is primarily a pragmatic distinction, for in either case, the generalization is an expression of a constant conjunction.

The search for causal relationships in political science is most profitably viewed as the search for and refinement of lawful relationships. This last point should be emphasized, for a conclusion that might be drawn at this point is that if we reduce cause to lawfulness, one observed relationship is as good as another. However, even without a concept of necessary connection to direct us toward final or ultimate causes, we can distinguish between sound empirical and spurious relationships. A discussion of the methods available for such analysis would take us far afield into the realm of research techniques.[33] The political scientist can work with empirical relationships in the form of statistical correlations; he can compare, sort through, and accept, reject, or refine them, and in so doing, roll back the frontiers of political knowledge—all within the framework of Hume's constant conjunction.

Let us conclude our discussion of generalizations and causality with a brief consideration of several types of causal situations, emphasizing those

---

[33] For a discussion of correlational techniques, see any good statistics book. Perhaps the best books but not necessarily the easiest, for social scientists is Hubert M. Blalock, *Social Statistics* (New York: McGraw-Hill, 1960).

that are especially relevant to political scientists.[34] Causal situations are usually analyzed in terms of sufficient and/or necessary conditions.[35] *A* is a sufficient condition for *B* when (1) if *A* occurs, *B* does, and (2) *B* might have other sufficient conditions. For example, based on historical observation we might conclude that economic rivalry between nations is usually followed by military conflict, but that, in addition, an arms race often precedes such conflict, even in the absence of economic rivalry. We have two independent sufficient conditions for military conflict.

If we observe that military conflict never occurs without economic rivalry preceding it, no matter what other factors are present, we would conclude that economic rivalry is a necessary condition for military conflict. Thus, *A* is a necessary condition for *B* when (1) if *B* occurs we know that *A* is present; but (2) *A* is not alone a sufficient condition for *B*. This notion of "necessary" can be handled within our constant conjunction framework, for it does not imply a necessary connection between *A* and *B*. It would be logically possible for *B* to occur without *A* preceding it. Observation has led us to conclude that, as a matter of fact, this never happens.

From what we have already said about political science, it would be reasonable to assume that the discovery of necessary conditions is as rare an occurrence as the discovery of sufficient conditions. It is even rarer to identify a condition *(A)* that is both necessary and sufficient; for if we do, we have found the one and only cause of *B*. Remember that a necessary condition need not be sufficient—we know it always occurs before a particular event but other conditions may also be necessary. But when a condition, economic rivalry, always precedes an event, military conflict, and military conflict never occurs without economic rivalry, we have an example of a necessary and sufficient condition.

Perhaps the kind of causal situation that has the most relevance for the political scientist is one where a combination of factors is sufficient for an event. In this case, we can call any one of them a *partially sufficient* condi-

---

[34] Some social scientists have attempted to develop notions of causality that are useful in the description and explanation of social and political phenomena. See Hubert M. Blaclock, *Causal Inferences in Non-Experimental Research* (Chapel Hill: University of North Carolina, 1961); and Herbert A. Simon, *Models of Man* (New York: John Wiley & Sons, 1957).

[35] For a discussion of "necessary" and "sufficient" conditions, see Stefan Nowak, "Some Problems of Causal Interpretation of Statistical Relationships," *Philosophy of Science,* 27 (1960), pp. 23–28. Also see Blalock, *Causal Inferences in Non-Experimental Research,* pp. 31–35.

tion to indicate that any single factor is not sufficient. Returning to the causes of military conflict, suppose we discover the economic rivalry and an arms race are *in conjunction* sufficient conditions. We can't say that economic rivalry alone is sufficient; but it is significant when other factors are added. There is evidence to suggest that this is the situation that confronts political scientists more often than not. With the recognition of the complexity of social phenomena and the acceptance of a research framework that assumes multiple causes, the single sufficient condition becomes an exotic idea, so exotic that most political scientists push it to the back of their research minds. The political scientist does his scientific work by sorting through a number of possible partially sufficient conditions, rejecting some, accepting others—in other words, by testing hypotheses.

CONCLUSION

In this chapter, we have discussed how concepts are combined in various ways to form generalizations. Without generalizations, description would remain at a basic level, and explanation and prediction, the topics of the next chapter, would be impossible. Generalizations are so important in scientific analysis that some scientists would argue that their formulation and testing define the central process of science. But, as was the case with concept formation, the development of sound scientific laws of politics is a difficult process.

CHAPTER

Explanation and prediction in political inquiry

T
HE philosopher of science Ernest Nagel has written that ". . . the distinctive aim of the scientific enterprise is to provide systematic and responsibly supported explanations."[1] If Nagel's view is representative of most students of scientific method, we can conclude that those doing political research and those reading the results of such research ought to know something about the nature of scientific explanation. Furthermore, it is evident that political scientists are forever trying to answer, explicitly or implicitly, "why" questions: *Why* did the Supreme Court make the *Baker* v. *Carr* decision? *Why* does the United States have a two-party system? *Why* do businessmen tend to vote Republican? *Why* did Gerald Ford pardon Richard Nixon? *Why* did Russia invade Afghanistan? When a question begins with *why,* an explanation is being asked for. In addition, such frequently used words as *consequently, hence, therefore, because, obviously,* and *naturally* are good indicators that one is face-to-face with, or in the midst of, an explanation.

---

[1] Ernest Nagel, *The Structure of Science* (New York: Harcourt Brace Jovanovich, 1961), p. 15.

EXPLANATION AND POLITICAL INQUIRY

Much of political science is descriptive and, as we have seen, many political scientists devote their energies to discovering and describing political facts. However, while recognizing the importance of description to a science, especially an immature one, we must not assume that it is the end of science. Emphasizing this point for behavioralists (but really for all political scientists) is Heinz Eulau: "No piece of political behavior research is content to describe the universe of politics. . . . The goal is the explanation of why people behave politically as they do and why, as a result, political processes and systems function as they do."[2]

One more justification of the political scientist's concern with explanation should be mentioned. A characteristic of scientific explanation which will be examined later in this chapter is its logical identity with scientific prediction. The logical structure of explanation and prediction is the same; the difference between them is pragmatic, that is, based on the way they are used. Is the objective to account for a past event or a present state of affairs (explanation), or is it to describe a future event or state of affairs (prediction)? If this identity is valid, then prediction, and therefore explanation, ought to be a major concern of political scientists. For one of their primary activities is to provide advice on policy matters, and policy decisions are always based on an expected outcome, a prediction about the best means for implementing a given end. In fact, David Truman has written, "we cannot . . . escape the necessity to predict. Governmental officials and private citizens anticipate as best they can the consequences of political actions with which they are involved."[3] Consider the two examples of a farmer trying to decide which of two senatorial candidates will be more likely to support his interests, and the President developing a policy to slow down inflation. In both cases, a prediction (whether realized or not) is necessary; in the first instance, about the behavior of potential senators, in the second instance, about the reaction of the economy to alternative policies.

There are some convincing methodological reasons for political scientists taking an interest in the logic of explanation. But there is a more common-

---

[2] Heinz Eulau, *The Behavioral Persuasion in Politics* (New York: Random House, 1963), p. 24.

[3] David Truman, *The Governmental Process* (New York: Alfred A. Knopf, 1951), p. 504.

sensical way of making the point. One merely has to consider how everyone, both the scientist and the man on the street, attempts to cope with the world. It is by trying to explain the things that happen to him. We argued in Chapter 2 that scientific knowledge is superior to common sense. This is not contradicted by the present argument, for we are now claiming that since explanation and prediction are basic human activities, it is not unfair to request that those dealing with the empirical world at more sophisticated levels have a basic understanding of the nature of the explanatory process.

The nomological model of explanation

Philosophers of science admit that there are many uses of the word *explain*. We can explain (describe) the structure of the Interstate Commerce Commission or explain (explicate) the meaning of "writ of certiorari." These are both acceptable dictionary uses of explain. Yet, neither gets at the basic nature of scientific explanation, the answering of *why* questions. The why can be answered only by showing that the fact to be explained either follows logically from premises or is highly probable based on the premises. One might say that a specific event causes another event, *X*. But we can explain *X* only by stating the general law that indicates the relationship is normal—to be expected under the circumstances. If this discussion seems a bit technical, let us make the basic point in a more down-to-earth way. This is possible because scientific explanation is based upon a commonsensical idea, that to explain something, one needs specific knowledge about the phenomenon and general knowledge that links it to other phenomena that preceded it. The soundness of our explanation will depend on how much general knowledge we have—no knowledge, no explanation. This point cannot be made strongly enough. As we will argue in the next section, almost anyone can construct a plausible account of why something happened. But a scientific explanation requires more than plausibility; it requires knowledge.

Political scientists appear to employ many kinds of explanation to account for political phenomena, but these are all patterns of one model of scientific explanation; they are variations on a single theme, not distinct logical types. This single logical type of explanation is usually called the "nomological" or "covering-law model." It claims that explanation is achieved by classifying what is to be explained under general laws. Most people say that Watergate

133

caused President Nixon to resign his office. But the events of Watergate cannot be used as causal factors unless we have available generalizations such as, "Whenever a President feels that he is about to be impeached, he will resign." If we really know nothing about why Presidents resign, if we have no laws linking presidential resignations to other factors, then we cannot explain.

Let us examine the structure of nomological explanation in more detail. Our objective, in addition to describing the model, is a demonstration that it is a flexible and realistic basis for explanation in political science. In addition to the fact that the nomological model can include many of the patterns of explanation used by political scientists, it is useful, even though it must be considered an ideal not yet fully realizable in political science.

In the first place, an explanation can be divided into what explains and what is explained; the former will be called the "explanans," the latter the "explanandum."[4] The explanans includes two kinds of statements: general laws, and sentences stating intial or antecedent conditions. Together, they imply the explanandum. More accurately, initial conditions are necessary only when the explanandum is an individual fact. For instance, the fact of the United States' two-party system might be explained by (1) the *generalization* that all political systems with single-member districts have two-party systems, and (2) the *initial condition* that the political system of the United States is one of single-member districts. However, suppose that we would like to explain the generalization. The point can be made if we translate the two arguments into simple deductive logic. If A = "single-member district system," B = "two-party system," C = "third parties are undercut," and $\supset$ = "If . . . then," the explanation of the singular fact would be:

$$
\begin{array}{ll}
\text{(1) } A \supset B, \text{ and of the law:} & \text{(2) } A \supset C \\
\quad\;\; \underline{A} & \quad\;\; \underline{C \supset B} \\
\quad\;\; B & \quad\;\; A \supset B
\end{array}
$$

What is so special about a deductive explanation? The answer lies in the logical connection between the premises and the conclusion, the explanans and the explanandum. To understand this connection is to grasp the power of deductive explanation. If the premises are true, the conclusion must be

[4] Carl Hempel and Paul Oppenheim, "The Logic of Explanation," in Herbert Feigl and May Brodbeck, eds., *Readings in the Philosophy of Sciences* (New York: Appleton-Century-Crofts, 1953), p. 321.

true.[5] Here is where the necessity of the argument exists. As Abraham Kaplan puts it, "In the deductive model the necessity does not lie in the premises, but rather in the relation between the premises and the conclusion which they control."[6] In addition, for an explanation to be truly explanatory, its generalizations must be well-confirmed by empirical evidence. This requirement refers to the generalizations, not to the logical structure of the argument. So, a sound scientific explanation accounts for a fact by showing that it is one instance of a general tendency. This is what a political scientist does if he explains a political phenomenon. If all sample surveys indicate that all businessmen are Republican, it is not surprizing that businessman X is a Republican; X is included in the generalization.

We must, at this point, make a distinction between two kinds of explanation, deductive and statistical-probabilistic. As the label implies, the former is an exercise in deductive logic. As already noted, in a valid deductive explanation, the logical connection between the explanans and the explanandum is such that if the former is true, the latter must be true. A deductive explanation employs universal laws or generalizations stating that *all* As are Bs. This is why the explanation can be deductive. Now, as we saw in Chapter 6, a universal law is never necessarily true. An empirical generalization must be testable and have the potential of being proven false. The difference between a universal law and a statistical law is the kind of claim we make about each based on the evidence. Neither is necessarily true.

A statistical or probabilistic explanation is one where statistical laws are employed. It should be of greater interest to political scientists because the generalizations that political science has generated have, up until now, been statistical. Unlike a deductive explanation, the inductive-statistical explanation of an individual event does not necessarily imply that event; the premises can be true and the conclusion can be false. The explanation consists not of showing why the conclusion is true, but why it is probable. Thus, the explanation of the voting behavior of a certain group or the behavior of Congress may be explained by statistical laws; their actions are accounted for by showing that they were highly probable based on the evidence con-

---

[5] For the nature of deductive logic, see any logic text. Two of the most highly respected are Irving M. Cope, *Symbolic Logic* (New York: Macmillan, 1954), and Patrick Suppes, *Introduction to Logic* (Princeton, N.J.: Van Nostrand Reinhold, 1957).

[6] Abraham Kaplan, *The Conduct of Inquiry* (San Francisco: Chandler Publishing Co., 1964), p. 339.

tained in the laws and initial conditions of the explanans. But let us repeat: A single event cannot be accounted for deductively by means of a statistical law. The law and initial conditions can be true and the event might not occur. Thus, even if we have a well-substantiated law that shows approximately 75 percent of all businessmen are strong Republican party-identifiers, we cannot *deductively* explain the Republican beliefs of a single Republican as we could if the law stated that all businessmen are Republican. Thus, his party identification is explained because it is highly probable or rationally credible that he is a Republican[7]—but he need not be, given the evidence, and this is what makes it a probabilistic and not a deductive explanation.

All this about inductive logic applies to statistical explanations accounting for individual events. What about the explanation of statistical laws? We have seen that universal laws are explainable by deductive logic. It is the same with statistical laws. That is, a statistical-probabilistic law can be explained with other laws, universal and statistical; yet, this will be a deductive argument—if the premises are true, the conclusion is true. For instance, the statistical law that 12 percent of all registered voters in city X are cross-pressured and identify with the Democrats can be explained by two other laws: (1) 30 percent of registered voters are cross-pressured, (2) 40 percent of registered voters who are cross-pressured are Democratic. This is a deductive explanation, since, if it is a valid argument and the premises are true (the probabilities are true), then the conclusion must follow. From the standpoint of logic, the explanation of universal laws and that of statistical laws exhibit no difference, since, in a sense, they are both "universal" statements. The distinction is that one states that in a certain universe all individuals exhibit a certain characteristic, while the other states that 60 percent have the attribute. So the tricky facet of statistical explanation is the explanation of the single event.

Other notions of explanation

We must consider an alternate notion of explanation and try to describe its shortcomings. Robert Brown speaks for many philosophers and social

---

[7] The concept "rationally credible" is Carl Hempel's. See "Deductive Nomological vs. Statistical Explanations," in Herbert Feigl and Grover Maxwell, eds., *Minnesota Studies in the Philosophy of Science,* 3 (Minneapolis: University of Minnesota Press, 1962), p. 149.

scientists when he gives the following definition: "All explanations are attempts to explain away impediments of some kind."[8] This implies an interpretation of scientific explanation that is psychological. That is, "to explain" means "to make understandable," to reduce the unfamiliar to the familiar.[9] In the words of the well-known physicist P. W. Bridgman, "Explanation consists merely in analyzing our complicated systems into simpler systems so that we recognize in the complicated system the interplay of elements already so familiar to us that we accept them as not needing explanation."[10] This notion of explanation is in opposition to the nomological interpretation advocated in this book, and it misses the point of what explanation is all about.

The power of scientific explanation lies in the logical connection between the evidence and the conclusion, not in the degree of psychological familiarity the argument has. According to Carl Hempel, "the covering-law concept of explanation . . . refers to the logic, not the psychology of explanation. . . ."[11] Thus, there is a distinction between *having* an explanation and *understanding* it. One can give a good explanation of a political phenomenon using unfamiliar concepts and newly discovered relationships. On the other hand, one might think he has explained a fact because his argument appeals to common sense, while in reality, no explanation has been provided; the required generalizations do not exist or those used do not properly imply the conclusion. Thus, their familiarity is neither a necessary nor a sufficient condition of valid explanations. The distinction can also be stated as one between a psychological and a cognitive meaning of explanation. In explaining an event to someone, we study her reactions as clues to her understanding of the explanation. She comprehends and accepts the explanation to a greater or lesser degree. This has to do with communicating a fact and depends in part upon my ability to articulate and her power of intellect and is thus psychological; it has no *logical* relation to the cognitive soundness of

---

[8] Robert Brown, *Explanation in Social Science* (Hawthorne, N.Y.: Aldine Publishing, 1963), p. 41.

[9] For an interesting discussion of explanation and understanding, see A. James Gregor, *An Introduction to Metapolitics* (New York: Free Press, 1971), chapters 7 and 8.

[10] P. W. Bridgman, *The Nature of Physical Theory* (Princeton, N.J.: Princeton University Press, 1936), p. 63.

[11] Carl Hempel, "Reasons and Covering Laws in Historical Explanation," in Sidney Hook, ed., *Philosophy and History* (New York: New York University Press, 1963), p. 147.

the explanation. In short, the soundness of an explanation and its psychological familiarity or attractiveness are distinct properties.

We have based our argument upon the requirements of scientific explanation; psychological understanding is neither a necessary nor a sufficient condition. There is a more pragmatic reason for rejecting this interpretation of explanation. It is the simple fact that an idea or argument will appear more or less familiar to different people and at different times. Thus, psychological familiarity cannot serve as an objective standard for assessing the soundness of an explanation. An explanation is objectively valid to one degree or another; its cognitive value can be uniformly evaluated by numerous analysts—each will reach the same conclusion. This is how a science operates. It does not base its knowledge on psychological familiarity. It must be admitted, however, that we would like our explanations to be understood. Even the soundest explanation is of limited use if only one person understands it.

The intersubjective nature of science seems to imply that scientists ought to be understood by other scientists, and hopefully by the general population. This is especially true of political knowledge, since it is often the basis of policy decisions that affect entire societies. However, the degree of understanding is another attribute of the explanation, independent of its soundness. This is the gist of our argument. A related model of explanation assumes that a fact has been explained when it can be fitted into a pattern[12] or system.[13] "According to the pattern model, then, something is explained when it is so related to a set of other elements that together they constitute a unified system. We understand something by identifying it as a specific part in an organized whole."[14] If this model proposes another mode of explanation that is not nomological, then one does not account for something simply by showing that it fits into a pattern. This might describe some of its relationships, but it doesn't answer the why question. On the other hand, the pattern model might be interpreted in a nomological sense if the relationships of the pattern or system are taken as manifestations of generalizations. In this case, it cannot be considered a distinct model.

There is another intellectual position that comes to mind in a discussion of

---

[12] Kaplan, *The Conduct of Inquiry*.

[13] Eugene Meehan, *Explanation in Social Science: A System Paradigm* (Homewood, Ill.: Dorsey Press, 1968).

[14] Kaplan, *The Conduct of Inquiry*.

the nature of explanation and psychological understanding. It is the argument that the nomological model of explanation does not really explain at all. Using the generalization "Workers tend to vote left" and the statement "*X* group is made up mainly of workers" to explain the group's voting left does not, according to this criticism, really show why the behavior occurred. Something else is required. For instance, W. G. Runciman has written, "Given that being a Catholic is correlated with being a Democrat, the question why is not so much answered as asked."[15] At one level, this is a version of the claim that no explanation is final. All explanations are, to use Abraham Kaplan's terminology, "indeterminate." That is, "every explanation is in turn subject to being explained."[16] This is a reasonable claim, and one that the practicing political scientist would do well to remember. However, it tends to cast doubt upon an argument such as Runciman's, for it makes clear that there are different levels of explanation. One of the tasks of any science is to search constantly for more refined laws to account for more variance (speaking statistically); in other words, to explain a wider range of phenomena more completely. But this does not mean that the initial rough generalization fails to provide an explanation of sorts.

Returning to Runciman's example, one can explain a group being Democratic (it is predominantly Catholic) using the law provided, and still seek to explain why Catholics tend to be Democrats. There is no contradiction here. The next step will simply be a more refined and inclusive law. Thus, if this argument merely boils down to a noting of the infinite regress of explanations, it need not trouble us. However, it can be pushed further. "There is a widespread notion that the hierarchy of explanations must ultimately ascend to the final comprehensive theory which is itself as ineluctable as a brute matter of fact."[17] What underlies this notion is a belief that the laws of nature represent the necessary order of the universe. That is, science's ultimate task is to show why things must be as they are. But as we have seen, this is not at all the objective of an empirical science. The laws of any science are contingent; they describe the relations of things as we observe them. Science cannot demonstrate their necessity.

---

[15] W. G. Runciman, *Social Science and Political Theory* (Cambridge, Eng.: Cambridge University Press, 1963), p. 92.

[16] Kaplan, *The Conduct of Inquiry,* p. 354.

[17] Ibid.

EXPLANATION AND PREDICTION

One of the reasons for a political scientist taking an interest in explanation is the fact that all policy scientists have to predict. This justification is valid because of the logical identity between explanation and prediction. The identity is based upon the fact that both explanation and prediction require laws and initial conditions. Thus, if one has a valid explanation, he should be able to employ it to predict, and vice versa. If, given the proper initial conditions, one could not have predicted the event that was explained, the explanation was not adequate in the first place. If it is possible to explain adequately without having a potential prediction, then the door is left open for any pseudoexplanation of a given phenomenon.

An explanation may be incomplete and yet be accepted by political scientists. This has led some to argue that while one can explain, using such partial explanations, prediction is impossible. Abraham Kaplan then raises the question, "What shall we say, because they do not allow for prediction, that they are not really explanations at all?"[18] In the strictest sense, they are *not* explanations, and so naturally they do not predict. In this period of a developing science of politics, we must often content ourselves with partial explanations, or even less. But this practical concession does not allow us to weaken the model of explanation to the point that it no longer explains.

Kaplan also implies that statistical laws can often explain better than they predict. However, once again, the explanation only appears sounder because the event has already happened. If the laws of voting behavior assert that it is 80 percent probable that county X will vote for candidate A, we can predict and explain the county's behavior with 80 percent certainty. The fact that it behaves in the *predicted* manner does not make the explanation sounder than a prediction.

There is another argument often used by those who claim explanation is possible without prediction. A well-worked example has to do with the explanation of earthquakes. We can explain them after they have occurred (using the proper laws and citing relevant conditions), but it is usually impossible to predict an earthquake. Rather, the last clause should read "technically difficult," because we are often unable to know about the initial condi-

---

[18] Ibid.

tions. Shifting the example to politics, we might have rather sophisticated laws accounting for revolutions and civil wars, but the initial social, political, and economic conditions existing right now in a small Latin American republic that would allow us to apply the laws may never come to our attention until after the revolution has occurred. This is a technical, not a logical, difficulty, and it in no way refutes the logical identity between explanation and prediction. Ernest Nagel has put it this way: "In many cases of physical inquiry we are ignorant of the pertinent initial conditions for employing established theories to make precise forecasts, even though the available theories are otherwise entirely adequate for this purpose."[19]

There is still another argument made by those who reject the logical identity of explanation and prediction. It is that we are often able to predict without being able to explain. This is a reversal of the argument just considered. Abraham Kaplan has presented the following as a case in point. "Analysis of voting behavior, for example, may have identified certain counties or states as barometers but making predictions from them is very different from having an explanation of the vote."[20] The prediction proceeds in the following manner:

If X counties vote Democratic, the Democrats tend to win the national election.
X counties have voted Democratic.
Therefore, the Democrats will win.

This is a rough prediction. If we apply it to a past Democratic victory, we have a rough explanation relative to the findings of survey research. Thus, the explanation and prediction are equally gross and neither is causal. Only mass election results can be predicted (and explained), and then without much confidence. The generalizations from the voting studies allow for better explanations (accounting for more variance and explaining at more refined levels) and more accurate and inclusive predictions. The X-county findings either represent accidental correlations or indicate that there are deeper causal factors at work. If the former is the case, we will have learned something; if the latter holds, an attempt would be made to discover these

---

[19] Nagel, *The Structure of Science*, p. 461.
[20] Kaplan, *Conduct of Inquiry*, p. 350.

factors, thus leading to the development of more refined explanations and predictions. For instance, if there are social characteristics, attitudes, or personality traits at work, it would be more fruitful to have laws relating them to voting behavior than laws showing a correlation between counties and national elections. But this goes for both explanation and prediction. What if the Democratic-type people make a mass exodus from the X-counties? The laws will no longer be useful for explanation or prediction since they were such low-level arguments in the first place.

THE COMPLETENESS OF EXPLANATIONS

In examining the nature of scientific explanation, we have not meant to give the impression that political scientists ought to sit on their hands until they have before them full-blown deductive or statistical explanations. At this stage, such a requirement seems unrealistic and overly restrictive. Thus, the arguments against the possibility of a science of politics (and therefore the scientific explanation of political phenomena), which we attempted to refute on methodological grounds in Chapter 3, are often of practical significance. For instance, while the complexity of political phenomena presents no *logical* barrier to nomological explanation, it can create difficulties for the political scientist conducting research. No claim is being made that political science is simple and that complete nomological explanation is immediately achievable. On the other hand, we have argued that explanation in any science must meet certain requirements, and it will only prove disillusioning to attempt to achieve explanation by drastically weakening these requirements. Taking a moderate position, one ought to realize that there are various degrees of completeness possible in explanation; one can make a series of distinctions between degrees of completeness and yet draw the line at inadequate explanations. In other words, if we are explicit, the class of incomplete but pragmatically acceptable explanation types can be distinguished from pseudoexplanations, arguments that have no explanatory value. The addition of one or several elements (usually laws) to an incomplete explanation makes it complete. But no addition could make a pseudoexplanation acceptable short of complete revision.

Carl Hempel has explicated this criterion of completeness for explanations rather thoroughly.[21] Using his analysis as a guide, we can spell out a typology of completeness for political scientists. First are *complete* explanations, those that explicitly state all laws and initial conditions. Hempel points out that such perfectly complete nomological explanations are rarely achieved by scientists. In the natural sciences, this is usually because the explainer assumes that certain laws will be presupposed, and so only the necessary facts are formally stated. "If judged by ideal standards, the given formulation of the proof is elliptic or incomplete: but the departure from the ideal is harmless; the gaps can readily be filled in."[22] In other words, if asked, the scientist could easily provide the missing laws (or initial conditions) that would completely account for the phenomenon in question. The number of *elliptical* explanations in political science is not great. The discipline is not well enough developed to allow a political scientist the luxury of assuming that others are aware of the laws he is implying. This is one reason for asking that political scientists explicitly formulate their generalizations.

Hempel's scheme has a category that is more relevant to political science. This he calls the *partial* explanation.[23] Like the elliptical type, it fails to explicitly formulate all the generalizations it is based upon. But even when the generalizations are made evident, the explanandum is not completely accounted for. All that is demonstrated is that something in a particular general class is to be expected. Thus, suppose we want to explain why a certain presidential decision *(S)* was to send troops to nation Alpha *(W)*. A partial explanation would only show (for example) that (1) *S* was an aggressive act (class *F*), (2) in these circumstances an *F* is to be expected, and (3) *W* is in the class *F*. Thus, the aggressive act would be explained completely, the partial sending of troops. As we have said, partial explanations are important for political science. An explanation is partial because its laws cannot completely account for its explanandum; this is the nature of most, if not all, laws about political phenomena.

One might have an explanation of sorts, but still not think it meets even the requirements of the partial explanation. In this case, we might classify

---

[21] See "Explanation in Science and History," in Robert G. Colodny, *Frontiers of Science and Philosophy* (Pittsburgh: University of Pittsburgh Press, 1962), pp. 7–33; and "The Function of General Laws in History," *Journal of Philosophy,* 39 (1942), pp. 35–48.

[22] Hempel, "Explanation in Science and History," p. 14.

[23] Ibid., p. 15.

the argument as an *explanation sketch*.[24] Such an argument is characterized by a lack of explicitness and logical rigor; yet it points to an explanation. Thus, it serves as a sort of outline or sketch to direct one's attention toward possible relationships and ultimately a more complete explanation. The social sciences, including political science, abound with such explanation sketches. They are valuable if it is remembered that a complete explanation is still far in the future. Take, for instance, Nathan Leites's explanations of Soviet politics, which begins with the maxim, "Character determines behavior."[25] They boil down to attempts at characterizing the Bolshevik-type personality and then relating it to political behavior such as decision making. Leites's explanations are speculative and, like most psychoanalytic analyses, a bit short on scientific rigor. But as explanation sketches, they are interesting and potentially useful, for they point out some possible explanatory factors—in short, a start is made. Once again, we must admit that in its present stage of development, political science must often be satisfied with the explanation sketch. But that is an empirical, not a logical, shortcoming. The formulation of explanation sketches is closely related to the development of hypotheses. Both involve speculation and educated guesses. An explanation sketch will have hypotheses as a major component which, if shown to be scientific laws, will allow the sketch to become a full-fledged explanation.

All of these incomplete explanation types can be distinguished from the pseudo or nonexplanation according to one main criterion: No matter how incomplete, it will be possible to test even an explanation sketch (admittedly, this may take some doing). That is, even in its rough state, the incomplete explanation makes some reference to empirical entities—to the world of experience. Such is not the case with nonexplanations. "In the case of nonempirical explanations or explanation sketches . . . the use of empirically meaningless terms makes it impossible even roughly to indicate the type of investigation that would have a bearing upon these formulations. . . ."[26] This distinction between incomplete and pseudoexplanations is important to our analysis. Many of the explanations that one finds in political

---

[24] Ibid.

[25] Nathan Leites, *A Study of Bolshevism* (New York: Free Press, 1954), and *The Operational Code of the Politburo* (New York: McGraw-Hill, 1951).

[26] Hempel, "The Function of General Laws in History," p. 42.

science are incomplete rather than pseudo. Thus, while they should be evaluated and criticized according to the standards of sound scientific explanation, they should not be dismissed as useless. To the contrary, their explication should lead to more complete explanations when more sophisticated laws are available. A framework for such explication will be discussed in the next section.

PATTERNS OF EXPLANATION

The first part of this chapter described the nature of explanation in political science. We argued that only nomological explanations can account for political scientists' *why* questions. What might appear to be different types of explanation are actually variations on a single logical model; they share the basic characteristic of employing laws to explain. This section will describe a typology of patterns of explanation based on a survey of political science literature. If it is at all inclusive, then the argument that every sound explanation in political science contains at least one law becomes stronger, for the nomological character of each pattern will be demonstrated.

There are six patterns. The first three, dispositional, intentional, and rational, employ human characteristics as independent variables. The others are macroinstitutional, system-maintaining, and genetic. It will become clear that a single criterion has not been used to classify patterns. For instance, dispositional explanations are distinguished from macroexplanations mainly by content, that is, the different types of concepts used as independent variables in their generalizations. On the other hand, a dispositional explanation and a genetic explanation have different structures. But we need not provide lengthy justification of this multiplicity of criteria, since our basic thesis is that all sound explanations are nomological. In this section, we are interested in describing the methods (patterns) of explanation used by political scientists.

Before moving to the patterns, one more point needs clarification. Each of the patterns is an ideal type of sorts. The explanations that one finds in the literature of political science are often mixed. However, in most explanations, either one pattern is dominant, or two or more coequal patterns are distinguishable; therefore, we are justified in speaking about six patterns and assuming that such discussion is useful for the practicing political scientist.

The dispositional pattern

The dispositional pattern in political science is so labeled because it uses dispositional concepts. A disposition is a tendency to respond in a certain way in a given situation. Included in the class of dispositional concepts are attitudes, opinions, beliefs, values, and personality traits. The dispositional pattern can be distinguished from the intentional pattern because the former makes no reference to conscious motives. In other words, the link between the disposition and behavior is not "out in the open."

May Brodbeck has pointed out that the dispositional definition may be employed as the generalization in an explanation.[27] Thus, we might explain an individual's electoral decision by stating the following definition: "A leftist is one who votes left" (voting left defines the disposition), and then claiming that the individual is leftist. However, the explanation is, in May Brodbeck's words, "vacuous and circular."[28] That is, useful dispositional explanations that tell us something about the world will relate the disposition to another factor, the result being an empirical generalization. Such an explanation is not vacuous and circular. Thus, the pattern's nomological nature becomes evident. Dispositions are antecedent conditions, independent variables that must be linked to resulting actions by covering laws before they can explain anything.

There are as many types of dispositional explanations as there are kinds of dispositions. Some of these have already been mentioned. However, there are several other dimensions according to which dispositional explanations can be classified. Dispositions may be attributed to individuals, decision makers, groups, types of people, classes, nations, or all men. The laws or relationships can be explicitly stated, consciously assumed, or unconsciously implied; and based on controlled analysis of statistical evidence, observation and experience, or commonsense speculation. A succinct statement of these dimensions can be made in a series of questions, the answers to which provide a clear categorization of any dispositional explanation:

1. What kind of dispositional concept?
2. Who has the disposition?

---

[27] May Brodbeck, "Explanation, Prediction, and 'Imperfect' Knowledge," in Feigl and Maxwell, *Minnesota Studies,* p. 268.

[28] Ibid.

3. How is it related to behavior (how well-developed and articulated are the laws)?
4. What kind of evidence is provided (how scientific)?

The last two questions can be asked of any pattern.

Let us consider an example. Lewis Dexter has attempted an explanation of the proposed fact that congressmen believe the mail they receive from their constituents is valuable and worthy of consideration.[29] The explanation is based on a number of attitudes and beliefs that Dexter thinks lead to the general disposition (the belief). He discusses five such dispositions. Included are values: "Most congressmen *genuinely treasure* the right of petition and the opportunity of the individual citizen to complain about mistreatment";[30] and beliefs: "Some congressmen actually *believe* and many others *like to feel* that on any issue of national significance rational communication between them and any constituent is possible."[31] Dexter characterizes these as dispositions peculiar to congressmen. In order to use them in explanations, they must be related as generalizations to the phenomenon being explained.

Dexter also uses another kind of dispositional concept. This is a general psychological attitude attributed to all or most people. "Most people seem to prefer to know what they are supposed to do"[32] helps explain the congressman's desire for indications of constituents' wishes. The statement containing dispositions concerning most people can be considered a generalization about most people. Since congressmen are people, the generalization applies to them. We can conclude that dispositions employed in explanations must be found in generalizations. For this reason, the dispositional pattern has explanatory power.

The intentional pattern

The existence of a dispositional pattern in our typology indicates that much political behavior is not intentional. Still, there is a class of actions that

---

[29] Lewis Dexter, "What Do Congressmen Hear?" in Nelson Polsby et al., *Politics and Social Life* (Boston: Houghton Mifflin, 1963), pp. 485–95.

[30] Ibid., p. 487.

[31] Ibid.

[32] Ibid., p. 486.

seem to manifest such purposive behavior. This is the basis for the inclusion of an intentional pattern. The term *intention* refers to all actions (not necessarily successfully carried out) that are consciously purposive. Political scientists often attempt to explain political phenomena by showing that the explanandum is the result of some intentional action.

The simplest kind of intentional explanation can be schematically presented: "*X* does *Y* because he intended to do it." But this is not a complete explanation of *Y,* because no grounds are given for expecting its occurrence. Just because *X* intended to do *Y* doesn't mean *X* will actually do it, unless we have a law, based on empirical evidence, that such a person as *X* acts upon his intentions. Thus, this simple law is necessary: intentions need not result in actions. Some sort of statement is required that provides grounds for explaining the action. Thus, for instance, saying that Senator Smith lent his support to the Civil Rights Act of 1969 because that was his intention doesn't explain anything unless we include the general law that "When a senator intends to support a bill, he usually does." Even in this overly simplified case, a generalization is necessary for sound explanation.

Usually, however, what we have called an intentional or purposeful explanation includes more justification of its explanandum than "because he wanted or intended to," and "he who intends to, does." If we want an intentional explanation of a political phenomenon *(X)* that goes beyond this trivial argument, we will probably have to refer to goals or objectives. It can be asserted that another important characteristic of most intentional explanations is that there is some reference made to goals, purposes, or objectives. The structure of the pattern then becomes, "*X* did *Y* because he wanted *G,*" based on the generalization "people who want *G* tend to do *Y* under these particular conditions."

We have noted two kinds of intentional explanations based on two kinds of intentional generalizations. The second clause is important because intentional explanations, whether of the simple (because he intended to) or more important goal-seeking (because he had *X*-goal) type, require laws that relate the intention to the explanandum phenomenon and demonstrate why it is as it is. The mere stating of an intention or a goal does not explain (unless there are laws implied and we accept it as a partial or elliptical explanation).

Lewis J. Edinger's explanation of why the nonpolitical elite in postwar Germany were not anti-Nazi is intentional because it is based on the proposed fact that the costs of a purge of pro-Nazi officials would have been more than the Allies were willing to pay.[33] Edinger explains the lack of a purge by setting forth the conditions for the decision to carry one out—that is, recruiting an entirely new group of anti-Nazi, nonpolitical leaders. His explanatory law is, "The more extensive the purge the more it will cost. . . . On the other hand, the less the victor is willing to pay one or the other price, the more difficult it will be to carry through such a purge."[34] Clearly, the term that makes this a variation on the intentional theme is "willing." If *X* is not willing to pay the price, it will not carry out the purge. The explanation is not, "*X* failed to carry out the purge because it didn't want to," but, "because it didn't want to pay the price required." The lawful relationship exists between purging and willingness to pay the price. In short, goals are cited to explain the action.

So intentional explanations, like all other sound explanations, are nomological. They differ from the other patterns only in the type of concepts used and the way in which generalizations are arranged. However, some philosophers of social science see in intentional explanation a unique way of accounting for social phenomena—a method of explanation logically distinct from the nomological model. The basis of this position is a belief that a citing of intentions explains by showing the meaningfulness of the behavior in question. "The explanatory force of learning the agent's intention depends upon the author's familiarity with intentional behavior; the explanation must solve a puzzle and in order for the puzzle to exist there must be a 'previous stock of knowledge and beliefs' with which the perplexing event is at variance."[35] This interpretation of intentional explanation is based upon an assumption that we tried to refute in the first section. We contended that the psychological fact of familiarity has nothing to do with the logical requirements of explanation. There seems to be an added attractiveness in viewing intentional explanation as being somehow more "meaningful" than other kinds. However, an intention explains a political fact only insofar as it is lawfully related to it. That the fact is made psychologically meaningful is neither a necessary nor sufficient condition of the explanation.

---

[33] Lewis J. Edinger, "Post-Totalitarian Leadership: Elites in the German Federal Republic," *American Political Science Review*, 54 (1960), pp. 58–82.

[34] Ibid., pp. 80–81.

[35] Brown, *Explanation in Social Science*, p. 66.

The rational pattern

A rational-type explanation is based on the presumed or demonstrated rationality of men (all or types of men). This pattern may be considered as a special case of intentional explanation in the most general sense. However, it is sufficiently distinct and in wide enough use among political scientists to justify separate consideration.

A rational explanation has the form "*X* because *Y* is rational" or, bringing out its nomological nature, "*X* because *Y* is rational and in situation *S,* a rational man does *X.*" There are many points in this basic characterization that require explication, but first a preliminary definition of rationality is in order.

Most definitions talk about rational behavior or action; thus, people are rational insofar as they behave rationally. Robert Dahl and Charles Lindblom have stated what seems to be the consensus definition of rational behavior: "An action is rational to the extent that it is correctly designed to maximize goal achievement, given the goal in question and the real world as it exists."[36] An individual is rational if his pursuit of goals is as efficient as possible. The importance of goals to rationality indicates why we could say at the outset that rational explanation is, in a way, a special kind of intentional explanation. According to the definitions we have been considering, all rational behavior is goal-seeking. The only difference between it and the intentional pattern is the claim that rational action is the *best* way to achieve a goal. An intentional explanation makes no such claim; it merely states that *X* has goal *Y* and in situation *S,* people with *Y* tend to do *W* to achieve it—*W* is not necessarily the *best* method. J. W. N. Watkins has succinctly made his point: "If we define purposeful behavior as trying . . . to do or achieve something, it follows that fully rational behavior is a limiting case of purposeful behavior."[37] We can see why the rational pattern is often confused with intentional explanation.

We have referred to the nomological nature of rational explanation. Let us now show in more detail why this pattern shares the basic logical structure of all adequate scientific explanations. Saying that "A man, *M,* voted

---

[36] Robert Dahl and Chalres Lindbolm, *Politics, Economics, and Welfare* (New York: Harper & Row, 1953), p. 38.

[37] J. W. N. Watkins, "Ideal and Historical Explanation," in Feigl and Brodbeck, *Readings,* p. 742.

for candidate X because M was rational," while providing the outline of an explanation, does not really account for the behavior. It lacks the information that relates the initial condition, "M is rational" to the explanandum, "M voted for candidate X." This is provided by the generalization that, "A rational man in situation S (the available candidates) would vote for X (or an X-type candidate)." Given the condition that M is rational, the direction of voting is explained (or predicted). If we adopt the consensus definition of rationality—the rational seeking of given goals—then the explanation takes the form: "M has goal G (to have his interests acted upon); M is rational; in situation S, a rational man with goal G will vote for an X-type candidate; X is an X-type candidate; therefore, M will vote for X." The structure of the two is the same, the second case is simply more refined.

According to Carl Hempel's formulation of the rational pattern, rationality becomes a sort of dispositional concept, for it presents A's action as a manifestation of his general disposition to act in characteristic ways—in ways that qualify as appropriate or rational—in certain situations.[38] To have the disposition of being rational is not *logically* different from identifying with the Democrats (attitude) or being authoritarian (personality trait). We have previously classified rational explanations as a special case of the intentional pattern. Now "being rational" has been characterized as dispositional. These two ideas can be integrated, with the result being an interesting formulation of the rational pattern. We can say that explaining rationally consists of stating an agent's goal; attributing a disposition, rationality, to the agent; and, finally, formulating a law relating them to the action being explained. "If X has A goal and is rational, then he does C."

Another portrayal of the rational pattern is Graham Allison's attempt to explain Soviet and American decisions during the 1962 Cuban Missile Crisis.[39] According to his formulation, (this is one of three patterns Allison tries out) one begins with an action, the decision of the Soviets to place missiles in Cuba, then makes the assumptions that Premier Krshchev made the decision and that he was rational. The explanation would invovle determining what the goal of a rational leader making such a decision would be. After sifting through a number of possible goals and considering the potential gains and

---

[38] Hempel, "Reasons and Covering Laws in Historical Explanation."

[39] Graham Allison, *Essence of Decision: Explaining the Cuban Missile Crisis* (Boston: Little, Brown, 1971).

losses of each, Allison concludes that Krushchev was trying to close the missile-gap—decrease American superiority in nuclear weapons by placing Russian missiles at America's doorstep. According to this rational account, this is the only goal that was worth the great risk of an American retaliation.

This is apparently a reasonable explanation of the Soviet decision, yet we don't actually know what the intentions of the Soviets were. Thus, as Allison would point out, he has not actually explained that decision, but he has instead given it a rational reconstruction: it might be that Krushchev had other goals and/or was not rational. We might view this example as an explanation sketch; *if* Krushchev was rational, *if* his goal was to close the missile gap, and *if* there is a generalization that indicates leaders in this kind of strategic situation will usually take great risks to improve their nation's position, then we have begun to explain the decision.

The macro pattern

We have now analyzed three patterns of explanation. Each pattern accounts for political phenomena in a different way, on the basis of different types of independent variables. Yet, all are similar in that (1) they are nomological, and (2) the concepts, and subsequently the generalizations containing them that account for the explanada, explicitly refer to human characteristics, whether individual or group. The pattern of explanation which will be analyzed in this section parts company with the first three patterns on the latter point. That is, the generalizations that a macroinstitutional explanation employs have as antecedent factors or independent variables institutional or physical concepts, so that in an institutional law $A \rightarrow B$, the A is such a concept. There are, consequently, two variations of the macro pattern, the institutional and the physical.

The dispositional pattern already analyzed includes some group properties—group dispositions—such as public opinion and national character. These are properly considered as statistical averages of many individual opinions or individual personality traits. Thus, since we have classified such concepts as dispositional, they will not be included in this section. What we are saying is that there is a difference between an institution (admittedly made up of individuals and properties of individuals) and a group property such as public opinion. The opinion of a group is a direct disposition of the individuals who make up the group. When an institution such as the party system is cited as the cause of a political phenomenon, a property of that institution, its decentralized nature, for instance, is usually being referred to implicitly or explicitly. Thus, one might want to call decentralization a disposition of a party, since its existence is determined by observing certain behaviors of political parties in given situations. This is not incompatible with our macro pattern, even when we add the additional assumption that such dispositions as party decentralization and group cohesion are ultimately reducible to laws about individual behavior. That is, we can give this interpretation of party decentralization and still opt for the usefulness of a macro pattern of explanation in political science because the decentralization of a party is not a direct characteristic of its members as is a public's opinion. While according to methodological individualism this concept is definable in terms of individual behavior, an individual is not cohesive; but an individual has opinions or personality traits. Therefore, we talk about the decntralization of the *party,* or the *institution.* This is because, while the party's decentralized nature is in part a result of human dispositions, these interact to give the institution a characteristic that none of the individuals possess.

One of the best-known explanations in the literature of political science is the accounting for of the U.S. two-party system. One of the first formulators of such an explanation was E. E. Schattschneider.[40] The general hypothesis he operates from is "The American two-party system is the direct consequence of the American election system, or system of representation."[41] Two institutional features of the electoral system in particular are cited as antecedent conditions—single-member districts and plurality elections.[42] The French sociologist Maurice Duverger has stated his version of the law: "The simple-majority single-ballot system favours the two-party system,"[43] and he says about it, "Of all the hypotheses that have been defined in this book, this approaches the most nearly perhaps to a true sociological law."[44] These arguments are important to us because they represent straightforward

---

[40] E. E. Schattschneider, *Party Government* (New York: Holt, Rinehart & Winston, 1942), pp. 67–84.

[41] Ibid., p. 69.

[42] Ibid., p. 74.

[43] Maurice Duverger, *Political Parties* (New York: Science Editions, 1963), p. 217.

[44] Ibid.

institutional explanations. The fact of having a two-party system is adequately accounted for by laws relating it to institutional properties of the electoral system.

We have sketched the general nature of the macro pattern and provided a justification for its consideration as a separate kind of explanation. One kind of macro explanation uses institutions and properties of institutions. There is another subclass of the macro category. Besides institutional explanations, there are those explanations employing physical characteristics of the environment. Thus, David Easton identifies three categories of, as he calls it, situational data: "(1) the physical environment; (2) the nonhuman organic environment; and (3) the social environment or patterns of human activity flowing from social interaction."[45] The latter is close to the institutional category we have just discussed, and the former refers to our present concern. Easton also says that "Our physical environment influences our activity, regardless of the kind of people we are. Our nonorganic resources, topography, and spatial location, such as being near or distant from the seat of government, influences the kind of political lives we lead."[46] A physical explanation in political science in simplest terms takes the form "*A;* if *A* (a physical fact), then *B;* therefore *B* (explanandum)." Physical facts include geographical variables and characteristics of the political system; for instance, the type of electoral ballot can be considered as a physical explanatory factor.

Some students of politics have noticed a relationship between the type of ballot and the incidence of straight-party voting. Angus Campbell states the association in the following manner: "We find, in the states which make it relatively easy for the voter to mark a straight ticket, that the number of straight tickets marked is some 20 percent higher than in those states where the ballot requires a series of separate decisions among the candidates for each of the various offices."[47] In a study of the impact of the Australian Ballot on voting behavior in the United States, Jerold Rusk concludes that "institutional properties of the electoral system, considered either as an entity or as a network of component parts, have played and continue to play

---

[45] David Easton, *The Political System* (New York: Alfred A. Knopf, 1953), p. 194.

[46] Ibid., pp. 194–95.

[47] Angus Campbell, "Recent Developments in Survey Studies of Political Behavior," in Austin Ranney, ed., *Essays on the Behavioral Study of Politics* (Urbana: University of Illinois Press, 1962), pp. 31–46.

a crucial role in influencing and shaping voting behavior—in essentially defining the conditions and boundaries of decision making at the polls.''[48]

Enough has been said to indicate that the macroinstitutional pattern is, like all sound explanatory types, nomological. In fact, macro explanations are perhaps more readily recognized as such than many other patterns because they claim that a political phenomenon is associated with a certain institutional characteristic or physical fact. That this association has to be expressed in a law seems evident.

The system-maintaining pattern

There are many activities in political science called *functional* or *system-maintaining*. Some of these will be examined in Chapter 14. Our pattern includes only those that attempt to provide sound explanations of political phenomena. Thus, several types of functional analysis have been rejected for inclusion in this section because they are not explanatory.

An important case of presumably sound but actually invalid explanation must be distinguished from the potentially sound variety of system-maintaining explanation. In it the behavior pattern or institution that is the explanandum is supposedly explained by showing that it is necessary for the performance of functions that are required by the system. The application of the label *teleological* can be seen as justified, for the present existence of a political phenomenon is being explained by its end. This kind of functional-teleological explanation is not sound. It is difficult enough to demonstrate that a certain function is necessary for the maintenance of a system—for instance, the allocation of values. However, it is another thing to prove conclusively that a particular political institution or activity is the only thing that can perform the function. Thus, we might be able to present evidence that a certain political function is necessary for the maintenance (continued existence) of the social system. But one cannot show that a particular political institution is the only one that could perform the function.

At this point, we can discuss the sound type of system-maintaining expla-

---

[48] Jerold G. Rusk, ''The Effect of the Australian Ballot Reform on Split-Ticket Voting: 1876–1908,'' in Richard G. Niemi and Herbert F. Weisberg, eds., *Controversies in American Voting Behavior* (San Francisco: W. H. Freeman, 1976), p. 512.

nation. Its main feature is the assertion and perhaps demonstration of a causal relationship between variables and a system. "It should be apparent that functional explanation is essentially causal; if it is concerned with the effects of a given activity or practice on a system, its purpose must be the establishment of cause and effect relationships."[49] Based on the analysis in Chapter 6, it seems reasonable to assume that if causality has any significance at all, it is because "to show cause" means "to subsume under general laws"; the concept of cause is reducible to the covering-law model. It follows that to explain functionally or to use the system-affecting pattern is to employ laws; thus, there is no difference in this respect from other sound patterns of explanation. In explaining a certain change, state, or maintenance of a system, we show what factors help produce it. The causal relationship can only be accounted for by citing a law that indicates the resulting state of affairs is expectable under the circumstances. The distinctive feature of system-maintaining explanations is the dependent variable, system maintenance. Such an explanation demonstrates that certain functions are necessary for the maintenance of the system and that specific variables fulfill these functions.

The genetic pattern

Of the six patterns of explanation we have distinguished, the one that is the most distinctive structurally is the genetic pattern. Each of the other patterns can be reduced to the admittedly oversimplified schema, "If *A* (representing laws and initial conditions), then *B* (the explanandum)." But, in Ernest Nagel's words, "The task of genetic explanations is to set out the sequence of major events through which some earlier system has been transformed into a later one."[50] Thus, a genetic explanation does not fit the above schema because it involves several stages. Its basic pattern (in its simplest form, involving only two stages) is, "If *A* (factors at time 1), then *B* (consequent factors); and if *C* (*B* plus other factors at time 2), then *D* (explanandum)." It is clear that the factors in the schema occur at different times. This

---

[49] Vernon Van Dyke, *Political Science: A Philosophical Analysis* (Stanford, Calif.: Stanford University Press, 1960), p. 32.

[50] Nagel, *The Structure of Science*, p. 25.

is why we said the genetic pattern is characterized by stages. A simple causal explanation, "If *A* then *B; A,* therefore *B,*" involves a time sequence. However, a genetic explanation is marked by at least two explanation stages, each of which can be considered a separate explanation, which together show why a political phenomenon is as it is or was what it was.[51] In other words, an explanation fitting the genetic pattern first explains a state of affairs *X* and then proceeds to explain, on the basis of *X,* another state of affairs, and so on.

Thus, the genetic pattern accounts for the present state of a political phenomenon by showing how it developed over time from previous stages. It differs from other patterns because of this developmental element and the multiplicity of stages. From what we have said so far it seems reasonable to conclude that the genetic pattern is often identified with historical explanation. It is also interesting to note that much of the methodological analysis of the genetic pattern has been carried out by philosophers of history.[52] Many of the explanations provided by political scientists that can be classified as genetic are actually historical. In these instances, the political scientist functions as an historian in accounting for political events or situations. For instance, Wilfred E. Binkley traces the development of the office of the Presidency using a narrative style that mentions the key historical occurrences that Binkley believes influenced the formation of the office.[53] But genetic and historical explanations are not identical. There are genetic explanations that are not historical in the technical sense, for instance, the explanation of the development of party identification in *The American Voter.*[54]

A main characteristic of many genetic explanations is a narrative style or chronicling of events. However, in accounting for a political phenomenon, not every antecedent event is relevant. We can say that genetic explanations account for political phenomena by describing a series of *relevant* events which, in a chain-like fashion, determine the state of the explanandum.

However, there is more to genetic explanation than a listing of relevant stages in the development of a political phenomenon. A genetic explanation

---

[51] A genetic explanation can be cut off at any point, so that the origin at one time may be a stage at another, and a stage may become the explanandum if we push the analysis back in time.

[52] See W. B. Gallie, "Explanations in History and the Genetic Sciences," in Patrick Gardner, ed., *Theories of History* (New York: Free Press, 1959).

[53] Wilfred E. Binkley, *President and Congress* (New York: Vintage Books, 1962).

[54] Angus Campbell et al., *The American Voter* (New York: John Wiley & Sons, 1960).

accounts for a political phenomenon by showing how it was changed or influenced at various stages in its development. The important point is that each stage supposedly has some influence on the following stage, and so on until the explanandum is reached; one talks about "necessary conditions." The question is how can each stage be linked to the next? Our answer is through the use of generalizations. That is, a law explains why the phenomenon changed from *A* to *B,* and then another law relates some part of *B* to *C,* and so on. Thus, we see that if a genetic explanation is to be of any value, it must be nomological, for it depends on the demonstration that one stage has an effect on the next.

An example will help clarify our argument. William Riker's explanation of the decline of judicial review can be interpreted as a genetic explanation.[55] Taking some liberties with his analysis, we can present the following as an explanation of the phenomenon in question: (1) the Supreme Court's experience with the "Court-packing" bill of 1937 persuaded it to practice judicial restraint; (2) one manifestation of its judicial restraint was its periodic restriction of doctrines that had been used to justify striking down acts of Congress; (3) therefore, when acts of Congress that previously were affected by such doctrines come before the Court, it does not employ the doctrines. Thus, it does not practice judicial review. The explanation is genetic because the explanandum is the result of the relationships between three stages of the Court's history. And each relationship must be expressed in the form of a law; for instance, "a judicial body which is trying to divest itself of a power will give up devices that justify the exercise of the power."

In addition to laws, nomological explanations contain initial conditions. The upshot of this fact is the realization that each stage of a genetic explanation is a separate explanation. Thus, using the example from Riker, we see that the explanation of the Supreme Court's adoption of judicial restraint (because of the fear engendered by the attack of Roosevelt in 1937) is logically independent of the next step. Each of the consequent steps can be pulled out of context and made to stand as a complete explanation of a single development. The realization that initial conditions are a part of genetic explanations provides the foundation for an important caveat about the pattern. It is that the genetic pattern should not be thought of as an historical

---

[55] William Riker, *Democracy in the United States* (New York: Macmillan, 1965), pp. 260–64.

theory of society like Spengler or Marx. A genetic explanation merely states that, "At stage I, *A* happened, which, because of events 1 and 2 at stage II, helped cause *B,* which, because of events 3 and 4 at stage III, helped cause *C.*" In other words, the explanation does not read A → B → C (or as it would in Marxian theory, feudalism → capitalism → communism). This is because we are noting how a combination of conditions at each stage influences the next stage. There is nothing inevitable about the outcome C, because events 1, 2, 3, and 4 did not have to happen (although they were caused). Again, contrast this with Marx's inevitable historical stages.

COMBINATIONS OF PATTERNS

We have now identified six patterns of explanation and their subpatterns. Each was presented as an essentially pure pattern. We analyzed a number of explanations as if each were only dispositional, only intentional, only system-maintaining, etc. However, practically speaking, one notices many explanations in political science that are really combinations of patterns; in fact, most explanations are not pure, in the above sense. One could take the position that a pattern is characterized as dispositional, for instance, because dispositional laws are dominant but not exclusive; it is dispositional to a greater *degree.* In saying this, however, we should not overlook political science explanations that are pure; in short, this section is designed to refine or add to, not correct, the typology of patterns that was presented in the previous section.

In discussing combinations of patterns, one of our patterns, the genetic, is naturally a mixture of sorts. We pointed out that the stages of a genetic explanation can be analytically viewed as a series of separate explanations. Thus, a dispositional explanation may account for the movement from one stage, and an intentional explanation may account for the movement to the next stage. If a genetic explanation uses dispositional generalizations at each stage, it might be classified as both genetic and dispositional.

The system-maintaining pattern is distinctive as it is characterized by the nature of its explananda or dependent variables, namely, the maintenance of systems. As we have seen, various sorts of laws can account for this phenomenon. Thus, for instance, dispositional or macro concepts can be cited as antecedent conditions for the maintenance of systems. It is trivial to say that system-maintaining explanations employ differnt kinds of concepts. This is a reiteration of the assertion that our typology of patterns lacks a single distinguishing criteria.

If this last point is kept in mind, the discussion to follow will be more meaningful. We will examine several ways that patterns can be combined (in addition to the sequential combining that occurs in genetic explanations). First, the types of laws that characterize several patterns may be employed jointly to account for a single explanandum. Take, for instance, V. O. Key's tentative explanation of the U.S. two-party system.[56] He argues that instead of a single-factor explanation, "A more tenable assumption would be that several factors drive toward dualism on the American scene."[57] The factors he cites (with appropriate generalizations stated or implied) are: (1) the persistence of initial form—this implies both institutional and dispositional explanations; (2) the influence of institutional factors, such as the single-member district; (3) the existence of "systems of beliefs and attitudes"—this implies a dispositional explanation.

Another way of combining patterns in an explanation is to relate several of them in one of several ways. Instead of showing how a number of factors independent come together to influence the explaandum, the political scientist often attempts to demonstrate how several variables *interact* to bring about the phenomenon to be explained. The simplest type in this category is characterized by a linking of several factors in a "causal chain." John H. Fenton and Kenneth N. Vines' explanation of why blacks register more in southern than northern Louisiana is an example.[58] The explanandum is accounted for by the permissive-attitude differential between the two regions. The more permissive attitude of the southern area is accounted for by an institutional property, the traditions of the Catholic church, which is dominant in that area. The structure of the explanation is "Registration because of attitudes; attitudes because of the Catholic church." This might be thought of as a genetic explanation, but there is a difference. A genetic explanation is constructed of a series of distinct stages in a temporal sequence. The "mixed" explanation under consideration is not characterized

---

[56] V. O. Key, *Politics, Parties, and Pressure Groups* (New York: Thomas Y. Crowell Co., 1958), pp. 227–31.

[57] Ibid., p. 227.

[58] John H. Fenton and Kenneth N. Vines, "Negro Registration in Louisiana," *American Political Science Review,* 51 (1957), pp. 704–13.

by such distinct stages. Correlations have been discovered between two sets of factors and they have been combined to explain the political behavior in question. Furthermore, the implication is that the process continues to operate. In short, there is structural difference between "The Supreme Court is as it is today because X happened at stage I, which caused Y to happen at stage II, and so forth" and "Blacks in southern Louisiana register more because the Catholic church lays the foundation for more permissive attitudes."

Besides horizontal causal chains, patterns may be combined in more compelx arrangements. Thus dispositional, institutional, and intentional laws may interact in many complicated ways, determinable only by equally complicated statistical tests. A simple example is Robert Dahl's explanation of "why political influence is always distributed unevenly in political systems."[59] Dahl uses three factors, "the unequal distribution of resources, variation in the skill with which different individuals use their political resources, and the variations in the extent to which different individuals use their resources for political purposes."[60] These factors involve dispositions, intentions, and physical characteristics. While Dahl calls his explanation a causal chain, it differs from Fenton and Vines's in that it includes a notion of feedback. Thus, while differences in political skills and motivations lead to differences in political influence, the latter helps determine the amounts of the former two factors. It can be seen why such an explanation is more complex.

CONCLUSION

We have now distinguished three kinds of pattern-combination structures: the merger of several independent variables; the arrangement of several variables in a causal chain; and the more complex arrangement of several variables, with provisions for interaction and feedback. The conclusion from this discussion is that rarely will a political scientist discover a sound explanation that uses a single causal factor. It could probably be argued that

---

[59] Robert A. Dahl, *Modern Political Analysis* (Englewood Cliffs, N.J.: Prentice-Hall, 1970), p. 17.
[60] Ibid.

a basic tenet of scientific analysis is that few scientific explanations use a single factor. Most employ several laws containing different factors. But, to repeat the main point of this chapter, all explanations, from the most straightforward, single-factor type to the most complex, multifactor variety, depend on the discovery of sound scientific laws.

Theories and models: Explanation and discovery

AMONG the activities that are probably essential to the development of a scientific discipline, two that seem especially interesting to political scientists are model-building and theory-construction. There are several reasons for analyzing them in the same chapter. Models and theories are structurally and to a certain extent functionally similar. In a general sense, they take us to next level of scientific analysis, after the formulation of concepts and hypotheses. Both models and theories combine concepts and generalizations in various ways. On the other hand, their similarity often leads to the unwarranted conclusion that they are identical. For instance, social scientist Herbert Simon once began a paper entitled "The Uses and Limitations of Models," with these words: "In contemporary usage the term 'model' is, I think simply a synonym for 'theory.' I am to speak, then, on 'Theories: Their Uses and Limitations.'"[1]

It is useful to make a methodological distinction between theories and models because, as they are used by political scientists, they have different purposes, and the failure to realize this difference can lead to confusion and

---

[1] L. D. White, *The State of the Social Sciences* (Chicago: University of Chicago Press, 1956).

even disillusionment. Thus, in addition to analyzing the nature of models and theories, each important in its own right, this chapter will attempt to demonstrate that the student of politics is aided in his studies if he understands the difference between them.

The distinction between models and theories is in many ways not a hard and fast one. However, given the normal activities of political scientists—all scientists, for that matter—the following proposition is in order: theories are used primarily to *explain* political facts, models to *discover* them. This implies a more basic distinction between scientific *explanation* and *discovery*, a distinction that will be analyzed in more detail later in the chapter. At this point, let us remember that how a political scientist develops an hypothesis (discovery) and how he goes about confirming and explaining it are logically distinct activities.

THEORY

It might be useful to begin an analysis of scientific political theory with two distinctions, one important but often ignored, the other misleading yet widely circulated.

The first distinction points out that the political theory now under consideration is not the same as that venerable activity that often goes by the same name but which in Chapter 1 was labeled *political philosophy*. Let us recall the normative charcter of political philosophy, its emphasis on *ought* questions. What *should* be the goals of the political system? What is the *best* political system? These activities can be contrasted with the scientific-empirical nature of political theory, which has to do with *is* questions. Confusion arises from the traditional interchangeability of political philosophy and political theory. While an ever-increasing number of political scientists are accepting one form or another of the distinction just mentioned, the confusion lingers. This is attributable not so much to the failure of political scientists to understand the nature of scientific theory, although this is one source of difficulty, as to the continued substitution of theory for philosophy, based on the unquestioned assumption that the two refer to the same activity. They don't; the subject of this section is *empirical* political theory, not *normative* political philosophy.

A second distinction, the misleading one, is often made between theory and practice. As manifested in the popular statement "That's fine in theory, but it won't work in practice," it assumes that theory or theoretical thinking is false or unrealistic. A student of political theory, Arnold Brecht, put it another way: "The relation between practice and theory is well indicated in the popular saying that we learn best through 'trial and error.' Trial is practice; error refers to theory. When theory miscarries in practical trials it needs correction."[2]

This chapter will demonstrate that there is no divorce in the above sense between theory and practice. Rather than being unrealistic or false, a *sound* theory is the basis for reliable knowledge of politics. Theories help us explain and predict political phenomena, and ultimately help us to make well-founded, practical decisions.

A second related and more sophisticated interpretation of the "theory versus practice" distinction views the former as the result of speculation. Its key phrase is, "That's fine in theory, but will it work in practice?" The distinction is still a fundamental one, but theory is given a higher status. Now, at least, a theory is not necessarily false, for according to this interpretation it is an elaborate hypothesis, a set of guesses to be tested. Thus, to be theoretical is to be hypothetical, *potentially* true. While this view is more generous than the first, it is misleading in ways that will become more evident as we move along.

The nature of political theory

Having discussed what political theory is not, it is time to discuss what it is.[3] There seem to be several variations that are popular among political scientists. Quentin Gibson has given a definition of theory that is basic: "Sets or systems of statements logically inter-connected in various complex ways."[4] In a similar vein, Nelson Polsby et al. have written that, "A scientific theory . . . is a deductive network of generalizations from which expla-

---

[2] Arnold Brecht, *Political Theory* (Princeton, N.J.: Princeton University Press, 1959), p. 19.

[3] For a good introduction to social science theory, see Paul D. Reynolds, *A Primer in Theory Construction* (Indianapolis, Ind.: Bobbs-Merrill, 1971).

[4] Quentin Gibson, *The Logic of Social Enquiry* (London: Routledge & Kegan Paul, 1960), p. 113.

nations or predictions of certain types of known events may be derived."[5] The simplest interpretation of theory views it as a set of related empirical generalizations. Therefore, several generalizations about a particular area of politics can be classified as a theory. Take, for instance, the laws derived from voting studies.[6] Since each law describes the relationship between a social, economic, political, or psychological variable and a type of voting act (men tend to vote more than women), the conjunction of several can explain voting behavior in a more general way. Or, one may view David Braybrooke's "miniature axiomatic system" as a theory, at least a potential theory, of party behavior.[7] It is an attempt to relate a number of generalizations from the literature of party behavior and organize them into a systematic theory.

The notion of political theory as a collection of empirical generalizations about a particular field or subject is a popular one among many political scientists. To others it represents a simplified version of the interpretation of theory that is more commonly accepted by the scientific community at large. According to this interpretation, a theory is characterized by the use of theoretical constructs, which we spoke about in Chapter 5. Thus, a theory might be defined as "a set of generalizations containing concepts we are directly acquainted with and those that are operationally defined; but, more importantly, theoretical concepts that, although not directly tied to observation, are logically related to those concepts that are." This provides the basis for a distinction between theories and empirical generalizations. While the latter can be empirically tested (confirmed or rejected), because their concepts are directly tied to observation, we can't test in the same way a generalization that contains theoretical (or, by definition, nonobservable) concepts. However, this is not to say that theories cannot be tested and evaluated.

Despite their characteristic use of theoretical concepts, sound theories are empirical. We can say that a scientific theory has two features, one structural, the other substantive; one referring to the relationship between

---

[5] Nelson Polsby et al., eds., *Politics and Social Life* (Boston: Houghton Mifflin, 1963), p. 69.

[6] See the list of propositions in Bernard R. Berelson et al., *Voting* (Chicago: University of Chicago Press, 1954), appendix A. This does not include the significant generalizations developed in Angus Campbell et al., *The American Voter* (New York: John Wiley & Sons, 1960).

[7] David Braybrook, "An Illustrative Miniature Axiomatic System," in Polsby et al., *Politics and Social Life*, pp. 119–29.

its concepts, the other to its empirical content. Carl Hempel has provided a more technical description of the elements of scientific theory: "Any . . . scientific theory may be conceived of as consisting of an uninterpreted, deductively developed system and of an interpretation which confers empirical import upon the terms and sentences of the latter."[8] We might begin with a purely formal logical system such as Euclidean geometry, where concepts are implicitly or internally defined, and then directly define (tie to observables) *some* of its concepts. This would then give the other concepts, those we have labeled theoretical, indirect empirical import. There is a difference between an uninterpreted mathematical or logical system and a scientific theory, and the difference is the latter's empirical nature.

The functions of theories

Since theories are empirical, they can be evaluated according to their soundness. A close analysis of a proposed theory should indicate whether it is properly constructed and empirically based. But perhaps a more fruitful approach to the nature of scientific theory is through an examination of the functions it performs, for one way to evaluate a theory is to determine how well it is doing what it is expected to do. Several comments have already suggested that a theory's major function is explanation—to explain singular facts and occurrences, but perhaps more importantly to explain empirical generalizations. This latter function is what gives the scientific theory its power.

Briefly, a theory can explain empirical generalizations because it is more general, more inclusive than they are. The great power of Newtonian mechanics, demonstrated over the centuries, is based upon the ability of a rather small set of theoretical laws to explain a great number of empirical laws about bullets, missiles, and other moving objects. "Explain," following the logic of the last chapter, means that the empirical generalizations are deductively implied by the theory. The same situation could exist in political science, although it is presently misleading to talk about an existing theory of politics (in the second, more sophisticated sense of theory). Let us suppose

---

[8] Carl G. Hempel, *Fundamentals of Concept Formation in Empirical Science* (Chicago: University of Chicago Press, 1952), p. 34.

that general stimulus-response learning theory can explain a wide range of empirical laws, all the way from the voting behavior of individuals to the military activity of nation-states.[9] The point is that if learning theory were a sound theory of political behavior, a set of general laws using such theoretical concepts as "demand" and "habit" would explain or imply a number of genralizations that previously had appeared to be independent, or at least not closely related.

This implies that in one sense a theory is not to be judged true or false, but more or less useful as an explainer of empirical laws. Since laws describe our knowledge in a particular field, the sound theory explains the knowledge more generally and completely, indicating to use the interconnection between seemingly isolated facts.

In taking this position, we cannot overlook a controversy that exists among philosophers of science over the status of theories.[10] Some say they are true or verified in the sense that empirical laws are. That is, they are real descriptions of the world of observation. This position, usually labeled the *realist*, recognizes no logical or philosophical distinction between theoretical and nontheoretical concepts, since they both refer to *real* entities. The opposing school of thought, the *instrumentalist*, takes another position, closer to one we adopted in the last paragraph. It argues that there is no point in trying to determine whether a theory is true or false, since it is neither. It does not describe the world, but explains or predicts worldly phenomena. A theory is tested according to how well it performs its major functions; thus, the label "instrumental." This is close to our notion of theory. However, the strict instrumentalist's complete rejection of the reality of theories is questionable. While a theory contains theoretical concepts, it is also tied to observation through an empirical interpetation. Thus, it more or less describes the world. The theoretical concepts fill in the gaps and allow the theory to explain in more general terms what has been explained by individual empirical laws.

Lurking behind explanation is another function of theories. Scientiss use theories to organize, systematize, and coordinate existing knowledge in a particular field. According to the first notion of theory, a set of related

---

[9] See Chapter 10 for an analysis of learning theory.

[10] For a thorough discussion of this controversy, see Abraham Kaplan, *The Conduct of Inquiry* (San Francisco: Chandler Publishing Co., 1964), chapter 8.

empirical generalizations, a theory is a systematization. A theory of voting behavior would be a set of relevant generalizations that have been collected and put into logical juxtaposition. According to the higher level notion of theory, a theory organizes as it explains. As several diverse generalizations are accounted for by the theoretical propositions of the theory, they are also related and made parts of a system of knowledge.

Theories explain and organize existing knowledge. They also suggest potential knowledge by generating hypotheses. A theory can, on the basis of its highly abstract generalizations, often predict an empirical generalization— predict that a particular relationship holds. The hypothesis can then be tested and accepted or rejected. Thus, in addition to its explanatory and organizational functions, theory has an heuristic one—to suggest and to generate hypotheses.

The place of theory in political science

In determining the role of theory in political science, we ought to remember the two notions of theory, for a different conclusion may be arrived at in regard to each. The first question that confronts us is: Do we have any scientific theories in political science? From what has been said in this chapter, the answer would appear to be no, if we are talking about the higher-level notion of theory. But if this is the case, is there any point in talking about theories? There are probably other methodological topics more significant to contemporary political scientists. While, because of limited resources and time, there is some wisdom in this position, it is perhaps too restrictive. For even without a sound scientific theory in hand, the political scientist is not wasting his time if he takes an interest in theory-construction. There is a payoff in asking such questions as: What would we have if we had a sound high-level theory? What would be its structure and what functions would it perform? Given the characteristics of scientific theory, are there any potential or near-theories awaiting further development in political science literature? The first set of questions has been touched upon in this chapter; the last question will be of some relevance to the more substantive analyses contained in Part 3.

If "theory" means a collection of empirical generalizations, then our answer to the original question about the existence of political theories can be more generous. For there are theories, or at least near-theories, of certain kinds of political behavior—consider our knowledge of voting behavior. Finally, recall the relationship between the lower- and higher-level notions of scientific theory. The implication is that a collection of laws can serve as the foundation of an abstract theory. Thus, if the higher-level notion is accepted as the standard of theory, the collected laws of voting behavior can be classified as a near-theory. In any case, the condition of theory in political science is not as bleak as it might appear, although at this point in the discipline's development the political scientist's time and effort might be more profitably spent on pretheoretical activities, such as those discussed in Chapters 5 and 6.

MODELS AND THE PROCESS OF DISCOVERY

Philosopher of science May Brodbeck notes in answer to the question, "What exactly is a model and what purposes does it serve?" that "I venture to suggest that 10 model builders will give at least five different, or at least, apparently different answers to this question."[11] It is probable that definitions of model are so numerous that we cannot mention all of them. However, there is one notion of model that merits initial consideration. It is more rigorous than the others and usually serves as their foundation, often in an indirect way. However, in its fully developed form, this notion of model is not the most widely accepted (or even recognized) in political science.

The technical, or the professionally acceptable meaning of model is based on the notion of *isomorphism,* which refers to the similarity between one thing and another (its model). More technically, isomorphism requires: (1) that "there must be a one-to-one correspondence between the elements of the model and the elements of the thing of which it is the model," and (2) that "certain relations are preserved."[12] Models of this sort are found in all areas of life (for instance, scale-model airplanes); in science, the ismorphism is usually thought to hold between two theories, or more explicitly, their laws. This is what we will take as the core meaning of model. If the elements

---

[11] May Brodbeck, "Models, Meanings, and Theories," in Leonard Gross, ed., *Symposium on Sociological Theory* (Evanston, Ill.: Row, Peterson, 1959), p. 374.
[12] Ibid.

(generalizations or concepts) of one theory are in one-to-one correspondence to the elements of another theory and the required relations hold, the one may be called a model of the other.

This type of model—an isomorphism between two empirical theories—is nonexistent in political science; the reason is the lack of any sound scientific theories of politics. However, following May Brodbeck, we can mention another notion of model that also involves isomorphism, this time between an empirical theory (in the sense of a set of empirical generalizations) and a set of purely arithmetical truths. "If this is the case, then the latter is called an arithmetical representation of the empirical theory."[13] This meaning may be more relevant to political science, largely because of the increasing use of game theory, which is an "arithmetical representation." We will have more to say about this later in this chapter and in Chapter 11.

Besides these isomorphic models, there are, as Brodbeck notes, several other common usages of the term, none of them directly involving isomorphisms.[14] (1) "Any as yet untested or even untestable theory may be dubbed a 'model.' "[15] (2) Model may also be used to refer to abstracted theories, like those about economic man. (3) Theories making use of ideal entities such as perfectly straight lines are often called models. (4) When numbers can be attached to the concepts of a theory, it is often called a model. Brodbeck calls these uses of model unnecessary. However, it would seem that they, or combinations and variations of them, are what political scientists have in mind when they use the term *model*. For instance, in speaking of model-building activity, William Riker writes, "The essential feature of this method is the creation of a theoretical construct that is a somewhat simplified version of what the real world to be described is believed to be like."[16] Riker's idea of model doesn't appear to emphasize an isomorphic relationship; this is the key point. Rather, he, along with many other political scientists, uses model in the idealizing and abstracting sense mentioned by Brodbeck (usages two and three).

The basic argument of this section, that models are unlike theories in that they do not explain, assumes that model means either arithmetical represen-

---

[13] Ibid.

[14] Ibid., p. 381ff.

[15] Ibid., p. 381.

[16] William Riker, *The Theory of Political Coalitions* (New Haven, Conn.: Yale University Press, 1962), p. 7.

tations or idealized or abstracted theories in the general sense just described. Isomorphism of theories will not be considered because, as we have already noted, there are few, if any, theories in political science. Some might say we are subverting the real meaning of model. However, we are primarily interested in what political scientists attempt to do with models. Furthermore, even the subverted notions of model are remotely based on isomorphisms. An idealization or simplification of something is a rough isomorphism, because the former resembles the latter to a greater of lesser degree. Perhaps a way out of this controversy is to substitute another word for model; "conceptual scheme" is one in widespread use. Thus, "model" would be saved for cases where there is an isomorphism between theories. However, because most political scientists continue to use the term model, we will also.[17]

The use and misuse of models

Our argument begins with the realization that those political scientists who construct models often characterize them as unrealistic or idealized. This seems to be the most popular use of model or conceptual scheme in political science (although it diverges from the more technical meaning). While asserting its idealized nature, the political scientist will often attempt to use his model to explain phenomena. Or, more accurately, the creator of a model realizes its limitations as an explanatory device, while those who come after and use the model for their own purposes are prone to make more extravagant claims about its explanatory usefulness. These claims, in their extravagance, are unfounded.

We will now attempt to show why the function of models is not to explain. Let us first consider arithmetical representations. Our primary example will be game theory, since it is one of the most popular and promising models in political science. Game theory is arithmetic because it defines rationality—maximizing one's gains and minimizing one's losses—in terms of probability calculus and set theory. It is supposedly isomorphic because the political scientist attempts to connect it to laws about political behavior. In this

---

[17] See Ralph M. Stogdill, ed., *The Process of Model-Building in the Behavioral Sciences* (New York: W. W. Norton, 1970), for a practical guide to model building. Also see Charles A. Lave and James G. March, *An Introduction to Models in the Social Sciences* (New York: Harper & Row, 1975).

regard, Anthony Downs has provided a model of party politics,[18] William Riker has provided a model of coalition formation,[19] and L. S. Shapley and Martin Shubik have provided a model of power in a committee system.[20] However, as May Brodbeck has noted, "The trick for the social scientist . . . is to find appropriate descriptive terms which when coordinated to the arithmetical ones result in true empirical laws of human behavior."[21] We would argue that, thus far, the confirmed empirical laws have not been discovered. But more importantly, the model-builders usually admit that their models are unrealistic. For instance, Anthony Downs says of his model of rational decision making, "The model is not an attempt to describe reality accurately. Like all theoretical constructs in the social sciences, it treats a few variables as crucial and ignores others which actually have some influence."[22] Notice that besides the model's isomorphic nature (not obvious from this quote) there is reference to idealizing and abstraction. Returning to our central point, even while admitting that his model is unreal, Downs claims that, "It proposes a single hypothesis to *explain* government decision making and party behavior in general."[23] At another point, he argues that "Theoretical models should be tested primarily by the accuracy of their predictions rather than by the reality of their assumptions."[24] Our criticism of this argument rejects the explanatory power of models. In admitting that his model is ideal, unreal, and so forth, Downs has articulated its inability to explain political phenomena. Constructing a theory of rational behavior and then stating that no one really behaves rationally undercuts the model's explanatory value.

We can draw several preliminary conclusions about models and explanation. First, attempts to make arithmetic theories, such as game theory, models of actual political behavior force the political scientist to frame unrealistic assumptions. In admitting that his model does not fit the real world, the model-builder admits, consciously or not, its lack of ex-

---

[18] Anthony Downs, *An Economic Theory of Democracy* (New York: Harper & Row, 1957).

[19] Riker, *The Theory of Political Coalitions.*

[20] L. S. Shapley and Martin Shubik, "A Method For Evaluating the Distribution of Power in a Committee System," *American Political Science Review,* 48 (1954).

[21] Brodbeck, "Models, Meanings, and Theories," p. 391.

[22] Downs, *An Economic Theory,* p. 3.

[23] Ibid., p. 33.

[24] Ibid., p. 21.

planatory power. A mathematical model such as game theory can explain if the actual political world operates in accordance with it—if the two are isomorphic.

Furthermore, models such as game theory contain *idealizations* referring to concepts like "rational political behavior." Insofar as they are unreal—because they leave out variables—they cannot explain. May Brodbeck has said of such ideal types in economics, "The better the theory, the more knowledge we have about the conditions under which the neglected variables do or do not make a difference. If there are no economic men or if the ideal type of capitalism does not exist, then certain suggested theories are false. Calling the models will not make them truer."[25] This is the heart of the matter; the formulators of such models often use them as if they were theories; in other words, they confuse models with theories.

Let us recall the nature of scientific theory. If a theory is viewed as a system of related empirical generalizations, we must conclude that models are not theories, for the former are not constituted of confirmed empirical generalizations. Since confirmed generalizations are essential to explanation, models cannot be granted the same explanatory status as theories. However, what about the more refined and more widely held conception that views a theory as a system of generalizations containing directly observable and operationally defined concepts, and theoretical concepts, which although not observable are logically related to those that are? Are the idealizations and speculations of models logically similar to theoretical concepts? This is the crux of the issue; for if they are, then it would seem that theories are not entitled to a superior explanatory status.

Our answer is that idealized concepts which are admittedly unreal cannot be equated with theories that contain theoretical concepts. A theoretical concept is so labeled, not because it is divorced from reality, but because it is derived from observational terms within a theory: "Theoretical notions cannot be understood apart from the particular theory that implicitly defines them."[26] Furthermore, to be explanatory, such a theory must have some empirical content, so that the theoretical constructs are linked, at least indirectly, to observational phenomena. The theoretical concepts are not non-

---

[25] Brodbeck, "Models, Meanings, and Theories."

[26] Ernest Nagel, *The Structure of Science* (New York: Harcourt Brace Jovanovich, 1961), p. 87.

empirical, idealized, or admittedly unreal, but instead, they are not observable; they fit within the empirical theory.

Thus, we see that a model (in the idealizing sense) is not an empirical theory. Idealized concepts are not equivalent to theoretical concepts. Insofar as they are ideal they are unreal. The gist of this is that empirically sound theories refer to experience; thus, they can explain experience. If a mathematical model is truly isomorphic with a segment of political phenomena, it will have empirical referents, and so be able to explain; at this point, it becomes a theory.

We have now argued that models, as they are usually construed by political scientists, do not explain as theories can; this includes both notions of theory—a set of related observational-empirical laws, or a set of theoretical laws. But, in criticizing the assumption that models in political science explain, we have not meant to detract from their overall scientific value. Models such as game theory can be of *heuristic* value. It is not difficult to see how. If the political scientist is trying to accumulate basic knowledge in his field, it probably helps to have something available that stimulates his imagination and sharpens his insight. It is probably not an exaggeration to say that in a relatively immature discipline like political science, such stimulation and sharpening is absolutely necessary. These functions are admirably performed by some models. If the model is a simplified interpetation of reality, the researcher is forced to consider what the situation would be like if the model did describe reality and to what extent the model is unreal. If the model if based on a formal theory such as game theory, there is a host of relationships suggested that can be tested. If a model of politics is based upon a structure or theory in another area, a biological model for instance, the researcher has a potentially rich supply of hypotheses generated as he compares his field with the other.

The reason for our earlier assertion that all models are basically isomorphic now comes to the surface. Actually, models in political science are suggestive primarily because they are representations of something else. The heuristic use of models generally takes the following form: we observe theory or system *A;* we see certain similarities between it and our own area of interest, *B* (they appear to be isomorphic to some extent); so we begin to wonder if some of the relationships that hold in *A* also hold in *B*. We recognize that certain adjustments and additions are probably necessary, but at least the model we derive from *A* will provide a basis for the formulation of hypotheses and the organization of our study of politics. It is at this point that the "familiarity" argument, which we rejected in Chapter 7 as a sound criteria for explanations, becomes relevant. If we use a familiar system, say the game of poker, to organize our study of an unfamiliar situation or area, international politics for instance, then progress has been made. The model, in this case simple game theory, opens the door.

The distinction between the explanatory and heuristic value of theories and models is based upon the more fundamental distinction between scientific justification and discovery.[27] Throughout our analysis of the nature of generalizations, explanation, and the function of theories in political inquiry, we have been dealing with scientific justification, the relationship of evidence to hypotheses. As we have seen, this is amenable to logical analysis. There are methods of distinguishing between a good and a bad explanation or no explanation at all, between a sound or unsound theory, and between an acceptable and unacceptable generalization. Scientific discovery, on the other hand, has to do with where the concepts, hypotheses, and theories come from; how the scientist conceives of them. This deals with the psychology of scientists and is an activity that emphasizes creativity, imagination, even genius. Therefore, it is a more difficult process to analyze; so difficult that some have concluded it is impossible. Donald Schon, in writing about those who have studied the subject of innovation in science, notes that their "theories on the subject fall into one of two categories: either they make the process mysterious and therefore intrinsically unexplainable; or they regard novelty as illusory and, therefore, requiring no explanation."[28] However, since models are an integral part of the process of discovery, and since models can be analyzed, certain aspects of the process can be analyzed.

If models are mainly of heuristic value, if their primary function within the scientific enterprise is to suggest relationships between concepts—to generate hypotheses—then they belong in the realm of scientific discovery and not explanation. This is our major conclusion. The objective of our analysis has not been to question the importance of models, but to point out that they

---

[27] Hans Reichenbach analyzes the two scientific activities in greater depth in *Experience and Prediction* (Chicago: University of Chicago Press, 1938).

[28] Donald A. Schon, *Invention and the Evolution of Ideas* (London: Social Science Paperbacks, 1967), p. 3.

have a different role in the development of scientific knowledge. Given the fact that there are few, if any, developed theories of politics, the significance of any device that suggests possible relationships cannot be exaggerated.

Models and other heuristic devices in political science

We have evaluated game theory in general terms as a model of politics. But there are others less explicit and more speculative. Part 3, which begins with the next chapter, discusses some of the more popular and promising models, conceptual schemes, and approaches used in the study of politics. But we will consider a few models here to make the argument more meaningful. Several are rough attempts at isomorphism, while others are idealized models or conceptual schemes. Their inability to explain, often realized by their creators, will become obvious, but their possible heuristic value will be emphasized.

Kenneth Boulding has examined several models of social conflict. He labels two of them the "ecological" model and the "epidemiological" model.[29] The former draws attention to "the similarity between the conflict of groups in human society and the competition of species in biological ecosystems."[30] The latter compares the spread of contagious diseases through a population to certain types of group conflict, such as conversion.[31] The chapters that Boulding devotes to these models are provocative discussions of suggestive similarities between different systems of phenomena. No explanations or potential explanations are forthcoming. This Boulding admits. "In applying simple mechanical models such as we have explored in this and in previous chapters to the enormously complex dynamics of conflict in society, we should look for insights rather than for exact correspondences."[32] The key word is "insights," for it indicates the heuristic emphasis of model-building.

More ambitious claims have been made by some social scientists inter-

---

[29] Kenneth Boulding, *Conflict and Defense: A General Theory* (New York: Harper & Row, 1962), chapter 6 and 7.

[30] Ibid., p. 123.

[31] Ibid., p. 124.

[32] Ibid., p. 137.

ested in general systems theory.[33] The comparing of systems of social behavior with chemical systems and biological systems, for instance, seems to some to lay the foundation for explanation. "Models and theories are never perfect but simply approach the limit of correct explanation."[34] But we would argue that the mere noting of similarities between systems explains nothing. Analogies and metaphors are often enlightening, but they account for no facts. Once again, we return to the heuristic value of models. Anatol Rapaport has written in this regard, "Metaphor and analogy, although they cannot be accepted as scientific 'explanations' are sometimes important aids in the sense that they prepare the mind to make more precise investigations."[35] This also applies to the much more sophisticated systems analyses of political scientists such as David Easton.[36]

There is another kind of model-building in political science that is seemingly remote from isomorphic analysis. It is characterized instead by idealized sets of assumptions about given areas of political phenomena. As we implied at the beginning of this section, this activity is perhaps the most prevalent of those that go under the name of model building. A sophisticated example, the decision-making approach of Richard C. Snyder and Glenn D. Paige, will be discussed in Chapter 12.[37] Less elaborate models, this time of party systems, are analyzed by Samuel Eldersveld.[38] He clearly uses them in a heuristic fashion to suggest relationships that can be tested. This use of ideal models can be traced back to German sociologist Max Weber's notion of ideal types. In his studies of bureaucracy, Weber found that if he began with an idealized or perfect concept of bureaucracy, he could use it as a

---

[33] One attempt to apply general systems theory to the study of society is James G. Miller, "Toward a General Theory for the Behavioral Sciences," *American Psychologist,* 10 (1955), p. 513–31.

[34] Ibid., p. 531.

[35] Anatol Rapaport, "Various meanings of 'Theory,'" *American Political Science Review,* 52 (1958), p. 984. For a thorough analysis of various uses of metaphors in political science, see Eugene F. Miller, "Metaphor and Political Knowledge," *American Political Science Review,* 73 (1979), pp. 155–70.

[36] David Easton, *A Framework of Political Analysis* (Englewood Cliffs, N.J.: Prentice-Hall, 1965).

[37] Richard C. Snyder and Glenn D. Paige, "The Decision-Making Approach to the Study of International Politics," in James N. Rosenau, ed., *International Politics and Foreign Policy* (New York: Free Press, 1961), pp. 186–92.

[38] Samuel Eldersveld, *Political Parties: A Behavioral Analysis* (Skokie, Ill.: Rand McNally, 1964), part 3.

standard to compare real world bureaucracies against. By "idealized" Weber meant "intentionally unreal." Likewise, the ideal models of modern political scientists are not meant to be descriptions of reality but useful heuristic devices.

As we have already implied, some political scientists call the kind of model we have just discussed a "conceptual scheme." The term seems to imply a set of ideal assumptions about a given subject area. Thus, William C. Mitchell has said in introducing his own "structural-functional" conceptual scheme: "A conceptual scheme or framework is an essential tool in all scientific investigation for it provides the elementary concepts, assumption, ideas, and directives that guide the selection and interpretation of facts."[39] Again, models or conceptual schemes are more important for their suggestiveness than their explanatory power.

In addition to idealized or speculative models, there are other heuristic techniques or strategies of discovery that are available to political scientists. These are alternatives to models, but they can often be used in a complementary manner. We will conclude this chapter with a brief discussion of some of them. This will, it is hoped, clarify the heuristic nature of models and indicate that there are alternatives available. A popular heuristic device is *Verstehen* or empathic understanding.[40] According to its users, *Verstehen* suggests possible relationships by somehow "getting into" other people's heads to speculate about how others would behave in certain situations. There are several related techniques of discovery in political inquiry. One of the most popular techniques is the construction of "alternative futures," gounded speculations about what the world will be like in 10, 20, and 50 years, based on present trends. One of the most famous practitioners of this method is Herman Kahn. In the 1950s and 60s, he predicted what the world would be like in the 1970s. That his predictions were not always accurate should not detract from the heuristic usefulness of his work; "as if" speculation is meant to be suggestive rather than predictive.[41]

---

[39] William C. Mitchell, *The American Policy* (New York: Free Press, 1962), p. 3.

[40] For a methodological critique, see Theodore Abel, "The Operation Called *Verstehen*," in Herbert Feigl and May Brodbeck, eds., *Readings in the Philosophy of Science* (New York: Appleton-Century-Crofts, 1953), pp. 677–87.

[41] Herman Kahn, "Alternative World Futures," (New York: Hudson Institute, 1964). Also see *On Thermonuclear War* (Princeton, N.J.: Princeton University Press, 1960). For a wider-ranging example of Futurist literature, see Albert Somit, ed., *Political Science and the Study of the Future* (Hinsdale, Ill.: Dryden Press, 1974).

A strategy somewhat similar to "as if" speculation but probably more empirically grounded has been described by Alexander George: "The analyst rehearses in his mind the different possible versions of a missing piece, trying to decide which version is more plausible, given the values of the pieces already known to him."[42] This might be interpreted as the first step toward theory *building,* but note that it has to do with the *discovery,* not justification, of facts. It is one type of a broader category of heuristic techniques, generically called mind experiments. We have all performed such experiments while sitting at our desks, driving our cars, or daydreaming in class. Let us quote J. A. Laponce, one of the few social scientists to think seriously about mind experiments:

> In such an experiment the mind is treated as one would a laboratory; it is emptied of unwanted ideas, of unwanted variables, it is made to relate only the factors under study which are either left free to play and interact among themselves—or on the contrary have to interact according to specific rules. These experiments in the mind, these anticipatory experiments which, in a writer, produce plays and novels, in a social scientist result in theories, formulae, and computer simulations.[43]

A more sophisticated, yet less widespread heuristic technique is the mathematical and logical demonstration that a given type of political behavior is logically possible. This is usually done in regard to rational political behavior. For instance, William Riker has shown, by means of mathematical reasoning, that "Congress may act irrationally and probably does so occasionally."[44] Riker defines rationality as transitivity of preferences and then presents a mathematical proof that shows how congressional preferences can be intransitive.[45] Thus, this scientific technique indicates to the political

---

[42] Alexander George, "Prediction of Political Action by means of Propaganda Analysis," in Polsby et al., *Politics and Social Life,* p. 850.

[43] J. A. Laponce, "Experimenting: A Two-Person Game between Man and Nature," in J. A. Laponce and Paul Smoker, eds., *Experimentation and Simulation in Political Science* (Toronto: University of Toronto Press, 1972).

[44] William H. Riker, "Voting Methods and Irrationality in Legislative Decisions," in John C. Wahlke and Heinz Eulau, eds., *Legislative Behavior* (New York: Free Press, 1959), pp. 97–108.

[45] The basic work in this area is Kenneth Arrow, *Social Choice and Individual Values* (New York: John Wiley & Sons, 1951). Also see Robert A. Dahl, *A Preface to Democratic Theory* (Chicago: University of Chicago Press, 1956), pp. 41–42.

scientist that certain political outcomes are logically possible and so are potential explananda.

We will consider one more heuristic strategy in political inquiry. It is the increasingly employed technique of simulation.[46] In a simulation run, an artificial political situation is fabricated or an actual situation is reproduced, and either individuals act out political roles or a computer makes a series of decisions based on data and decision-criteria that have been programmed into it.[47] The result in either case is a possible outcome given the data. Simulation is important both in producing such possible outcomes and in providing hypotheses about how decisions are made. However, some political scientists seem to equate simulation runs with empirical experiments.[48] According to our analysis, this is slightly misleading, for the simulation situation is not analogous to the experimental laboratories of the physicist and chemist.

The analysis of this chapter has attempted to draw a distinction between explanatory theories and heuristic models, a distinction based on the difference between scientific justification and discovery. Part 3 will devote more time to the latter. The next few chapters will examine a number of approaches, ways of organizing our study of politics, which are somewhat sophisticated models and somewhat potential theories of politics.

---

[46] A good book of readings on simulation is Harold Guetzkow, ed., *Simulation in Social Science: Readings* (Englewood Cliffs, N.J.: Prentice-Hall, 1962).

[47] For an example of the latter type of simulation study, see Ithiel deSola Pool et al., *Candidates, Issues, and Strategies* (Cambridge, Mass.: MIT Press, 1964).

[48] For a stimulating presentation of this view, see J. A. Laponce's "Introduction" to Laponce and Smoker, *Experimentation and Simulation in Political Science* (Toronto: University of Toronto Press, 1972).

PART

3

APPROACHES TO THE
STUDY OF POLITICS

Approaches to the study of politics

AN approach in political inquiry is a general strategy for studying political phenomena. The next six chapters examine some of the most important approaches in contemporary political science. This chapter introduces that examination. Approaches are formulated and used for a number of reasons. They can function at both heuristic and explanatory levels. That is, an approach might provide the framework for, or even take the form of, a model or conceptual scheme or it might serve as the impetus for the development of a theory of politics. Thus, in evaluating an approach, we will consider its promise as an explanatory or potentially explanatory device.

But the central point which anticipates our analysis of specific approaches is that they are of more heuristic than explanatory value. That is, an approach is probably used most often to suggest hypotheses that can then be tested. Approaches to the study of politics are therefore more an aspect of scientific discovery than of explanation. Part 3 meshes with the second section of Chapter 8 because of the close *functional* ties between models and approaches. In many instances, the two labels are synonymous.

However, this does not mean that approaches are never of explanatory value. As we have already suggested, they may stimulate the formulation of theories. There is, in addition, a lower-level explanatory function of approaches that is related to their heuristic functions. In suggesting hypotheses, an approach might be instrumental in generating an explanation sketch or perhaps even a partial explanation of a political phenomenon without providing the foundation for a theory.

In this regard, approaches and patterns of explanation overlap to some extent. This is not surprising when we realize that both approaches and patterns attempt to deal with the world as it is. If, for instance, dispositions are *as a matter of fact* a significant kind of political variable, then we would expect there to be dispositional approaches and a dispositional pattern of explanation. However, while there is overlap in content and function, the notions of pattern and approach refer to different methodological entities. A classification of patterns describes the kinds of concepts political scientists use to explain and the forms nomological explanation can take. Approaches, on the other hand, are attempts to develop strategies for directing the research activities of the political scientist.

It should now be clear how important the process of discovery is in any science, especially a developing one like political science. While discovery puts a premium on imagination and creativity, it is a process that can be systematically examined; there are tools available that are useful in opening the political scientist's mind to new concepts and hypotheses. These tools, what we have labeled *approaches,* but also called *conceptual schemes, frameworks models,* and *paradigms,* articulate the basic assumptions that shape research.

Many historians of science have emphasized the role of approaches in scientific discovery. The major point is that great "change is brought about, not by new observations or additional evidence in the first instance, but by transpositions that were taking place inside the minds of the scientists themselves."[1] This psychological change is usually manifested by a change in approaches—in physics from Newton's to Einstein's, for example. An overt approach is not necessary for the discovery of new concepts and relationships, at least for the scientific genius. For others it is crucial; for in articulating the basic assumptions they have about human nature, about the factors that are causing the events being studied, scientists, including political scientists, begin to move beyond the mere collection of facts. A list of all the observations one makes in a day is useless unless the observations are

---

[1] Herbert Butterfield, *The Origin's of Modern Science* (New York: Free Press, 1957), p. 13.

selected and organized according to a set of assumptions; in other words, an approach. In the case of the genius the approach may lie below the threshold of consciousness; for others, it should be clearly articulated. In all cases, the model is there—we all start with assumptions.

An approach may involve the attempt to locate an organizing concept or set of concepts that can orient research and coordinate empirical data from several sources. An approach is designed to include as wide a range of political phenomena as possible within a single set of concepts. The political scientist has to determine how much scope the conceptual scheme has and how much revision is required if it is to include an even wider range. Or it may be realized that it applies only to a limited range. This activity involves both conceptual analysis and empirical research as the conceptual scheme is refined and expanded or reduced in scope. In the process, the political scientist will be able to organize the study and may have hypotheses suggested to him. The ultimate success would be the generation of an empirical theory.

Let us now describe the substance of Part 3 in light of what we have just said. Some of the approaches to be examined are more highly developed than others. Some are broad conceptual schemes, while others are narrower models revolving around a single central concept. Some are sets of empirical generalizations, while others are formal models.

The organization of Part 3 can be viewed as a continuum of levels of analysis. The idea is one of cutting into politics at a number of points to examine different slices of political life. Thus, no approach is right or wrong; but some may be more useful than others. Because we do not have a finely honed knife available, there is some overlap between the approaches. But there are differences to be drawn that are meaningful for the political scientist.

One difference deals with assumptions about basic human motivation— theories of human nature. Some approaches assume that political behavior is rational, that is, conscious and goal-seeking. Others view it as the result of unconscious motivations, factors unknown to the actor. There is an equally important distinction, of ancient origin, between humans as social and cooperative animals (consensus theory) and as selfish and competitive animals (conflict theory).

Perhaps the most important distinction for political scientists is between micro and macro approaches. This distinction refers to the level of analysis that the researcher selects as a starting point for the study of politics. A micro approach begins with the smallest unit—in politics, with the individual; a macro approach begins with the largest unit—the political system. How we label approaches that are somewhere in between, those that emphasize interest groups for instance, has never been definitively answered. Heinz Eulau has provided a pragmatic answer. Since the main objective of science is to discover relationships, hopefully causal ones, among concepts, it makes sense to consider the relationship between independent (cause) and dependent (effect) variables.[2] Eulau labels the former the *subject-unit* and the latter the *object-unit* and suggests that if, within a particular approach, the object is larger than the subject, then the approach is micro; if the object is smaller, the approach is macro. The common-sense idea is that if we use smaller- or lower-level units to explain higher-level ones, such as the personalities of senators to explain the decisions of the Senate, we have a micro approach; if we use higher-level units to explain lower-level ones, like the structure of the Senate to explain the voting behavior of individual Senators, we have a macro approach.

Several major evaluative criteria will be employed as approaches are examined. Among them are: how appropriate the approach is for political analysis; how effectively it organizes existing knowledge; how fruitful it is in suggesting new insights and hypotheses. The last is the one we are the most interested in, for it speaks directly to the role of approaches in the process of discovery.

Using the micro-macro distinction as our point of departure, we begin with those approaches that make the individual and his or her psychological characteristics the center of attention. Chapter 10 deals with approaches that emphasize dispositional behavior. These include such specific approaches as learning theory and personality theory. Intentional and rational approaches, which see behavior as conscious and goal-seeking, are considered in Chapter 11. This includes an analysis of the most fully developed rational model of politics—game theory. Chapter 12 continues the discussion of rational models initiated in Chapter 11, but it concentrates on how economic models have been applied to politics.

---

[2] Heinz Eulau, "The Legislative System and After: On Closing the Micro-Macro Gap," in Oliver Walter, ed., *Political Scientists at Work* (Belmont, Mass.: Duxbury Press, 1971), pp. 137–50.

Chapter 13 moves the analysis to a more macro level in emphasizing the importance of institutional roles and the impact of the small group on individual decisions.

Chapter 14 examines approaches based on that central concept of politics—power. Elitism and pluralism (group theory) are approaches that begin with the question: How is power distributed in a political system? In so doing, attention is shifted from the individual to the group.

Approaches that stay at the level of political systems are the topic of Chapter 15. The main part of the analysis focuses on the most important offshoot of systems theory, functionalism, which bases its approach to the study of politics on the functions of political systems.

Chapter 16 considers an aspect of political systems which is attracting the attention of more and more political scientists, namely, communication. Communications theory asserts that any approach to the study of politics is incomplete without a consideration of how political information is transmitted within and between political systems.

Before we examine contemporary approaches to the study of politics, it might help if, for a moment, we turned our attention to a classic approach. Marxim is an easy choice for several reasons: first, the influence of Marxism both as an ideology and as approach to social, economic, and political analysis is unparalleled in modern times; second, to many it provides an alternative to the scientific method outlined in this book; third, despite its complexity and varied interpretations, Marxism is based on a fairly compact set of assumptions. Our main concern is with the scientific dimension of Marxism, not its ideological impact.[3] This is consistent with Marx's interpretation of his work as an empirically sound description and explanation of historical development.

Marxism is a macro approach. It begins with the assumption that every characteristic of a society can be traced back to its economic structure. A capitalist economic system produces a capitalist class system (with capitalists exploiting the workers), which produces a capitalist state and a capitalist ideology. Individuals gain their identity from the class they belong to; they function as capitalists or workers, as landowners or peasants. People behave

---

[3] For a discussion of Marxian methodology, see Bertell Ollman, "Marxism and Political Science: Prolegemenon to a Debate on Marx's Method," *Politics and Society* (Summer 1973), p. 491–510.

in a competitive fashion not because they are naturally competitive but because they live in a competitive capitalist society. Marx suggests that humans are social beings, characterized mainly by the motivation to produce. What better basis for ultimate communism—a classless, stateless, conflict-free society where people contribute what they can and use only what they need.

Marx's approach includes assumptions that specify how historical change takes place. It is widely known that Marx believed in the necessity of violent class revolution. More important for us is the theory that Marx used to account for this process—the dialectical process, to Marx the source of all historical change places conflict at its core. Every ruling class produces its antithesis, and the two must eventually come into conflict. Out of this struggle comes the next stage of history. The Marxian approach assumes that conflict is normal and inevitable in human society because societies are always based on class and classes have irreconcilable interests. Since everything is attributable to economic class divisions, it follows that when classes cease to exist, so does conflict. Since the state exists only to maintain the dominance of the ruling class, the end of classes implies the end of the state and politics.

Marx and the Marxists who have followed him have been accused of making a number of methodological errors. The most basic error is that the empirical and ideological become intertwined to such an extent in Marxism that they cannot be separated; this, according to the critics, undercuts the significance of Marxism as an empirical approach to political analysis. Marxists tend to view their approach as an irrefutably accurate description of history and, at the same time, an expression of what ought to be the course of history. What is going to happen (the Communist revolution) should happen because it is going to happen; or, the other way around, what should happen will happen because it should happen. Critics have accused Marxists of making both methodological errors, each based on the failure to distinguish between facts and values.

A Marxist would probably reply that it is misleading to apply the criteria of scientific methodology to Marxism, since the latter presents an alternative and superior route to social, political, and economic knowledge. The historical dialectical process describes not just a series of events that could have moved in several directions, but a set of predictable historical stages, beyond the manipulation of human actors—this is "objective reality" to the Marxist.

Most modern political scientists would probably argue that the most meaningful way to evaluate Marxism as an approach to political analysis is to set aside its ideological content and look only at its empirical assumptions and hypotheses. Marxism is not an alternative to the scientific method; its value to students of politics must be based on the ability of its assumptions to generate testable and potentially useful hypotheses about politics. Some of them might be: All political conflict is the result of economic class conflict; in all pre-Communist societies there is a ruling class; violent revolution is, with few exceptions, the only method of economic, social, and political change. Each of these statements is a testable hypothesis; each is implied by Marx's basic assumptions. Thus, Marxism can be considered a useful approach to political analysis; whether the hypotheses can become laws is another matter.

There is another question about approaches and models that ought to be considered. It asks if the assumptions which are at the heart of every approach will bias the conclusions drawn by the political scientist using it. If the researcher starts out assuming that a micro approach is best, then he or she will probably look only at the behavior of individual political actors. This will surely color the "picture" of politics he or she finally comes up with. The implication is that all scientific truth is relative to the approach it springs from. To some, this is one of the costs of using models; sometimes it is an unacceptable cost. To others, it is not the result of models, but an inescapable fact of human thinking. We must always begin with assumptions, stated or unstated, conscious or unconscious. The question then becomes, in making the assumptions overt, laying them on the table, perhaps in the form of an approach, can we evaluate the relative impact of different approaches? In short, can we develop criteria for sorting out biased and nonbiased conclusions? Ultimately, is there such a thing as "knowledge" of politics that would be independent of a particular approach? The basic premise of this book is that such knowledge is possible. The question is a real one, however, and should be remembered as we work our way through the next six chapters.

Underlying this analysis of the role of approaches in political science is a broader question, one that has attracted the attention of historians of science

for countless decades. How does science develop? Is it through an incre-
mental and accumulative expansion of knowledge, with little reliance on
conscious approaches? Is it through the gradual improvement of scientific
approaches? Is it through the competition of several approaches? Or, as the
most influential contemporary historian of science, Thomas Kuhn, argues, is
it through the overthrow of one dominant model, which he calls a *paradigm,*
by another?[4] In looking at contemporary political science, it seems that there
is no universally accepted paradigm. Instead, we find a number of alternative
approaches, each with its own claimed advantages. This portrait of a pluralist political science provides the backdrop for the analysis contained in the
ensuing chapters.

----

[4] Thomas S. Kuhn, *The Structure of Scientific Revolutions* (Chicago: University of Chicago
Press, 1962).

Individualistic-psychological approaches

ERNON VAN DYKE has written: "The basic point about political phenomena is that they consist of or result from the actions of human beings."[1] It would seem difficult to deny, no matter what one's philosophical position, individualism or holism, that humans are the fundamental stuff of politics. Groups are composed of individuals; so are political institutions. Whether working at the macro or micro level, with individual political actors or large nation-states, the political scientist will be concerned with human behavior in one form or another. Therefore, it seems proper to consider first those approaches that focus upon concepts referring directly to human characteristics.

Individualistic approaches can be sorted into two general categories. The first views political behavior as nonintentional, that is, the result of psychological factors that influence the political actors at the subconscious level; included are such factors as attitudes, opinions, and personality traits. The second individualistic approach bases its examination of politics on the assumption that political behavior is intentional, that is, characterized by the

---

[1] Vernon Van Dyke, *Political Science: A Philosophical Analysis* (Stanford, Calif.: Stanford University Press, 1960), p. 23.

conscious seeking of goals. One type of intentional behavior can be thought of as rational, that is, designed to achieve a particular goal in the most efficient manner possible. Dispositional or nonintentional approaches—including the two most impressive examples, learning theory and personality theory—are analyzed in this chapter. The intentional approach and its most highly developed representative, decision-making theory, are discussed in the next chapter. The other subject of that chapter is the rational approach, with special emphasis on its increasingly popular offspring, game theory.

We will examine and evaluate the basic assumptions and methodological foundations of each approach. How suggestive is the approach as a heuristic device? What are its prospects as an explanatory theory, or at least as the core of a theory of politics? These are critical questions we will ask of every approach.

DISPOSITIONAL APPROACHES

The great political thinkers of the past recognized that to understand political phenomena, one has to study human nature. While their conceptions vary, from Aristotle's cooperative social animal to Hobbes's self-centered and competitive beast, there remains the assumption that individual psychological motivations and politics are inexorably linked. Yet, until the 19th century, philosophers tended to view humans as rational, that is, conscious and goal-seeking beings. However, at that point, social thinkers began moving from rational approaches to those that emphasize the darker side of human behavior. Darwin suggested that a human is simply a more developed animal. The philosophers Schopenhauer and Nietzsche portrayed us as irrational actors in an irrational world, unable to discover meaning and able to create order only through the imposition of superior will. Following in their footsteps, Freud dug even deeper into the human psyche and found a bundle of needs, desires, and anxieties struggling to get out. Simultaneously, in the United States, the psychologist Watson was establishing a quite different school of psychology, which nevertheless began with the same assumption, that human behavior is not consciously rational. He argued that human activity is the result of conditioning; we tend to continue activities that are followed by rewards and to cease activities that are not.

But it was not until 1908, when the English political thinker Graham

Wallas refuted rationalism and intellectualism in political analysis and emphasized unconscious attitudes, that the groundwork was laid for dispositional approaches to political phenomena.[2] While primitive, his work is all the more important because it provided an impetus to the scientific study of politics. But of primary relevance here are his insightful remarks about the dispositional approach. If one were able, Wallas argues, to photograph a man's activities for an entire day and then present him with the film

> He would, of course, see that much of his activities consisted in the half-conscious repetition, under the influence of habit, of movements which were originally more fully conscious. But even if all cases of habit were excluded he would find that only a small proportion of the residue could be explained as being directly produced by an intellectual calculation.[3]

This plea to emphasize nonrational dispositions in political analysis did not fall upon deaf ears. Since Wallas wrote his groundbreaking book *Human Nature in Politics,* social scientists have done much to advance our understanding of dispositions, and many have opted for their use in the explanation of political phenomena. For instance, the political scientist Robert Lane has written: "Explanations of political decisions which rely wholly upon analyses of the social environment, while they may have high predictive value, neglect a vital link; they never explain why an individual responds to the environment the way he does."[4] It is this link that interests us.

The nature of dispositions

A disposition is a tendency to respond in a certain way in a given situation. To say that a person has the attitudinal disposition, that is, the attitude "Democratic" means that when asked, "With which party do you identify?" the answer is, "Democratic." In this case, the situation is the asking of a question and the response is a particular answer. There is another feature of the disposition that distinguishes it from its relation—the intention. What we call dispositions can be thought of as psychological characteristics or factors that are unconsciously related to other political phenomena.

---

[2] Graham Wallas, *Human Nature in Politics* (Lincoln: University of Nebraska Press, 1962).
[3] Ibid., p. 47.
[4] Robert Lane, *Political Life,* (New York: Free Press, 1959), p. 98.

For instance, the individual voter with attitude X doesn't perceive its influence on the direction of his vote. He doesn't say, "I voted for candidate Y because I have attitude X," although empirical research may discover a strong relationship between the attitude and the type of voting decision. If he says, "I voted for Y because I want Z to happen and I think Y's party also wants Z to happen," we have a case of intentional behavior.

Dispositions can be more or less unconscious. Thus, we are completely unaware of many dispositions that influence our behavior. On the other hand, we might know we have attitude X—we are certainly aware of our Democratic or Republican leanings. The important distinction between intentions and dispositions is that the *relationship* between the latter and behavior is not "out in the open," even though we are aware that we have the disposition. Note that an acceptance of this distinction does not require one to advocate a mentalistic psychology that proposes looking into people's heads to find unconscious motives. Dispositions are defined behaviorally, in terms of observable actions. Again, it is the link between the disposition and relevant political phenomena that is below the surface, and not necessarily the knowledge that one has the disposition.

Types of dispositions

We are now ready to consider the major types of dispositional concepts used by political scientists. Those in widespread use are opinions, attitudes, ideologies, values, and beliefs. An opinion has been defined as "an implicit verbal response or 'answer' that an individual gives in response to a particular stimulus situation where some general 'question' is raised."[5] An opinion is usually distinguished from an attitude on the basis of generality. That is, an opinion has to do with a specific issue, for instance, price supports for farmers, while an attitude is broader; one would have an attitude toward the government's role in the economy. Thus, an attitude can be thought of as being manifested in a number of opinions.[6] The political scientist Lewis

---

[5] Carl I. Hovland, Irving L. Janis, and Harold H. Kelley, *Communication and Persuasion* (New Haven, Conn.: Yale University Press, 1953), p. 6.

[6] This distinction between opinions and attitudes is made in H. J. Eysenck, *The Psychology of Politics* (London: Routledge & Kegan Paul, 1954), p. 111ff.

Froman has defined attitude in this manner: "A predisposition of an individual to evaluate some aspect of his world in a favorable or unfavorable manner, that is, a predisposition to approve or disapprove, like or dislike, some social or physical object."[7] An attitude is probably more stable and durable than an opinion; one would expect opinions toward government aid to farmers to change more often than attitudes toward governmental regulation of the economy.

There is one more dispositional level directly related to opinions and attitudes. This is usually labeled "ideology." Perhaps the best way to think of an ideology is to imagine a cluster of attitudes. Eysenck has called it a "super-attitude."[8] Thus, a person's attitude toward the government's role in the economy might be part of an overall conservative ideology.

There are a number of well-known ideologies—conservatism, liberalism, socialism, Marxism. These are the ones that have been studied the most often by political scientists and historians, usually in a philosophical or impressionistic manner. The underlying assumption of this approach is that ideologies are rather elaborate and highly structured sets of attitudes with certain core values and readily recognizable labels. If this conception is used, there is evidence from survey data that few Americans are ideological—few Americans have well-defined and structured sets of attitudes.

In recent years, behaviorally inclined social scientists have used more rigorous techniques to identify and measure ideologies.[9] This has entailed a somewhat different approach to the identification and measurement of ideology. Instead of examining classic ideologies, behavioralists have attempted to find statistical correlations among a number of attitudes in various publics. Thus, Eysenck identifies an ideology by statistically correlating a number of attitudes.[10] We have three important dispositional levels. A quick survey of political science literature tends to indicate that opinions, attitudes, and, to a lesser extent, ideologies are used extensively to orient the study of politics and explain political behavior. Furthermore, explaining the

---

[7] Lewis Froman, *People and Politics* (Englewood Cliffs, N.J.: Prentice-Hall, 1962), p. 20.

[8] Eysenck, *The Psychology of Politics,* p. 113.

[9] See David E. Apter, ed., *Ideology and Discontent* (New York: Free Press, 1964); and Robert E. Lane, *Political Ideology: Why the American Common Man Believes What He Does* (New York: Free Press, 1962).

[10] Eysenck, *The Psychology of Politics,* chapter 4.

dispositions, that is, treating them as dependent variables, is becoming an important task of political scientists.

Closely related to attitudes and opinions are values. "A value is a statement of 'good' or 'bad,' 'right' or 'wrong,' something which is desired or thought desirable."[11] A value is less specific than an attitude. Political scientists have often emphasized the importance of political values (values pursued politically) when explaining political behavior. For instance, Harold Lasswell has identified a number of values that are sought in politics: power, wealth, well-being, skill, enlightenment, affection, rectitude, and respect.[12] There is a methodological point about values that should be mentioned. In Chapter 1, the distinction between fact and value was drawn. We emphasized that our analysis of the scientific study of politics deals only with how we know facts; description and explanation, as we understood their relevance for political inquiry, have to do with empirical, not normative, questions. However, while "values" are not true or false, it is a fact that people have one value or another; an assertion attributing the holding of a value to someone can be empirically tested (if it is properly formulated). Thus, values in this empirical sense are fair game for political scientists.

Beliefs have to do with matters of fact. "Beliefs are defined as cognitions with an extra feeling of credibility which distinguishes them from cognitions which are not believed."[13] Thus, a belief can be true or false. But a false belief is no less a belief, for its truth or falsity is logically independent of the psychological certainty of its believer. The relevance of beliefs to political behavior is obvious. What people believe is often the main determinant of what they do and what their attitudes are. But there need be no logical consistency among attitudes, values, and beliefs. Values and beliefs might seem to differ from attitudes and opinions in that the former are less obviously dispositional. But while an opinion is clearly a response to a situation, so is a value. An individual responds to certain objects or ideas with approval or disapproval. We characterize them as dispositional because their existence is determined (by definition) by measuring responses—if X does Y in situation Z, he has disposition D.

---

[11] Froman, *People,* p. 18.

[12] Harold Lasswell, *Psychopathology and Politics* in *The Political Writings of Harold D. Lasswell* (New York: Free Press, 1951), p. 74–77.

[13] Lester W. Milbrath, *Political Participation* (Skokie, Ill.: Rand McNally, 1965), p. 31.

Using dispositions

Having described the main varieties of concepts used in the dispositional approach to the study of politics, we can examine the nature of the approach itself. Actually, there are several ways political scientists use dispositions in the discovery and explanation of political phenomena; thus, we can talk about variations on the dispositional approach.

Perhaps the most straightforward dispositional approach views dispositions as antecedent conditions of political phenomena. In other words, the assumption is made that it is possible to formulate hypotheses that express such relationships, and that these generalizations can provide a foundation for useful models and, hopefully, explanatory theories of politics.

It is not difficult to find examples of low-level dispositional models or potential theories of politics. We will examine only two, one constructed by Lewis Froman, the other by Seymour Martin Lipset. Froman has speculated about the differences between leaders and nonleaders in interest groups; for instance, in regard to their group loyalty.[14] Starting from a dispositional approach, he hypothesizes that there are relationships between interest group leaders' behavior and their attitudes, values, and beliefs.[15] A behavior differential is related to a dispositional differential. For instance, Froman argues that, "Nonleaders have fewer values relating to why they are in the group."[16] Thus, the group is more important to the leaders. A number of similar generalizations are suggested by the dispositional assumptions of Froman's model. Together they explain (or provide an explanation sketch of) the membership differential.

Another explanation based upon the dispositional approach has been provided by Lipset.[17] He is interested in the fact that extremist movements are often backed by the lower classes. After supporting this fact with much

---

[14] Froman, *People,* pp. 43–48.

[15] It should be made clear that we are not drawing a logical distinction between dispositions and behavior. By definition, a disposition is a type of behavior, a response to a situation. But when using dispositional models, there are practical reasons for such a distinction. These boil down to the need to emphasize that the dispositions are being used as independent variables and so are antecedent conditions of political behavior (which might include other dispositions).

[16] Froman, *People,* p. 43.

[17] Seymour Martin Lipset, *Political Man* (Garden City, N.Y.: Doubleday Publishing, 1959), p. 97.

empirical evidence, he attributes a psychological trait, a disposition, to the lower classes:

> The social situation of the lower strata . . . predisposes them to view politics as black and white, good and evil. Consequently, other things being equal, they should be more likely than other strata to prefer extremist movements which suggest easy and quick solutions to social problems and have a rigid outlook.[18]

There is always the danger of giving ex post facto explanations. It is especially tempting to use dispositions to account for political phenomena *after the fact*. In a sense, this is what Lipset has done. Noticing the relationship between lower classes and extremism, he speculates and formulates a disposition which, if possessed by the lower classes, would account (at least partially) for their extremism. An ex post facto explanation should not be condemned as long as its creator realizes that he is speculating, playing with his data, and not producing a substantiated explanation. In the present context, the significance of such analyses as Froman's and Lipset's lies in their demonstration of how a general dispositional approach to politics can (1) lay the foundation for an explanatory theory; (2) generate hypotheses to be tested, and in general act as an impetus for discovering new relationships. The dispositional approach fulfills one of the classic functions of the scientific heuristic device. It directs the political scientist's attention toward certain variables that might account for the facts that interest him, and at the same time suggests hypotheses that can be tested.

A more highly developed model based upon assumed relationships between dispositional concepts and political behavior has been rpesented in *The American Voter*.[19] The authors of this highly praised voting study argue that to describe, explain, and predict electoral behavior, a sound and economical approach is needed. It assumes that although past experiences and situations influence an individual's political behavior, the most efficient method of accounting for voting and voting preference is through the measurement of dispositions that are directly related to the final decision. Their model does not fail to take into account sociological and economic factors. It only, in the authors' words, "maximizes explanatory power while dealing with a minimum number of variables."[20] Their "funnel of causality" ap-

---

[18] Ibid., p. 100.

[19] Angus Campbell et al., *The American Voter* (New York: John Wiley & Sons, 1960).

[20] Ibid., p. 33.

proach is so labeled because the factors which lead to the voting act are examined as if they existed in a temporal funnel. The funnel broadens as we go back in time, away from the actual moment of decision; moving in the direction of causality, we find the funnel becoming narrower, indicating that as we come closer to the act of voting fewer factors have a direct causal impact. The moment of decision and the tip of the funnel are reached, in a metaphorical sense, simultaneously; at this point the fewest number of factors are operating. These are the factors that ought to be emphasized in the most economical model of voting; in *The American Voter,* they are attitudes toward such factors as "the issues of domestic policy; the issues of foreign policy; and the comparative record of the two parties in managing the affairs of government."[21] The attitudes serve as a link between socioeconomic factors and the voting act. We see how a general dispositional approach can suggest a strategy of explanation, and if reasonably successful, as in this case, provide the basis for a low-level theory of political behavior.

A more recent application of the dispositional approach to voting behavior attempts to explain the downturn in voting turnout that has occurred in American elections since the early 1960s.[22] This is a significant development, since classical democratic theory implies high levels of political participation. After sorting through a number of factors, the authors of the study conclude that most of the decrease can be explained with an attitudinal theory that combines the factors of *strength of party identification* (the more strongly we identify with a political party, the more likely we are to vote) and *political efficacy* (the more we feel that our vote can have an impact on government policy, the more likely we are to vote). Analysis of survey data collected during the 1960s and 1970s suggests that both party identification and political efficacy declined; the conclusion is that they were the major reasons for the downturn in turnout. In light of our emphasis on the heuristic value of models, it is interesting to note that the authors point out several ways that their model could lead to future research.

---

[21] Ibid., section 2. They are able to explain and predict the voting decisions of 86 percent of their sample, using a law that is the multiple correlation of six attitudinal factors with voting choice.

[22] Paul R. Abramson and John H. Aldrich, "The Decline of Electoral Participation in America," *American Political Science Review,* 76 (1982), pp. 502–21.

Other views of the dispositional approach

An alternative interpretation is sometimes made of the dispositional approach. It is not nomological in that it rejects the assumption that a dispositional model deals with generalizations relating dispositions and other political phenomena. Instead, this interpretation suggests that dispositions refer to the characteristics of specific individuals and do not require generalizations. Philosopher of history William Dray has argued along these lines in claiming that the dispositions of material things (the breaking of glass) are different from human dispositions (such as the trait ambition). "For ambition is not a general characteristic of men (or even perhaps, of politicians) in the way being brittle is of glass.[23] According to this reading of the dispositional approach, the political scientist works with the normal behavior of *individuals*.

There are several ways of showing the weakness of this position. Perhaps the simplest is to first admit that political scientists usually explain individual actions with descriptive statements about the individual—particular statements describing the general behavior of one person. However, the use of dispositions indicates that one is employing general concepts that ultimately imply laws about all men or, more likely, a class of men. May Brodbeck makes this point in regard to the explanation of action by means of personality characteristics. Referring to the social scientist or historian engaged in such explanatory activities she says, "He just uses laws about his particular man. It would be odd, though, if he were to say that another man of similar character in similar circumstances would nevertheless behave very differently. 'Character' after all, refers to a certain *kind* of man though possibly, just possibly, there might be only one of the kind."[24] While one may speak of one man, he must ultimately refer to all men of a particular type. While political scientists continue to analyze the President's, a Senator's, or Hitler's personality and attitudes, each disposition is ultimately useful as a heuristic or explanatory device only insofar as it can be related to other variables in generalizations.

---

[23] William Dray, *Laws and Explanation in History* (New York: Oxford University Press, 1957), p. 146.

[24] May Brodbeck, "Explanation, Prediction, and Imperfect Knowledge," in Herbert Feigl and Grover Maxwell, eds., *Minnesota Studies in the Philosophy of Science,* 3 (Minneapolis: University of Minnesota Press, 1962), p. 270.

LEARNING THEORY

The assumptions of the dispositional approach can be expressed more theoretically in the language of psychological learning theory. Many view it as the most promising dispositional model currently available to political scientists. In addition, learning theory seems to explain the formation of dispositions, usually through socialization. Until now, our discussion has concentrated on the impact of attitudes on political behavior. A consideration of learning theory turns our attention in the opposite direction. What determines the attitudes and opinions that we have at the time of our political action? *The American Voter's* funnel of causality model speaks to this question. Learning theory provides an answer. It is no small accomplishment to discover that party identification is a main cause of voting preference. It is even more significant to understand the process that produces the party identification.

First of all, psychologists have accumulated an extensive body of experimental data on learning and have subjected this data to some rigorous methodological analyses. The result has been the development of a well-honed scientific tool. Political scientists thus have a useful model available if, and this is the crucial question, learning theory is related to the behavior of political actors. That an impressive model exists is one thing; to be able to use it is another. Indications are that political scientists can use learning theory. The matter of relevancy is the second reason for a political scientist's taking an interest in learning theory.

This section examines each of these reasons. The next few paragraphs describe some of the major elements and assumptions of learning theory. We hope that a foundation of sorts will be laid for the evaluation of attempts to apply learning theory to the politics that follows.

What is learning theory?

Scientist and philosopher Anatol Rapaport defines learning as the "selective accumulation of behavior patterns."[25] Let us begin our analysis of learn-

---

[25] Anatol Rapaport, "Mathematical, Evolutionary, and Psychological Approaches to the Study of Total Societies," in Samuel Z. Klansuer, ed., *The Study of Total Societies* (Garden City, N.Y.: Doubleday Publishing, 1967), p. 136.

ing by unpacking Rapaport's definition. "Accumulation" refers to the fact that the learner leaves the learning process with something that he doesn't have when he goes in. But what? The obvious answer is "behavior patterns," including dispositions; or in the more technical language of learning theory, associations between stimuli and responses—upon receiving a particular stimulus, a public opinion question, for instance, the individual gives a particular response, a no answer. But why is accumulation selective? This gets to the heart of learning theory, for it is another way of asking why only some behavior patterns are learned; it is at this point that a systematic presentation of the basics of learning theory seems in order.

There are two varieties of learning theory—two ways to account for stimulus-response connections.[26] The first, which is called *association* theory, says that people learn through observing or experiencing associations or relationships of various kinds. A child watches its parents behave or react to situations and learns to behave in a similar manner. An example from politics might clarify the process. We know that there is a strong correlation between the American voter's party identification and that of his parents.[27] How might we explain this? Association learning theory tells us that a child observes his parents' political activities, listens to their political discourse, and becomes aware of their attitudes. If they identify with the Democratic party, he will come to associate "Democratic" and "political party." There need be no attempt, and there usually is none, by the parents to instill in the child their own political attitudes. Instead, because of the observed relationship, it is second nature for the child to think of "Democratic" whenever he hears "party."

A second brand of learning theory begins with the assumption that a connection between stimulus and response usually requires reinforcement if it is to be established. Mere association is not enough in most cases. *Reinforcement* theory argues that we learn to make certain connections when we are rewarded and not to make other connections when the result is punishment. The first is an example of positive reinforcement. Psychologists know that rats can be taught to push (response) a lever (stimulus) if the response produces food (positive reinforcement). Conversely, they can be taught not

---

[26] For a survey of learning theories, see Winfred F. Hill, *Learning* (San Francisco: Chandler Publishing Co., 1963).

[27] Angus Campbell et al., *The American Voter*, pp. 146–47.

to push the lever if the result is an electric shock (negative reinforcement).

We know less about the relevance of learning theory to human behavior. But we can, based on some fairly sound data, speculate about its potential value and also make the distinction between association and reinforcement theory.[28]

We have already considered how association theory accounts for the learning of party identification. The point was that the child forms the association between "party" and "Democratic" without any overt attempt on the part of his parents to instill in him a particular disposition through reward and punishment. That is, if a mother buys a toy for her six-year-old son every time he calls himself a Democrat, or if a favorable response to his father's question, "Which party is the best?" leads to a trip to the zoo, the learning that occurs is based on reinforcement. This example is absurd, because few parents would resort to such strategies to teach their children a party identification. Political attitudes, in most cases, are not that important. The learning of party identification is incidental to the main experiences of childhood. But because of the pervasiveness of the parents' influence, the association is formed.

Are there, however, dispositions relevant to political science that can be explained by reinforcement theory? The answer is probably yes; it is likely that most political behavior can be accounted for in this way. Once again, an example might prove useful. An interesting question is why do some people change their attitudes, including party identification, after they become adults? There is, for instance, the case of the moderately strong Democrat, Smith, who enters a business corporation, works his way up to a fairly responsible administrative position, moves out of the central city, and buys a house in the suburbs. At each point in his new environment, our Democrat is subjected to Republican influence. As he advances, Smith finds that an increasing number of his business associates and friends are Republican. When he moves to the suburbs, he discovers that his neighbors are predominantly Republican.

A dispositional approach to political behavior based on reinforcement theory would probably predict a shift in Smith's party identification. Let us

---

[28] For behavioral applications of learning theory, see Froman, *People,* and Neal E. Miller and John Dollard, *Social Learning and Imitation* (New Haven, Conn.: Yale University Press, 1941). Also see the controversial speculative application by the most famous learning theorist, B. F. Skinner, *Walden Two* (New York: Macmillan, 1948).

see why. First of all, Smith will no doubt talk about politics with his new friends and neighbors. He soon discovers that any favorable comment about the Democratic party is met with ridicule, criticism, or at best an uncomfortable silence. In addition, Smith begins to notice that while there are a few Democrats at the lowest occupational levels of the corporation, as status and income increase they become fewer and fewer, until upon reaching the middle levels there are none to be found. At this point, the long-standing Democrat begins to wonder if Republican identification is an unwritten requirement for advancement in the company.

Given these conditions, it would not be surprising if Smith became a Republican. In terms of reinforcement theory, there are many reinforcing agents at work that tend to teach Smith to make the association between the stimulus "party" and response "Republican." He discovers that he is rewarded—he forms friendships, he is treated cordially by associates and neighbors, and he finds it easier to climb the occupational ladder—if he responds correctly. On the other hand, an unfavorable response leads to punishment.

What can this oversimplified but realistic example tell us? First of all, because humans are far more complex than rats, it follows that reinforcement theory must be more subtle and flexible in its approach to political behavior than to the behavior of rats. Even our simplified example describes a situation where the possible reinforcing agents are numerous and intertwined. As a model of politics, reinforcement theory must simplify—reduce the variables to a manageable few. But this is the strategy of any conceptual scheme. Its success is evaluated on the basis of how suggestive it is, or, if it is proposed as the rough draft of a theory, how it might explain political phenomena.

The same could be said of association theory. Let it be made clear that neither brand of learning theory has all the "good" on its side. At this early stage, it seems prudent to think of general learning theory with its two variants, each with its own areas of applicability. So there is reason to speculate that in some situations—the learning of party identification by children, for instance—a mere association is at the root of the learned response. On the other hand, there are dispositions more effectively accounted for by reinforcement theory; probably many of the more highly developed dispositions—attitudes, personality traits—ought to be included in this category. One preliminary conclusion is that a parochial interpretation of learning theory as an approach to the study of politics is counterproductive. The political scientist, remembering the general principles of learning theory, ought to first see how his model fits the world—how useful it is in generating hypotheses and how it might at some future time explain and predict—before refining it to a "reinforcement" or "association" theory.

The uses of learning theory

It is clear that we are evaluating learning theory on two levels: first as a heuristic device, which organizes our thoughts and suggests that we look for particular factors and relationships. We have seen, for instance, how reinforcement theory focuses our attention on reinforcing factors when the phenomenon being considered is attitude change. There is no doubt that learning theory can function as a useful *model* of politics, if, as we have assumed, the value of a model lies in its suggestiveness.

But how would we evaluate learning theory on the second level, as an explanatory theory of politics? To answer this, we have to distinguish two theoretical-explanatory functions that learning theory might perform.

First, learning theory can perhaps explain dispositions, that is, account for attitudes and opinions in terms of association and reinforcement. But the explanatory scope of learning theory is potentially much broader. Thus, it is not unrealistic to look forward to the development of a theory of general politics based on stimulus-response connections that could, in addition to explaining dispositions, account for such phenomena as political change, stability, and conflict, to name a few.

Let us consider several examples of research devoted to the pursuit of such a theory. Then we will discuss a field of political analysis that some political scientists believe will produce the theory. Kenneth Boulding has made the following observation and suggestion: "Up to this point in the development of the social sciences, learning has been treated largely on an individual basis. The time now seems to be ripe for the development both of theoretical systems and of empirical studies of learning on the scale of the large society, or what might be called the 'macrolearning' process."[29] In

---

[29] Kenneth Boulding, "The Learning Process in the Dynamics of Total Societies," in Klansuer, *The Study of Total Societies,* p. 111.

other words, it might be fruitful to begin thinking about learning done by communities, cities, or interest groups, and how to measure the accumulation of behavior patterns by such large-scale political systems. Several political scientists have directed their attention toward this significant question.

Richard M. Merelman has examined the relationship between "learning and legitimacy" in political systems.[30] He analyzes the nature of the moral support that a people gives its political regime—how legitimate the regime is perceived to be—through the assumptions of reinforcement theory. He conceptualizes the problem and justifies his use of the approach in the following manner: "This process of learning, in which the government acts as the provider of a learning stimulus to a population and the population responds, is possible because the government attaches a series of sanctions or, in learning theory terms, reinforcements to each policy."[31] Merelman argues that material reinforcements are replaced by symbolic ones, which become symbols of legitimacy. In other words, the support that is given the system is ultimately based on, and therefore explainable in terms of, the rewards and punishments allocated by the decision-making process. There is nothing surprising about the hypothesis that the legitimacy of a political system is a function of the policies it makes and enforces. It surely has prima facie validity. What makes the hypothesis significant to us is how it was generated: by the principles of learning theory.

SOCIALIZATION THEORY

The principles of learning, discovered by psychologists in their laboratories, have been used by sociologists and political scientists to explain how people acquire social and political attitudes and beliefs. The result is socialization theory; its basic assumption is that Democrats and Republicans, Communists and Fascists, and radicals and conservatives have the orientations they do because of a series of learning experiences. The major ques-

---

[30] Richard M. Merelman, "Learning and Legitimacy," *American Political Science Review*, 60 (1966), pp. 548–61.

[31] Ibid.

tions asked by socialization theorists are: What is learned? When is it learned? How is it learned?[32]

Through the socialization process, people learn both specific political attitudes, such as party identification, and more general orientations to the political system. On a day-to-day basis, the former are more familiar; they are what we read about in the Harris and Gallup polls. But in the long run, the way people feel about their political system, whether they consider it responsive or unresponsive, just or unjust, efficient or inefficient is more important. If a generation learns not to trust its political leaders, the potential for massive change, even revolution, increases.

The next two questions are intertwined and cannot be answered separately. They deal with the when and how of the socialization process. Most socialization theorists hypothesize that the most important learning occurs during the formative years of childhood. It is at this time that basic values and attitudes are shaped, values that are retained into the adult years. Thus, at the center of socialization theory is the assumption that adult political behavior is largely the result of childhood learning experiences. To some students of socialization the link is not an obvious one; they argue that important learning continues to take place in the adult years. The upshot of this debate is a consideration of the agents of socialization, those people and institutions that are instrumental in the learning process.

As might be expected, the family is usually given primary emphasis. If most basic learning occurs in early childhood, it seems to follow that the family is the most important socializing agent. In the United States and other Western cultures, family means "nuclear family," defined as "a small group composed of husband and wife and immature children which constitutes a unit apart from the rest of the community."[33] Since most socialization research has been conducted in Western societies, mothers and fathers have been presumed to be the prime teachers of political values. However, in many non-Western cultures, family refers to the "extended family," a much

---

[32] Two of the leading books in this field are the groundbreaking Herbert Hyman, *Political Socialization* (New York: Free Press, 1954); and David Easton and Jack Dennis, *Children in the Political System* (New York: McGraw-Hill, 1969). The best introduction to political socialization is Richard Dawson and Kenneth Prewitt, *Political Socialization* (Boston: Little, Brown, 1977).

[33] G. Duncan Mitchell, *A Dictionary of Sociology* (Hawthorn, N.Y.: Aldine Publishing, 1968), p. 77.

broader grouping that includes two or more nuclear families related in a number of complicated ways and numbering perhaps in the hundreds. That both types of families are important agents of socialization is undeniable. But the different processes that occur in each must be recognized; perhaps the differences are so great that few generalizations can be produced that apply to both.

The next socializing agent is the school. Again, there is no doubt a difference between its role in industrialized systems and less-developed systems. In the former it seems to function mainly as a reinforcer of values already learned in the family. In the latter, where highly institutionalized educational systems are not as prevalent, the function may be more to change the values of those who go to school. In some societies the peer group, one's circle of close acquaintances, is the most important agent. Some theorists argue that the peer group is becoming even more important than the family and school in more developed societies. In another sense, it is not easy to separate the role of these various agents. For instance, in the school setting, do children acquire their values from teachers or from their fellow classmates? This question is one of great importance for socialization theory, and is still being sorted out.

It has become fashionable to argue that the most important agent of socialization in today's world of mass communications are the mass media. Almost irresistible is the notion that, as children spend more and more time watching television and less time interacting with their parents, television becomes the main source of values. While there is great common-sense appeal to this assertion, it must, at this point, remain an interesting hypothesis, since little research has been done to directly test it.[34] Another hypothesis which is generated by an emphasis on the mass media as socializing agent is that adult attitudes toward most issues are the result mainly of newspaper, television, and radio reports. Some critics of the mass media have argued that we are at their mercy. The implication is that if the media are biased, if they have a point of view, the mass public will naturally come to have the same point of view. Let us reiterate that the role of the mass media remains the least explored but perhaps the most interesting area in the field of political socialization.

---

[34] Wilbur Schramm, *Television and the Lives of Our Children* (Stanford, Calif.: Stanford University Press, 1961).

What is the role of government in the socialization process? This is a reasonable question, especially for students of politics. For several reasons, it is not an easy one to answer. First, in most societies, government has become involved in most activities of life. This means that government is closely intertwined with the other socializing agents. How, for example, do we separate the public school system and the government? Each is really a part of the political system. A second reason for the difficulty in identifying the role of government in the socialization process is the wide variation in the types of governmental systems. Some governments take an active and conscious role in the teaching of political values. Thus, in Marxist systems like the Soviet Union and China, the political leaders view the political education of the masses as one of their prime functions. An attempt is made to influence the attitudinal atmosphere of all groups and to reduce the impact of other agents of socialization; thus, the deemphasis on the nuclear family and the rejection of religion. This type of directed socialization is not peculiar to Marxist and other totalitarian regimes, only more crucial to the success of the regime.

Directed socialization can be contrasted with the autonomous variety. The learning that occurs in the family, school, peer group, and secondary group is in most cases not intentional. That is, parents, teachers, and friends do not consciously attempt to instill a particular set of values; it just happens. In a socialization system that is operating autonomously, each generation passes on its values to the next generation. Association learning theory best accounts for this kind of socialization. In every society one would expect to find a combination of directed and autonomous socialization; differences result from the particular mix. One interesting hypothesis is that in a stable political system the autonomous process is dominant, while times of instability and change bring directed socialization to the forefront; revolutionary groups naturally attempt to resocialize the masses; and political leaders who rise to power during such times usually place high priority on the creation of a political culture that is favorable to the new regime.

COGNITIVE DISSONANCE THEORY

Another theory of attitude formation, really attitude adjustment, puts more emphasis on the cognitive or knowing side of the human mind. Cognitive dissonance makes more sense of many instances of adult attitude formation because it takes into consideration the attempt to organize one's ideas in a consistent manner.[35] However, it is not a rational approach like the ones in the next chapter. The drive at the heart of the theory of cognitive dissonance is toward a consistent set of attitudes—psychological peace is achieved only when one's attitudes are not in conflict with each other, as they would be, for example, if one believed in greater government regulation of the economy while, at the same time, feeling great respect and affection for Ronald Reagan. The assumption is made that human behavior is not directed primarily at maximizing the realization of goals, but rather minimizing the psychological tension that conflicting attitudes produce.

Cognitive dissonance theory is not at odds with socialization theory as an approach to the study of political attitude formation; actually, it adds to it. Socialization theory presumes that we learn political attitudes. Cognitive dissonance suggests that when we learn an attitude that seems to contradict others, adjustments will be made to bring the attitude set back into equilibrium. At another level, the two dispositional approaches are compatible. At its core, cognitive dissonance theory makes the same basic assumption that learning theory does: We tend not to continue doing or thinking anything that leads to physical or psychological discomfort.

Cognitive dissonance is a concept that has great commonsense appeal, yet, apparently not a great deal of utility to the political scientist. This suggests one of two explanations: Either the approach is nothing more than a set of intuitively satisfying but not overly fruitful ideas, or political scientists have not tapped its real potential. The truth probably lies somewhere between. Even if there is more truth in the first position, cognitive dissonance theory might prove to be as rich a source of hypotheses as have other simplified models of political behavior.

Like all approaches, cognitive dissonance theory begins with several basic assumptions. The first is that people naturally seek to avoid dissonant attitudinal situations. Second, for all of us, some attitudes are more important than others; the former are central, the latter peripheral. Now, the fundamental hypothesis that emerges is that there are typical strategies we use when inconsistency is discovered in our belief system. They all are ways

---

[35] The classic study remains Leon Festinger, *A Theory of Cognitive Dissonance* (Stanford, Calif.: Stanford University Press, 1962). For a critical discussion of the application of cognitive dissonance theory to political situations, see H. T. Reynolds, *Politics and the Common Man* (Homewood, Ill.: Dorsey Press, 1974), pp. 30–45.

to adjust the system so that more consistency is achieved. As might be expected, the theory predicts that the more peripheral attitudes will be adjusted to fit those that are more central.

An example should clarify the use of cognitive dissonance theory. In his study of the ideology of the John Birch Society, a far-right group formed in the late 1950s, Stephen Bennett shows that its ideology underwent change as dissonant situations were perceived.[36] The most important one arose as a result of President Johnson's escalation of the war in Vietnam. The problem was that one of the basic tenets of the Birch Society's ideology has always been that most American political leaders, including the President, are either Communists or Communist sympathizers. The task for the Society member was to explain how a pro-Communist President could be fighting Communists in Southeast Asia, and with such apparent fervor. Something had to be done to reduce the inconsistency and restore psychological peace. From his examination of writings contained in official John Birch publications, Bennett detected the classic strategies of cognitive dissonance at work. The most obvious and easiest to use is denial: "a direct attack upon one or both of the cognitive elements or the relation between them." Thus, the John Birch Society simply denied that the Johnson administration was really fighting communism. Instead, they argued that the American military action was a massive act of deception, designed to convince Americans that their leaders actually were anti-Communists, while providing a justification for more government regulation of the domestic society, something that all Communist conspirators have uppermost in their minds. If successful, this explanation, the denial of one of the inconsistent beliefs, would restore a sense of order to the belief system. It worked, but only partially, for as Bennett shows, ever more complex techniques were emplolyed by the John Birch Society as more cognitive dissonance was generated by this confusing situation.

THE FUNCTIONALIST APPROACH TO ATTITUDE FORMATION

There is another theory of attitude formation that should be mentioned. It

---

[36] Stephen E. Bennett, "Modes of Resolution of a Belief Delemma in the Ideology of the John Birch Society," *The Journal of Politics,* 33 (1971), pp. 735–72.

is usually called the *functionalist* approach.[37] Functionalists argue that we take on attitudes because they perform one or several functions for us. Among the functions are helping us adjust to new situations, protecting our sense of self-esteem, and explaining confusing situations to us. The main point of the functionalist approach is that attitudes are not selected because they are based on the truth, but emerge because they satisfy certain psychological needs. This theory provides a transitional link to the next section, which examines personality theory as an approach to politics.

PERSONALITY THEORY

There is another type of disposition, the personality trait, which forms the basis of another psychological approach to the study of politics. Much has been made of the distinction between attitudes and personality traits. It is usually based on a model that makes attitudes the result of learning and personality the result of heredity. The available evidence seems to blur this distinction, so it is probably more accurate to consider personality traits as more deeply ingrained dispositions. A politician is labeled politically aggressive (a personality trait) if he or she responds in a certain way in a certain situation. "Personality as we know it is an essentially social product, inconceivable in the completely isolated human being."[38] Personalities develop as people interact with each other. In short, both attitudes and personalities are acquired.

Although personality traits can be considered dispositions, they are viewed by personality theorists as different enough from other dispositions to constitute a separate approach.[39] Personality theory has developed within a tradition quite different from the other dispositional approaches. The latter have close ties to behaviorism, while the former receives its basic orienta-

---

[37] See Daniel Katz, "The Functional Approach to the Study of Attitudes," *Public Opinion Quarterly*, 24 (1960), pp. 163–204; and M. Brewster Smith et al., *Opinions and Personality* (New York: John Wiley & Sons, 1956).

[38] M. Brewster Smith, Jerome S. Bruner, and Robert W. White, *Opinions and Personality* (New York: John Wiley & Sons, 1956), p. 31.

[39] For basic surveys of the field, see Fred Greenstein, *Personality and Politics* (New York: W. W. Norton, 1975); Fred Greenstein ed., *A Source Book for the Study of Personality and Politics* (Chicago: Markham Publishing Co., 1971); Alan C. Elms, *Personality in Politics* (New York: Harcourt Brace Jovanovich, 1976).

tion from the Freudian tradition. This implies basic differences in both substance and methodology. The personality theorist argues that political behavior is the result of deep seated traits that are usually developed at an early age. Examples are hostility, submissiveness, and rigidity (or the opposite of each). All personality theories postulate one or more basic needs or drives that are supposedly the motivating force behind personality development. The most famous example of this sort is Freud's concept of sexual drive. If it is repressed at an early age, the personality will be affected and there will be a resulting impact on adult behavior.

The central assumption of the socialization theorist is that we learn our attitudes and beliefs directly from agents of socialization, such as parents and school. If parents and teachers are liberal Democrats, then the probability is great that their children and students will be liberal Democrats. According to the personality theorist, the acquisition of personality traits, while a social process, works differently. Children acquire their personalities because of the ways that their parents and other influential adults treat them. A classic example would be the child who is given extrinsic love (love as a reward for expected performance) instead of intrinsic love (love without strings). The personality theorist's prediction would be that such a child would develop low self-esteem and perhaps a competitive personality. The parents need not have the same type of personality to shape the children's. That is the crucial insight of the personality theorist.

The differences between the learning theory-socialization model and the personality model can also be seen in their varying methodologies. The behaviorist, employing the former model, uses the sample survey in measuring the attitudes of large groups of people. The personality theorist, however, uses techniques, such as projective tests and clinical interviews, which dig deeper into the psyches of much smaller numbers of people. In head-to-head clashes, the behavorist charges the personality theorist with being less that scientifically rigorous—after all, how can one generalize from such a small number of cases? The personality theorist returns the fire with the claim that socialization theory, in its desire to amass large samples so as to satisfy the laws of probability sampling, can examine only the most superficial psychological characteristics of political actors.

Actually, there is no reason why socialization theory and personality theory must be mutually exclusive. We learn many of our attitudes and acquire our basic personality during the same period of life. It is reasonable to assume that John Kennedy's personality was being formed through inter-action with his parents, brothers, and sisters while he was also learning to be a Democrat because of the partisan atmosphere of his household. However, personality theory might seem a bit more imperalistic, for typically its de-fender claims that personality has an impact on the acquisition of attitudes; the causal relationship does not work the other way around. For instance, in the classic study *The Authoritarian personality,* an attempt is made to dem-onstrate the impact of personality on the genesis of Fascist-type political movements.[40] It argues that there is a particular personality syndrome, the authoritarian, which makes people vulnerable to such ideologies. More spe-cifically, the fundamental hypothesis proposes that the Nazi party was suc-cessful in Germany mainly because of the large number of authoritarian individuals in the German citizenry.

The origins of personality theory: Freud and Lasswell

Almost all modern theories of personality begin with the concepts of the master, Sigmund Freud. Freudians, neo-Freudians and anti-Freudians either base their theories on his or feel compelled to show why they have departed from them.[41] There can be no greater respect than what comes from the opponent who must demonstrate why opposition is justified. We needn't get involved in the details of Freudian analysis to understand why it has exerted such a tremendous influence on the human sciences, including political sci-ence.

Freud rejected the classical rational model of human behavior, yet he refused to associate himself with those philosophers, Schopenhauer and Nietzsche are examples, who argued that because humans are not rational their actions are unexplainable. Freud was too much the scientist to accept this pessimistic conclusion. Instead, he proposed that humans act in predict-able ways; our behavior is caused. The causal force is the personality. J. A. C. Brown has written this about the genesis of Freud's breakthrough: "In his

---

[40] Theodore W. Adorno et al., *The Authoritarian Personality* (New York: Harper & Row, 1950); also see Richard Christie and Marie Johoda, eds., *Studies in the Scope and Method of the Authoritarian Personality* (New York: Free Press, 1954).

[41] For a useful introduction to Freud and the Freudians see J. A. C. Brown, *Freud and the Post-Freudians* (New York: Penguin Books, 1961).

early studies of hysterial patients he had been able to show that the apparently irrational symptoms which had puzzled physicians for centuries were meaningful when seen in terms of painful memories which had been repressed into the unconscious and were striving to find expression."[42]

This captures the core of Freud's theory. Each of us has a three-part personality; the *id,* that bundle of primitive biological drives, which is the motivating force; the *superego,* the set of values acquired from family and society, which is roughly equivalent to the conscience; and the *ego,* which keeps the personality functioning through a continual juggling act among the id, the superego, and reality. Sometimes the id can be satisfied; sometimes the limitations of the external world or the superego prevent such satisfaction. This fact of psychological life led Freud to formulate his concept of the defense mechanism to describe the repertoire of techniques used by the ego to redirect the energy of the id without actually satisfying it. Repression, displacement, projection, and regression (to name only a few) are all based on Freud's assumption that when the basic drives cannot be satisfied directly, the ego resorts to trickery and deception to reduce the psychological tension. Often they succeed. But just as often, such games lead to serious personality disorders. The ultimate payoff for the political scientist is the fruitful hypothesis that political activity is one of the ways that the ego satisfies the personality needs of political actors.

The earliest and the most compact example of this kind of theorizing was developed by Harold Lasswell in the early 1930s.[43] Coming out of the Freudian tradition, Lasswell argued that political behavior is the result of the political actor's personality displacing itself on a public object and then rationalizing its activities in terms of the public interest. Imagine an individual who grows up with deep hatred for his cold and domineering father. At the same time, he acquires from his culture the strong moral prohibition against hating one's parents. The result is psychological tension, which the ego tries to relieve. One way to do this, following Lasswell's formula, is to redirect or displace the morally unacceptable hatred for the father onto something more distant, such as the institutions of government. Thus, our subject comes to hate the most visible source of public authority. This strategy is psychologically functional because the need to hate has been partially

---

[42] Ibid., p. 3.
[43] Lasswell, *Psychopathology and Politics.*

satisfied, without having to violate one of the basic tenets of the superego. But, according to Lasswell's theory, there is more. The ego must make this nonrational behavior (because it is unconsciously caused) appear rational (conscious and goal-seeking). After all, Freud argues that the basic determinants of behavior operate at the subconscious level. Our subject does not say, "I hate government because I hate my father." Instead, he becomes an ideological anarchist, justifying his antiauthority position by citing a set of philosophical principles; this is the rationalization mentioned in Lasswell's formula. What appears to be the conscious acceptance of a political ideology is really an attempt by the personality to relieve some of its internal tension.

This explanation is admittedly oversimplified. Lasswell recognized this later in his career.[44] Yet it catches the basic thrust of the Freudian approach to political analysis. It also has several important implications for the study of political behavior. Perhaps the most important is that those individuals with unhealthy personalities, with great amounts of psychological tension, often find their outlet in politics. Thus, one would expect a sample of politicians to display a larger number of psychological disorders than a similar sample of the general population. Several recent studies have indicated there is no necessary relationship between politics and unhealthy personalities.[45] Instead, their examinations of nonextremists demonstrate that political activity can be the result of both healthy and unhealthy personality traits.

Lasswell formulated another closely related argument that has even more profound implications for political research. For centuries, political thinkers, such as Machiavelli, have defined politics as the exercise of power. Lasswell adds a psychological twist by suggesting that there is a basic political personality, characterized by a strong power drive. It is the opportunity to exercise power, to control other people that attracts political people to politics. What is it that power promises? In Lasswell's words, "it is compensation against estimates of the self as weak, contemptible, immoral, unloved."[46]

Just as research has tended to question the belief that political actors are likely to have less healthy personalities, so it is that the classic power-

---

[44] His work, written with Abraham Kaplan, *Power and Society* (New Haven, Conn.: Yale University Press, 1950), demonstrates the breadth of his vision of politics.

[45] Jeanne Knutson, "Psychological Variables in Political Recruitment: An Analysis of Party Activists" (Berkeley, Calif.: The Wright Institute, 1974).

[46] Lasswell, *Power and Personality* (New York: W. W. Norton, 1948).

hungry politician has been somewhat overrated.[47] Political scientists and psychologists have identified several other motivating factors that they believe lead to political activity. The two most widely used factors are achievement and affiliation; according to this research, some people get into politics because it gives them the chance to experience the feeling of success, while others find it provides the opportunity to receive affection and acclaim from others. The same basic framework is being used—people do what they do because of the need to satisfy certain personality needs. There are several needs, besides power, which are satisfied by political activity. In addition, these studies indicate there are other institutions and occupations, business for instance, which might be equally attractive to many power-seekers.

The psychobiography

The use of personality theory in political analysis can take several forms. First is the psychobiography, an in-depth study of a single, well-known political leader. The assumptions upon which such a study is based are that individuals make a difference in the political process, and second, that personality is the main determinant of the leader's behavior. The advantage of the psychobiography is the opportunity it provides for a deep understanding of an individual's political life. Its main disadvantage is the inability to generalize from a single case. A highly respected study of Woodrow Wilson, considered by many to be the benchmark psychobiography, persuasively argues that Wilson was a President who was motivated by a number of powerful psychological needs developed early in life; these needs caused him to perform political acts that appear, from the standpoint of a rational model, to be nonrational.[48] For example, how else can Wilson's self-defeating behavior during the League of Nations struggle be explained? However, because only a single President is being analyzed, it is impossible to formulate generalizations about how all or even most Presidents behave. We cannot tell if Wilson's often erratic behavior, or the relationship between his childhood experiences and his mature political behavior, is typical or not.

---

[47] Rufus Browning and Herbert Jacob, "Power Motivation and the Political Personality," *Public Opinion Quarterly*, 28 (1964), pp. 75–90.

[48] Alexander George and Juliette George, *Woodrow Eilson and Colonel House* (New York: Dover, 1964).

We know a great deal about a single President but little about Presidents in general.

Personality typologies: Barber's theory of presidential personality

In order to generalize, the personality theorist must retain the rigor of the successful psychobiography, while moving beyond the analysis of a single actor. The result is the second kind of personality approach, the formulation of a typology of personality types into which a number of political actors can be classified. The most interesting work of this sort is James Barber's study of presidential personality.[49] He begins with the assumption that presidential behavior is not the result of rational calculation, but it is the resolution of deep seated personality needs. Barber builds his theory of presidential personality along two dimensions: whether a President is active or passive, that is, how much energy is expended in carrying out political tasks; whether he is positive or negative, that is, to what extent does he enjoy the tasks he performs. Barber's analysis is a sorting out of the last 13 Presidents, from Taft to Carter, into four categories that are the logical combinations of the dimensions. According to Barber, each category is a distinct personality type, with its own genesis and impact. He proposes a three-stage causal model: certain types of childhood and early adult experiences lead to the development of a particular set of psychological needs, in short, a particular personality; then, at the other end of the causal chain, the personality colors the nature and quality of presidential decision making.

A brief discussion of Barber's typology will clarify the basic model. We will note the defining characteristics, typical development, and likely behavior patterns of each of Barber's types. A list of those Presidents who fall into each category will indicate how Barber uses his model to analyze presidential behavior. The most interesting types are the active-positive and the active-negative. The former category, which includes Franklin Roosevelt, Harry Truman, John Kennedy, Gerald Ford, and Jimmy Carter, represents those Presidents who were active in office and seemed to enjoy their presi-

---

[49] James D. Barber, *The Presidential Character* (Englewood Cliffs, N.J.: Prentice-Hall, 1977).

dential responsibilities. But, one might ask, isn't that redundant? Aren't active people naturally happy in what they do? According to Barber, all we need to consider is the active-negative to realize the superficiality of this point of view. Active-negatives, such as Woodrow Wilson, Herbert Hoover, Lyndon Johnson, and Richard Nixon, were as active as the active-positives, but for different reasons. The crucial difference lies in the motivation of each type; in fact, this is the heart of any personality approach. The active-positive is attracted to and finds satisfaction in politics because it offers the opportunity to succeed, to achieve goals. The active-negative, however, senses that politics and power go hand in hand, and it is the opportunity to control others that is subconsciously sought.

It is at this point that Barber explores the origins and development of presidential personality. His thorough examination of biographical materials convinces him that the active-positives are loved intrinsically and encouraged as children; they grow up feeling good about themselves—they develop high self-esteem—while also learning that it is satisfying to achieve. The active-negatives, though, are typically deprived of this kind of love and affection; the result is low self-esteem and the consequent need, growing ever stronger, to find ways to increase it. On the surface, the two active types appear similar in their high levels of energy. But at a deeper level, they could not be more dissimilar.

The real payoff comes when Barber relates psychological motivations and presidential behavior. An active-positive President like Franklin Roosevelt viewed the office as a vehicle to solve problems, to achieve success. But high-level politics is not the reason for living. This means that the typical active-positive retains his good humor during times of crisis and is able to remain flexible and conciliatory in the face of opposition. Perhaps more important, he can walk away from defeat with self-esteem intact because he has not personalized the problems that confront him. Take all that Barber has said about the active-positive, turn it on its head, and one is face to face with the active-negative. Serious, humorless, feeling constantly over-worked, the active-negative finds it difficult to bend politically because most significant political situations become tests, indicators of just how good he is; in short, chances to increase his self-esteem. Crises become *his* crises, to be won through the use of power; the point of the game is not solving the problem so much as it is dominating opponents. Barber points out that each of the active-negatives has an ultimate crisis that he cannot let go of, which finally destroys him politically and probably psychologically: Wilson, the League of Nations fight; Hoover, the Great Depression; Johnson, the Vietnam War; and Nixon, Watergate. It is interesting to note that Barber wrote his book before Watergate; thus, he was not explaining Nixon's crisis but predicting it. The fact that Watergate arose and was handled by Nixon in the typical active-negative, self-defeating manner adds credibility to Barber's approach. His credibility was on the line again with his prediction that Jimmy Carter's would be an active-positive presidency.

The other two personality types are identified by Barber as the passive-positive and the passive-negative. The former is characterized by a need for affection, not because of childhood deprivation but the contrary—because of an abundance of love received in the early years. In short, Presidents Taft and Harding learned to appreciate the affection of others and so found in politics an effective way to satisfy expectations for affection—what could be more satisfying for such a person than the outpouring of love from thousands, even millions, of citizens. However, because they were not encouraged to achieve as children, they did not approach the presidency with the active, goal-seeking mentality of a active-positive.

The passive-negatives do not really enjoy the presidency and do not become activists. The negative "I don't really want to be President approach" of Eisenhower and Coolidge is easy to identify. To explain why such a person would run for the office is not as easy. The first three types fall into three classic categories of psychopolitical motivation. The active-negative is driven by the need for *power* (really Lasswell's original political personality); the active-positive by the desire to *achieve;* the passive-positive by the need for *affection* and *affiliation*. What of the passive-positive? Barber suggests that a sense of duty is the main motivator. This seems to catch the feeling that people had about President Eisenhower. Here is a man who serves out of duty and loyalty, not a lust for power, nor the desire for great achievements, nor the need for constant demonstrations of affection from the populace.

We have described the heart of Barber's book. Much of his analysis, including some of his more speculative excursions into the relationships between personality and the psyche of the nation, have not been mentioned. But enough has been written to give the reader the flavor of this sophisticated use of the personality approach.

GROUP DISPOSITIONS

Our classification of dispositions has covered individualistic concepts; we have discussed the attitudes and personality traits of individual political actors. While this is the dominant interest of political psychologists, many attempt to use one dispositional approach or another at the group or aggregate level.[50] Thus, we see claims that the Democratic party is more liberal than the Republican party; the Senate favors a tax cut more than the House of Representatives; China is more Marxist than the Soviet Union. All of these statements have an implied assertion that groups, institutions, and even nations can be treated as if they were individuals with attitudes and even personality traits.

This tendency is perhaps most obvious when discussion turns to "national character."[51] It is not unusual to hear particular characteristics attributed to nations and ethnic groups: materialistic Americans, cynical French, authoritarian Germans. As an example, let us quote from a British author who, on the eve of World War II, wrote this about Germans: "The whole German soul was shot through with a megalomanic lust for power, dressed up in all the romantic trappings which appeal to it so irresistibly."[52] It is almost as if it were Freud or Lasswell using personality to explain the behavior of individual politicians.

National character has served as a useful concept in many studies of international politics. However, there is a fine line between such legitimate research and the casual use of national and ethnic stereotypes.

Such aggregate dispositional concepts as national character can be interpreted in several ways. To some, they refer simply to the distribution of attitudes or personality traits among the individuals of a society. Saying that Germany was authoritarian before World War II means that there was a large proportion of authoritarian individuals in the country. According to

---

[50] For a discussion of aggregate personality traits, see Fred Greenstein, *Personality and Politics,* chapter 5.

[51] For a thorough discussion of national character and political analysis, see Alex Inkeles, "National Character and Modern Political Systems," in Nelson W. Polsby et al., eds., *Politics and Social Life* (Boston: Houghton Mifflin, 1963), pp. 172–89. A useful bibliography is included.

[52] Harold Butler, *The Lost Peace* (New York: Harcourt Brace Jovanovich 1942), p. 93.

this interpretation, there is nothing special about an aggregate disposition; it is completely reducible to the dispositions of individuals.

The second approach to aggregate concepts does not allow for their reduction. It speaks of national character as if something called "the nation" has a set of dispositions independent of its citizens. This is a manifestation of holism, discussed in a previous chapter. To the holist, an authoritarian nation is not simply a collection of authoritarian citizens. There is something in the fiber of the nation, in its structure, which is authoritarian—this is an emergent property. If one were to sample the literature devoted to the study of national character, it would probably be discovered that the holist approach is less popular today than it once was. Contemporary political scientists are likely to use the concept, along with other aggregate dispositional concepts, to describe groups of individuals. They are not viewed as philosophically distinct but as convenient ways to describe large populations.

Intentional approaches:
The rational approach
and game theory

I T is often tempting to think of all human behavior as purposive, that is, intended. Political scientist Vernon Van Dyke has articulated this outlook: "The action of human beings . . . usually relates somehow to their desires. Human beings are purposive."[1] On the face of it, this probably goes too far. If Chapter 10 demonstrated anything, it was that much political behavior can be accounted for by dispositions of various sorts that are not consciously linked to the behavior. If an intention has the characteristic of being conscious, in the sense that objectives are intentionally pursued and therefore consciously linked to behavior, it follows that much political behavior is not intentional.

INTENTIONAL APPROACHES

Such a conclusion goes against the grain of a tradition in political thought that views political phenomena as explainable largely in terms of human

---

[1] Vernon Van Dyke, *Political Science: A Philosophical Analysis* (Stanford, Calif.: Stanford University Press, 1960), p. 23.

intentions. For instance, Thomas Hobbes bases much of his political philosophy upon the egoistic (intentional) nature of man. From this assumption, the political system is viewed as the result of intentional behavior. John Locke argues that men leave the state of nature to find more effective methods of protecting their natural rights. Perhaps the clearest example of a general political philosophy based on intentional behavior is the utilitarian calculus of Jeremy Bentham, which assumes that political behavior is ultimately a conscious calculating of needs and wants and the means for satisfying those needs and wants.

The nature of intentional behavior

A preliminary conclusion is that to understand fully the utility of the intentional approach, we ought to distinguish it from the dispositional approach. That is, the difference between unconsciously and consciously motivated political behavior must be clarified. Perhaps a brief analysis of the concept "motive" would help at this point, for it seems that this is what we are talking about, or at least around. "Motive" is being viewed as the label of the class of all factors that influence or lead to behavior. This definition includes both dispositions and intentions. Robert Brown has classified motives into three categories: intention motives, impulse motives, and dispositional motives.[2] Our own distinction follows Brown's rather closely, if an impulse is viewed as a sort of innate or unlearned disposition.

A classification of motives, this time a dichotomous one, has been formulated by Richard W. Snyder, H. W. Bruck, and Burton Sapin.[3] Because they are political scientists, their scheme is perhaps more relevant to our analysis. They label all intentions "in order to" motives, and what we have called dispositions, "because of" motives. In their own words, "*In order to* motives refer to an end state of affairs envisaged by the actor," while, "On the other hand, *because of* motives refer to the actor's past experience, to the sum total of factors in his life-history which determine the particular project

---

[2] Robert Brown, *Explanation in Social Science* (Hawthorne, N.Y.: Aldine Publishing, 1963), p. 83.

[3] Richard W. Snyder, H. W. Bruck, and Burton Sapin, "Motivational Analysis of Foreign Policy Decision-Making," in James N. Rosenau, ed., *International Politics and Foreign Policy* (New York: Free Press, 1961), pp. 247–53.

of action elected to reach a goal."[4] This gets at the basic distinction between unconscious dispositions and conscious intentions.

We should, however, be aware that an overzealous application of this distinction can lead us astray. To some, it implies that dispositions are explainable, while intentions are not—that dispositions are general tendencies, while intentions are *free* creations, "off the top of the head," so to speak. This position usually comes down to an application of the philosophical doctrine of free will to political behavior: There are some actions, namely intentions, which are born in the minds of men with no antecedent conditions. From this assumption is derived a fairly common criticism of psychological and sociological explanations of political behavior, especially voting behavior. There are certain mental activities, such as the decision to vote Democratic, which cannot be explained by general tendencies, yet they are accounted for by an assumption of free will.[5]

This conflicts with the assumption of determinism, a principle that we have argued is basic to any scientific activity. To one who accepts it as an operational rule, the belief in undetermined intentions is unfounded and overly restrictive. Why exclude, on a priori grounds, the possibility of scientific knowledge of intentions? If it is assumed that intentions are unexplainable, if they do spring newly born from the minds of men, then the argument might be advanced that they cannot be related to other factors—they cannot be placed in generalizations. But given the nomological nature of scientific knowledge, it follows that intentions are of scientific value only if they can be placed in generalizations. We are assuming that a "unique" intention is actually the result of a *combination* of general tendencies, including dispositions, which is unique.

Both dispositions and intentions are the result of general tendencies. The difference between them is not logical but pragmatic. Even though we make a distinction between conscious and unconscious factors, let us remember that the characteristic of consciousness has to do with the relationship between behavior and its determinants. This does not preclude the possibility of demonstrating the intention that is cited as the reason for a particular action is the result of other factors; this is what we would expect to be the

---

[4] Ibid., p. 252.

[5] See the chapter by Walter Berns on voting studies in Herbert J. Storing, ed., *Essays on the Scientific Study of Politics* (New York: Holt, Rinehart & Winston, 1962).

case. In other words, if intentional behavior is to serve as the foundation of an approach to political inquiry, the "free seeking of goals" must be viewed as behavior that is designed (intended) to satisfy a particular need, want, or desire that can be explained. Thus, an act of free will is not, in principle, unexplainable.

A related reason for not exaggerating the distinction between intentions and dispositions is based upon the fact that an intention (defined as we are defining it—a conscious act) often becomes a disposition. That is, a conscious intention may, in time, be transformed into an unconscious response. Take the case of a new legislator who performs certain acts consciously to build a foundation of power within his legislative body, but who after several years makes many of the same moves—responses out of habit; he has learned certain patterns of behavior. What was once intentional behavior could now be labeled dispositional.

There is an important characteristic of intentional behavior which, while lurking near the surface of this discussion, has not yet been straightforwardly stated. If we equate *in order to* motives with intentions, then the thrust of the definition is that intentional behavior is goal-directed. To say that a presidential candidate gave a speech because he intended to is not necessarily incorrect; nor is it very enlightening. What we probably want to add is that the candidate gave the speech because he wanted to *(in order to)* influence voters. Thus, intentional behavior usually involves the seeking of goals or objectives. While there is nothing illogical about replying, "Because I wanted to," to the question, "Why did you do that?", it would seem more reasonable to cite the objectives that motivated the action. This is usually the beginning assumption of the political scientist who uses the intentional approach to suggest, explain, and predict.

The uses of the intentional approach

Used heuristically, an intentional approach to politics can be suggestive. More than most approaches, the intentional seems to make political phenomena meaningful and thus susceptible to coherent analysis. However, when the political scientist begins visualizing the intentional approach as a potential explanatory and predictive theory of politics, certain limitations must be remembered.

While some political behavior seems to be explainable in terms of intentions and goals, there is a large portion that is not. Several reasons can be discerned: (1) Not all intentions are acted upon. If we are trying to predict behavior, the single assertion by Smith that he intends to start a riot will not be enough; Smith might be a liar or braggart whose speech is impressive but not indicative of behavior. (2) Intentions which are acted upon do not always realize successful completion. As we all know, it usually takes more than strong resolve to achieve a goal. The most dedicated and purposeful candidate does not always win the election. (3) Or, the results of intentional behavior are not always intended. Political strategies have been known to backfire. (4) And finally, much political behavior is the result of unconscious dispositions.

For these reasons, there is no place in political science for an all-inclusive theory that explains everything on the basis of intentions. One of these, conspiracy theory, appears to account for all kinds of political behavior on the basis of the intentional seeking of objectives by behind-the-scenes leaders. Because it has been a popular and, at times, a respected explanatory device within political science, it deserves mention and requires refutation. In Karl Popper's words, "The conspiracy theory of society cannot be true because it amounts to the assertion that all results, even those which at first sight do not seem to be intended by anybody, are the intended results of the actions of people who are interested in the results."[6] This summarizes what has already been said several times, namely, that intentions and goals alone do not usually account for political phenomena.

Something else is needed in conjunction with intentions. In any intentional theory or model, there will also be statements referring to other factors besides the intention, such as the intender's capabilities, beliefs about how best to achieve goals, and relevant environmental conditions.

DECISION-MAKING THEORY

We can tie up some of the loose ends which are still dangling by describing the most highly developed model of intentional political behavior. Our

---

[6] Karl Popper, *The Open Society and Its Enemies,* 2 (New York: Harper Torchbooks, 1962), p. 96.

brief analysis of decision-making theory will help us understand the general nature of the intentional approach, while indicating what can be done by suggesting and explaining when the basic assumptions of intentionality are worked into a systematic model.

Decision-making theory focuses upon the decision maker as the fundamental unit of political analysis. The basic assumption is not that every political act is intentional—this assumption has been laid to rest—but that ultimately, politics involves making decisions that are judgments about how to gain a particular objective in a given situation. Thus, the decision-making theorist does not claim that the model accounts for all political phenomena; rather, it is assumed that decision making is the most important aspect of the political system and is of primary interest to the political scientist.

While the decision maker is the focal point, he is not viewed as operating within a vacuum. His environment, the situation in which he finds himself, is recognized as an important factor, both as a shaper of the objectives that he is trying to achieve and as a set of limits that help determine what he can and cannot do in seeking his goals.

Many approaches to decision making leave the impression that the decision-making process is isolated from its environment. Others argue that the process must be linked to other factors and approaches. The latter position leads to the impression that decision-making theory lacks the preciseness of some models, especially its close cousin, game theory. A dilemma arises: The more the central concept of decision making is linked to the environment, the harder it is to isolate; yet, if decision making is to function as a useful model, it must be simplified. One does not want to include everything. Thus, the decision-making theorist must make a choice between the wider-ranging model that establishes numerous links with the political, social, and economic systems, and the more narrow, more focused approach that tends to view decision making as an internalized, self-perpetuating process run by goal-seeking decision makers. The distinction seems to revolve around the question of goals: The broader decision-making approaches include the question of where goals come from. The more narrow approaches take it as given—given a decision maker with goal X, what will be the decision?

Decision-making theory is a refined version of the general intentional approach. The decision maker's dispositions can be included in the model, although as decision-making theory is used by political scientists, they are sometimes de-emphasized. Thus, even though the President has his objective in mind, his decision about how to achieve it may be colored by his attitudes, opinions, beliefs, and personality, and this latter kind of influence will probably operate without his being aware of it. In short, political decision makers are no less subject to the influence of their dispositions than other people.

We can begin to see the heuristic value of decision-making theory. In focusing upon the decision maker and his activity, the researcher has his attention directed toward those factors that might be related to the focal points. The model provides an overall framework for analyzing certain basic aspects of politics and is the foundation for a potential theory of politics.[7]

Let us examine how decision-making theory can be used to explain a particular policy or event through an example from the literature of political science. Richard C. Snyder and Glenn D. Paige have provided an explanation of the decision by the United States to resist the invasion of South Korea by North Korean forces.[8] From decision-making theory comes their basic assumption: "Acts of a nation-state result from more or less deliberate and conscious choices by someone at some time, and a course of action is followed to serve certain purposes."[9]

Snyder and Paige argue that the decision to resist agression in Korea was made by our decision makers because of several basic objectives, including protecting our national security and avoiding World War III. While admitting the influence of other factors—environmental conditions, and the like—their argument boils down to the following: The United States intervened in Korea because President Truman and his advisers decided that certain basic values were worth protecting and these objectives have to be related to military intervention by generalizations. Perhaps the most generally appropriate law would be: If a national leader wishes to preserve his or her nation's security, he or she will intervene in any conflict that threatens this security. Other factors—beliefs and capabilities, for instance—would have

---

[7] For an evaluation of the uses of decision-making theory, see James N. Rosenau, "The Premises and Promises of Decision-Making Theory," in James C. Charlesworth, ed., *Contemporary Political Analysis* (New York: Free Press, 1967), pp. 189–211.

[8] Richard C. Snyder and Glenn D. Paige, "The United States Decision to Resist Aggression in Korea: The Application of an Analytical Scheme," in Charlesworth, *Contemporary Political Analysis,* pp. 193–208.

[9] Ibid., p. 195.

to be included. Snyder and Paige show that the specific objective-values are variations on the theme of national security and so included in the generalization. The result is an explanation using laws that relate goals and action taken. In other words an explanation is generated by the principles of decision-making theory. The assumption of intentionality is especially important, for it suggests the other relationships that might be significant. Assuming that President Truman has objective A and aims to achieve it, and given that action X was taken, what other factors would have to be present if X is to lead to A?

THE RATIONAL APPROACH

There is a particular kind of intentional behavior, usually called rational, which grounds another approach to the study of politics. The approach assumes that all political actors, or a particular class of them, are rational. From this premise, other characteristics of individuals or political systems are deduced; in other words, hypotheses are generated. If some of them are verified, then the indication might be that a rationalistic theory of politics is in the offing. Thus, rational approaches can be both heuristic and potentially explanatory.

We will begin our analysis of the rational approach to the study of politics with a discussion of rationality in general, its meaning and significance in political inquiry. Then we will consider the most highly developed rational model, game theory.

The concept of rationality

The first thing to do is to consider some proposed definitions of rationality. Most of them are behavioral in that "rational" implies a certain kind of activity. Robert Dahl and Charles Lindblom have summarized what many political scientists have in mind when they talk about rational behavior: "An action is rational to the extent that it is correctly designed to maximize goal achievement, given the goal in question and the real world as it exists."[10]

To be rational is to be efficient in the pursuit of goals; in the words of

---

[10] Robert Dahl and Charles Lindblom, *Politics, Economics, and Welfare* (New York: Harper & Row, 1953), p. 38.

economist Anthony Downs, "maximizing output for a given input, or minimizing input for a given output."[11] A politician is rational if, given a particular objective and situation, a course of action that is most likely to achieve the objective is chosen. The influence of economic theory on this notion of rationality is obvious. But it is not surprising when one realizes that many of its developers and users are or were originally economists.

There are other ways to characterize rationality. Philosopher of social science Quentin Gibson has equated "considering the evidence" with rational behavior.[12] If, in a given situation, an individual, in seeking an objective, bases her choice of means on all the available evidence, she is rational. This notion of rationality is perhaps more applicable to political situations, for it considers the possibility of a decision maker's having incomplete or imperfect evidence. Herbert Simon has been among the handful of political scientists who have attempted to work out usable concepts of rationality. He has advocated a move away from the concept, most often identified with economic theory, which revolves around the assumption of *ideal* rationality. Simon states that his task "is to replace the global rationality of economic man with a kind of rational behavior that is compatible with the access to information and the computational capacities that are actually possessed by organisms, including man, in the kind of environments in which such organisms exist."[13] With a more "realistic" notion of "rational," a greater number of social and political phenomena can be included within a rational model of politics. Robert Dahl and Charles Lindblom have taken the more realistic notion of rationality one step further with their concept of *incrementalism*. The idea is that the typical rational decision maker does not choose from among grand, comprehensive alternatives but instead makes a series of small, piecemeal adjustments to existing policies.[14]

At the heart of any definition of rational behavior lies some notion of using the best means to achieve a given goal. So far we have discussed rationality in general—any type of means to achieve any type of goal. But our central

---

[11] Anthony Downs, *An Economic Theory of Democracy* (New York: Harper & Row, 1957), p. 5.

[12] Quentin Gibson, *The Logic of Social Enquiry* (London: Routledge & Kegan Paul, 1960), p. 46.

[13] Herbert Simon, *Models of Man* (New York: John Wiley & Sons, 1958), p. 241.

[14] See Charles Lindblom, "The Science of Muddling Through," *Public Administration Review,* 29 (Spring 1959), pp. 79–88.

interest is rationality in politics. There are two possibilities: rational action designed to achieve political ends (a candidate dying his hair to make himself more attractive to the voters), or rational political action directed toward any ends (Congress passing a law to regulate the drug industry). Both situations are political and, in the real world, tend to blend together. Another complication results from the fact that real-world people often pursue political and nonpolitical goals simultaneously; and it is likely that the rational political choice will conflict with the rational nonpolitical choice. Anthony Downs provides us with an example: "Let us assume a certain man prefers party *A* for political reasons, but his wife has a tantrum whenever he fails to vote for party *B*. It is perfectly rational personally for this man to vote for party *B* if preventing his wife's tantrums is more important to him than having *A* win instead of *B*."[15] In Chapter 2, we examined representative definitions of politics, and these should help us single out the particular rational behavior that interests us.

Let us backtrack a bit. The definitions we have considered say that one is rational if he uses the best means to achieve his goals. This implies that while *means* are rational or not rational, there can be no such evaluation of what is being sought. We never label ends rational, only means. Thus, one can seek any goal—political order or disorder, for instance—rationally.

However, after having identified rational behavior and *means* activity, we must recognize that some political scientists have formulated notions of rational *ends*. That is, they claim or imply that an act is rational if it is designed to achieve certain ends.

The national-interest theory of Hans Morgenthau is a case in point.[16] Morgenthau states that nations seek their rational interest. Then he implies that this type of behavior is rational. A major difficulty with such an approach is its ambiguity. In making a political end rational, it is not quite clear if the basic assertion—all rational nations seek their national interest—is an empirical generalization of a definition of rationality.

Furthermore, in postulating an *end* as rational, the political scientist moves into the realm of normative political philosophy. That is, he is recommending that men or nations pursue an objective that is "good" or "best." It is fair to interpret Morgenthau's argument in this manner. He is saying

---

[15] Downs, *An Economic Theory*, p. 7.
[16] Hans J. Morgenthau, *Politics among Nations* (New York: Alfred A. Knopf, 1960).

that it is morally right for a state to seek its national interest. He makes seeking its national interest the ultimate moral good of a state; since it is rational to protect one's national interest, it is good for the state; "rational" is equivalent to "morally right." To be fair to Morgenthau, we must add that he makes this the good of politics, while arguing that there are different moral values in other spheres of human activity.

If our basic distinction between facts and values has any validity, then it seems fairly clear that this kind of rational analysis has no place in the empirical study of politics. One can probably trace this sort of normative rational argument back to theories of the "good order," which have always had an important place in political philosophy. William T. Bluhm has, in characterizing such theories, made evident their similarity to the contemporary rational-ends theorists. "Investigating the 'rational' or 'best' order, the theorist first of all seeks to determine the rational or 'right' order of human ends or values."[17] We can conclude that in political science, rational models and theories deal with the means that are appropriate for a given end. Theories that postulate an end as rational have probably moved into the realm of normative political philosophy.

How the rational approach is used

Rational approaches can be used both to suggest and to provide potential explanations of political phenomena, usually decisions. As the basis of a potential explanatory theory, the concept of rationality must be related to other variables in generalizations. As we saw in Chapter 7, the basic explanatory premise in rational theories takes the following form: "A rational man in situation S would perform act A." Or, more completely, a rational man with goal C and faced with alternatives A to Z will choose A. So, being rational or having the disposition of rationality is related to a particular decision. The useful rational theory of politics would expand upon this simple hypothesis as it added variables and relationships. But its basic nomological structure would remain intact.

In evaluating the usefulness of rational theories, one should begin by

---

[17] William T. Bluhm, *Theories of the Political System* (Englewood Cliffs, N.J.: Prentice-Hall, 1965), p. 5.

noting that much political behavior is not rational. Thus, rational theories are limited in their scope.

This implies that it is incumbent upon the political scientist who contemplates employing a rational theory to substantiate the claim that a political actor is rational. This calls for a clearly defined concept of rationality with empirical import. Before we can determine whether or not the President is rational, we have to remember what it means to be rational. If the concept is not properly defined, then, in Kenneth Boulding's words, "it can easily collapse to the empty proposition that people do what they do, for what they do is by definition the best choice.[18] Many political scientists are guilty of this tautological activity, despite its obvious shortcomings. The result is the unthinking attribution of rationality to everyone, which doesn't take us very far.

But an even more significant question, especially in regard to theory construction, is Are there empirical laws about rational men? Or, at least, are there well-constructed hypotheses that can be tested?

So we must have two kinds of knowledge to use the concept of rationality in theories and explanations; generalizations relating rationality to other variables, and evidence that relevant political actors are rational to demonstrate that the generalizations and theories encompass them.

At this point, we should mention a strategy that is apparently not bothered by the empirical limitations and methodological requirements of the rational approach. An appropriate label is the "commonsense rational" theory of politics. Take, for instance, the following argument of W. G. Runciman:

> There is nothing, in a sense, that needs to be explained about a South Wales miner voting Labour or an executive of General Motors voting Republican. The simplest model of rational self-interest is enough to explain these cases without being in defiance of Graham Wallas, exaggerating the 'intellectuality' involved.[19]

The basis of Runciman's "explanation" is either the assumption that everyone is rational until proven nonrational or that when behavior conforms to our expectations it is rational and requires no further explanation.

---

[18] Kenneth E. Boulding, *Conflict and Defense* (New York: Harper & Row, 1962), p. 9.

[19] W. G. Runciman, *Social Science and Political Theory* (Cambridge: At the University Press, 1963), p. 94.

Because of the limited time and resources available to political scientists, such arguments may be of temporary usefulness. In addition, the assumptions might be of some heuristic value. However, both assumptions are empirical assertions, and if they are to serve as explanatory premises, their particular manifestations must ultimately be tested against the world. In addition, the assumptions require that evidence be collected that demonstrates the rationality of the particular class of political actors referred to. So Runciman's argument might be valid in certain instances, but he is misusing the rational approach if he assumes that the burden of proof is on those who believe there is nonrational behavior. A rational theory does not have privileged status relative to other theories. It, too, must be evaluated according to how well it organizes and explains the world of politics.

While no model has privileged status, the rational approach has a certain down-to-earth appeal that many other models lack. This appeal is probably based on two main factors: the ease with which a simple rational model can be used, and the comforting thought that those decision makers who hold our lives in their hands are truly rational. In regard to the first point, one needs a minimal amount of information to "explain" behavior if it can be assumed that political actors are rational; if all acts are rational, then one must simply identify the goal that is sought. It is probably no accident that journalists usually give rational explanations of political events. There is not enough time to collect the data that might indicate other motivations. The second factor is psychological. It is functional for most of us to assume that important political decisions are made by rational beings. To admit to ourselves that President Reagan's foreign policy flows from his personality needs is painful, to say the least. So, too, is the recognition that a nuclear war could result from an ideological clash that is largely the result of divergent value systems, passed on, with little rational justification, through the socialization system. But simplicity and psychological appeal alone are not grounds for justifying an approach.

The building of rational theories of politics is no easy task. Their formulation and verification does not guarantee that more than a narrow range of political phenomena will be accounted for, because so much political behavior cannot be included within a concept of rationality.

Although theories of politics based on rationality may be difficult to develop and be limited in scope, the concept may serve as a foundation for models or conceptual schemes of politics. In short, while the explanatory power of rationality seems limited, its usefulness as a suggestive device for discovery is probably greater.

There is a heuristic gambit that some take. It revolves around the assertion that the "rational political man," like the "rational economic man" only an ideal. However, even though there are no rational men, a model making the unrealistic assumption that there are is useful in suggesting what men would do *if they were* rational. Based on this kind of information, the political scientist begins to formulate generalizations about the kinds of situations where men (or certain kinds of men) act rationally. The strategy generates data that can be used to map out the limits of rational theories—to see just how far one can go in developing rational explanations. Karl Popper has suggested such a strategy, which he labels the "zero-sum method." He means by this, "the method of constructing a model on the assumption of complete rationality . . . on the part of all the individuals concerned, and estimating the deviation of the actual behavior from the model behavior, using the latter as a kind of zero coordinate."[20] A concept of rationality at least serves as a focal point or standard against which behavior can be measured.

GAME THEORY

The most highly developed rational model of politics is game theory. Thomas Schelling has defined it as "the formal study of the rational, consistent expectations and that participants can have about each other's choices."[21] Game theory seems relevant to the study of politics because it analyzes conflict situations—situations where two or more actors are competing for values. A decision maker might use game theory to help formulate the best strategy in a particular situation. A political scientist might use it to suggest the possible behavior of political actors or explanations of various kinds of political decisions.

At the heart of game theory is an assumption of rationality. It is assumed that in a game situation, the players or decision makers are trying to maximize their gains or minimize their losses—they want to get as much as they

---

[20] Karl Popper, *The Poverty of Historicism* (New York: Harper & Row, 1964), p. 141.

[21] Thomas Schelling, *The Strategy of Conflict* (New York: Oxford University Press, 1960).

can out of the game. The assumption applies to poker, football, and political situations.

The elements of game theory

All games have a common set of charcteristics.[22] First, there are *players* or participants, each with *goals* and *resources*. A gambler without money cannot play cards, and a nation without military forces cannot play war. But in addition to resources, the players have goals or objectives that indicate what they want to get out of the game. In the most general terms, this is to win. But to be meaningful, the goals in any particular game situation must be specified, for they may differ from game to game, and within a game, from player to player. For example, imagine an election where one candidate wants to win but the other wants only to make a good showing to establish the legitimacy of his party or ideology.

A game involves players with goals and resources. Game theory makes the assumption that the players are rational. This leads to the formulation of another important concept, *strategy*. Strategy in game theory has much in common with the term we use in everyday conversation. It has something to do with planning, working out methods for success. In game theory, it refers to the plan that a rational player develops, telling him what to do given the possible moves of his opponent(s). In most games, a number of strategies are open to each side. The objective is to choose the one that maximizes gains and minimizes losses. The best strategy is not always the one which, if successfully completed, will lead to the biggest payoff; often one will be chosen that offers a good chance for modest gain and a slight chance of loss. The big payoff strategy might have another possible payoff—the disastrous loss.

Some games are commonly called games of skill, while others are labeled

---

[22] For discussions of the elements of game theory, see Richard C. Snyder, "Game Theory and the Analysis of Political Behavior," in *Research Frontiers in Politics and Government* (Washington, D.C.: Brookings Institution, 1955), pp. 70–103; and Martin Shubik, "Game Theory and the Study of Social Behavior: An Introductory Exposition" in Martin Shubik, ed., *Game Theory and Related Approaches to Social Behavior* (New York: John Wiley & Sons, 1964), pp. 3–77. Easy books on game theory are hard to find. Two of the more accessible ones are Steven J. Brams, *Game Theory and Politics* (New York: Free Press, 1975) and Henry Hamburger, *Games as Models of Social Phenomena* (San Francisco: W. H. Freeman, 1979).

games of chance. Strictly speaking, game theory includes neither. A game of pure chance, like the children's game of War, depends only on the random selection of cards. The outcome of the game is beyond the control or manipulation of the players. While it is wise to know the odds if one is going to play the more advanced game of roulette, the movements of the wheel and ball are again beyond the control of the players (assuming that the house is honest). A game of pure skill is the game of chance's opposite. Here, only the players' expertise counts. Chance or luck is absent from the equation. In the real world, it is difficult to find games of pure skill, but there are activities (target shooting, for instance) that come close (the most important factor is the shooter's skill). In such a game, one is competing only with oneself, not with other players. Here is a crucial difference between skill and strategy. A strategic game, the kind analyzed in game theory, assumes there will be other players trying to succeed and that what one does will affect what the others can do. Thus, not only must the participants consider themselves, they must always remember the moves of others; they must formulate strategies. The strategies, while based to some extent on incomplete information (thus allowing the play of chance), nevertheless make the game unlike a game of pure chance, because some predictions can be made about the other players' strategies.

So it is up to each player to select the most rational strategy. This is what the football quarterback does when he decides whether to run or pass from his own one-yard line; what the baseball pitcher does when he throws a fastball rather than a curveball; and perhaps what the presidential candidate does when he chooses to campaign only in the largest states. In each case, the rational player remembers the possible strategies of the opponents. The defense has a number of formations it can employ to cover all the moves of the quarterback. The batter may be expecting either a fastball or a curveball. The opposing candidate *B* can meet candidate *A* head-on or campaign unchallenged in the smaller states.

We have been referring to another basic element of game theory, the *payoff*. Each set of strategies has a set of values attached to it that constitutes the outcomes of the game—so much won or lost, given the combinations of opposing strategies. These are the payoffs. In a general sense, they describe in mathematical terms—dollars, votes, runs—the goals of the players. It is the tallying of payoffs at the end of the game that determines the winner.

There is one element of game situations that we have not mentioned. It has to do with the framework, the environment within which the game is played. This framework is usually described in a set of rules—a set of propositions indicating what the players can or cannot do. In poker, chess, and football, the rules are specific and unambiguous. In politics, they are more complicated. What are the rules of an election or a negotiation between two nations? There are rules, but they are not neatly summarized in a rule book. Instead, we have to look at customs, traditions, legal codes, constitutions, and, in addition, geographical, biological, sociological, and psychological limitations on the player's behavior. It is clearly more difficult to ferret these out. But this is one way of saying, "Politics is more complex than poker."

Types of game theory

When we think about game theory and its possible applications to politics, it becomes more and more obvious that there are actually several game models. They can be classified according to how many players the game has and what kinds of payoff the game provides.[23]

The two-person zero-sum game is the simplest type. It involves two participants competing in a game with rules that allow only strategies that lead to playoffs of the all-or-nothing variety. That is, the winnings and losses always cancel each other out. Two-handed poker is of this sort: if player A wins \$50, then player B has to lose \$50 $(50 - 50 = 0)$. There are probably political situations that can fit zero-sum conditions, if certain variables are left out, such as a two-man election. If we assume that each candidate is rational and is trying to win, then it is a zero-sum game, for one will win, the other will lose. This kind of a game involves head-to-head conflict, and while there are political situations that can be analyzed within a two-person zero-sum framework, there are probably more that require a more complex game model.

One such model defines the two-person nonzero-sum game. In this game,

---

[23] For a discussion of various kinds of games, see Shubik,, *Game Theory;* for a detailed discussion of two-person games see Anatol Rapaport, *Two-Person Game Theory* (Ann Arbor: University of Michigan Press, 1966).

the gains and losses of the two players do not cancel out, and they do not equal zero. This allows a wide variety of possible payoffs, including situations where both players gain and where those both players lose. The former is a positive game; the latter is a negative game. It is not difficult to think of political situations that might fit this model—certain situations in international relations come immediately to mind. What of negotiations between two nations where the payoff results in a gain, let us say, in territory for both, even though they are in conflict; or the converse situation of nuclear war, where neither nation wins?

An even more complex game model includes those games where more than two players participate, and where gains and losses do not cancel out. This is labeled the n-person nonzero-sum game. Take, for instance, the common situation where a number of states are competing for a new military base. If there are 10 states involved, 1 will win and the other 9 will lose; the sum of all their gains and losses will equal minus 8. This is another negative game. There are numerous examples of positive games—legislative vote trading is a good one. This game model is probably applicable to a number of political situations, including interest group behavior, international bargaining, and many coalition situations.

This suggests a further development of game theory, the mixed-motive game where the competing parties have some common interests and some conflicting interests. Such a situation is more difficult to analyze than more simple games, but it is probably more typical of the real world of politics. An important variation occurs when all important interests in a particular area are common, but because of a lack of information about each other, the parties involved in a political situation have trouble coordinating their activities. Consider the United States and the USSR as they attempt to reach an agreement on the limitation of nuclear weapons. It is in the interest of both to reach an agreement, but neither knows enough about the other to sign a treaty.

Because it is more complex than two-person games, the n-person game is probably applicable to a wider range of political phenomena. But its complexity, the greater number of variables and relationships it uses, calls for a high degree of mathematical sophistication on the part of its user, and makes it extremely difficult to employ. Thus, political scientists are faced with a dilemma: The game models that are the least complex and easiest to use are probably the least applicable to politics.

Using game theory

This leads to a more general observation about the use of game theory in political science. Richard Snyder has warned against the premature application of mathematical models, such as game theory, to social and political phenomena.[24] He sees the possible prematurity stemming from two sources: first, the fact that game theory, or at least certain kinds of game theory, might not yet be sufficiently developed. In this case, the political scientist should be aware of the limitations of the mathematical model. But, second, it is much more likely that the reverse is true. That is, political science is not yet ready to use many of the sophisticated models developed by mathematicians and economists. Before they are used, the political scientist must be ready to approach his data in a particular way, making assumptions that are often foreign to traditional political analysis. Even if he does prepare himself, there is no guarantee that game theory will be applicable to more than a narrow range of political phenomena.

The indications are, however, that game models are of more significance than this. Their main function for the present and near future is heuristic: suggesting explanatory hypotheses. Let us examine one highly respected example.

William Riker bases his *Theory of Political Coalitions* on an assumption of rationality. From this starting point, he develops a game model that he attempts to adjust to empirical realities. He then uses his modified game model to generate a hypothesis that can explain a relationship, discovered by V. O. Key, between the existence of a Republican minority in Southern states and the continuance of organized factions in Democratic parties.[25] The hypothesis which Riker labels the "size principle" states that "In social situations similar to *n*-person, zero-sum games with side payments, participants create coalitions just as large as they believe will ensure winning and no larger."[26] This principle can be translated into the following hypothesis about party behavior: Political parties try to win by the *smallest* possible

---

[24] Snyder, "Game Theory," pp. 72–73.

[25] V. O. Key, *Southern Politics in State and Nation* (New York: Alfred A. Knopf, 1949), p. 300.

[26] William Riker, *The Theory of Political Coalitions* (New Haven, Conn.: Yale University Press, 1962), p. 32.

margin. This is rational, because then the winnings have to be divided among a minimal number of party members.

Riker provides some empirical (both experimental and historical) evidence supporting the hypothesis that has been generated by his game model. He is then able to use his generalization to explain Key's discovery.

> When the Democratic party is a coalition of the whole, it is worth nothing. But when an opposition exists, the coalition is worth something. Hence, a majority faction inside the Democratic party appears to take charge of the winnings. It then expels some of these not necessary to win in order to divide the gains among fewer persons.[27]

This example demonstrates the usefulness of game models. Their rigor and sharpness make them a significant source of hypotheses. Game models will probably not be applicable to politics exactly as they come from the mathematician or economist. We noted that Riker modified the model to make it more relevant. But the basic assumptions remain the same. If game theory is to be fully exploited by political scientists, they will have to become familiar enough with its nature and limitations to be able to decide when it can and cannot be used, or how it might be adjusted to meet the complexities of particular political situations.

---

[27] Ibid., pp. 95–96.

CHAPTER

Economic models of politics

Ａ S previous chapters have indicated, political science has borrowed from and adapted the models and approaches of other disciplines
such as psychology and sociology. In this chapter, we will consider several
models that are derived from economics. Drawing upon economics has become a popular activity for more and more political scientists in recent
years. This takes us back to the previous century, when the distinction
between economics and politics was not as clear-cut as it is today. It is no
accident that the scholars of that era who studied government and economics were called political economists.

The perception of the close ties between the disciplines of political science and economics is initially the result of the integral, real-world relationship between political and economic systems. In the words of political economist Charles Lindblom, "In all the economic systems of the world, much of
politics is economic, and most of economics is also politics."[1] The relationship between politics and economics can be observed in many ways: huge
government budgets; the economic nature of most government policies; the
fact that even in capitalist nations, private economic enterprises look to

---

[1] Charles E. Lindblom, *Politics and Markets* (New York: Basic Books, 1977), p. 8.

245

government for a number of services (maintenance of a stable economy, protection from foreign competition).

Turning their attention to economics has reinforced another tendency in modern political science: political scientists have developed a greater concern with the outputs of political systems, which has led to a growing interest in the policymaking approach.[2] This is actually a rather broad category that includes a number of models and approaches designed to evaluate the degree to which government decision makers achieve the goals of their societies. What we are really dealing with is the analysis of instrumental judgments—decisions about the best ways to achieve objectives. This usually entails the use of various measurement techniques often associated with economics. Thus, there is a second reason for the close ties between economic and political analysis.

This brings to mind several characteristics of economics that seem so appealing to political scientists interested in the policy process—its apparent ability to measure phenomena with mathematical precision and the degree to which it has produced deductive models of economic behavior. Economics comes across as a more scientific enterprise than political science—the goal is to capture some of the economist's rigor by adapting his models and techniques.

Some observers have suggested that political scientists should not view the use of economic models as a panacea for the shortcomings of political science, because the scientific rigor of economics is more apparent than real. They point out that economists have oversimplified the world to make it fit their models. It is true that economic models typically begin with ideal, simplifying assumptions that are somewhat unrealistic. But, as we have already seen, the use of ideal assumptions is often helpful in generating hypotheses and suggesting new areas of research. All models are by necessity simplifications of the real world.

Perhaps the best-known ideal assumption in economics is "economic man," the rational, goal-oriented human who makes decisions based on a calculation of costs and benefits. Economic man is the cornerstone of classical economics, the assumption that gives credibility to the notions of supply and demand and the market system. This also suggests that most of the

---

[2] The parameters of policymaking were first explored in Daniel Lerner and Harold Lasswell eds., *The Policy Sciences* (Stanford, Calif.: Stanford University Press, 1951).

economic models that have influenced political science are *micro* in nature.

It has been argued that it is the assumption of rationality that best characterizes the field of economics. One leading economist claims "that economic . . . theory is in a fundamental sense more nearly a theory of rational behavior than a theory of material goods."[3] He is saying that the concept of economic rationality is applicable to a wider range of social situations than those typically considered economic. In the last chapter, we saw how game theory begins with an assumption of rationality. In this chapter, we return to rationality because many political scientists have recently been impressed with the elegant models constructed by economists using such ideal assumptions. About 15 years ago, one such political scientist made these predictions about the next several decades of political analysis: "Theory will become increasingly logical, deductive, and mathematical. In terms of its content, we will make increasing uses of economic theory, decision theory, welfare economics, and public finance. Models of political systems analogous to types of economies and markets will proliferate."[4] Proliferate may be a bit of an exaggeration, but economic analysis has had an impact on significant numbers of political scientists.

COST-BENEFIT ANALYSIS

There are two basic ways that economics can be used to analyze politics. The first concentrates on the outputs of political systems and evaluates them using various economic measuring techniques. The second applies some of the theoretical assumptions of economics to political situations.

Let us begin with the former. There are several techniques that have been applied to distributing public goods, that is, performing the basic political function of deciding who gets what. The most popular techniques are cost-benefit analysis, operations research, and program planning-budgeting.[5] As

---

[3] Mancur Olson, "The Relationship between Economics and the Other Social Sciences: The Province of a Social Report," in Seymour Martin Lipset ed., *Politics and the Social Sciences* (New York: Oxford University Press, 1969), p. 142.

[4] William C. Mitchell, "The Shape of Political Theory to Come: From Political Sociology to Political Economy," in Lipset, *Politics and the Social Sciences,* p. 129.

[5] For a useful discussion of how some of these techniques are applied see Fred A. Kramer, *Contemporary Approaches to Public Budgeting* (Cambridge, Mass.: Winthrop, 1979).

tools in the making of real-world decisions, such rational techniques have received mixed reviews from public administration specialists. Our main concern, however, is not so much their applicability to actual problems as their use as models of political analysis.

Let us spend a few minutes describing cost-benefit analysis.[6] Its basic operating principle is simple enough: the best way to make public policy decisions is to measure the benefits and costs of each policy alternative. Things get tricky when attempts are made to construct indicators and measures of the benefits and costs. Sometimes it is possible to examine them directly, but often only indirect measures are possible.

Cost-benefit analysis is considered an economic model of politics because the costs and benefits of public policies are measured in monetary terms. An attempt is made to apply the logic of private business to decision making in government. But because the private and public sectors are based on different assumptions, there is an initial problem. Whereas classical economics tells us that *profit* is the main objective of the private economic enterprise, governments are supposed to work for the *public good*. When the leaders of General Motors make an economic decision, which of several new car models to build, they subtract projected costs from expected revenue—revenue minus cost equals profit. General Motors should build the car that will produce the greatest profit.

When government leaders make a decision, the cost-benefit approach assumes that they also consider the costs of proposed policies. But because governments do not exist to earn a profit, they do not compare revenue and cost; instead, political decision makers subtract the cost from the benefit, giving them the *net benefit*. The policy that produces the greatest net benefit should be selected.

While this can be a useful approach to decision making, in reality, problems begin to arise primarily because it is so difficult to translate benefits into quantifiable economic measures. What is the market value of clean air, for instance? How do we compare the benefits of a clean environment with those of unfettered industrial development? Or, on a broader level, how do we compare the benefits of a strong national defense with the benefits of

---

[6] For a good introduction to cost-benefit analysis see William N. Dunn, *Public Policy Analysis: An Introduction* (Englewood Cliffs, N.J.: Prentice-Hall, 1981), chapter 7. For an application to basic political questions see Joyce and William Mitchell, *Political Analysis and Public Policy* (Skokie, Ill.: Rand McNally, 1969).

social programs? Since both are costly, choices will have to be made. What we have realized is that in making public policy choices, government decision makers must go beyond economic costs and benefits. They must also consider moral values, attitudes, and the distribution of power.

Let us look at an example. Suppose that a government is considering supporting the construction of a nuclear power plant. The heated discussion that follows will revolve around a disagreement over its relative benefits and costs. Even if we assume that all participants in the dispute are rational, a clear resolution will probably not emerge. On the one hand, a nuclear plant provides a source of energy whose economic costs can be measured. But on the other hand, what about the potential hazards, both short- and long-term, so difficult to measure, yet so significant if they are real. As students of politics, we must not ignore another potential cost, a psychological one. If a nuclear accident occurs, will the populace ever trust this mysterious source of energy again? Even if nuclear scientists and engineers are unanimous in arguing that the accident presented no real dangers and was a once-in-a-million occurrence, the emotional harm that might be done to large groups of anxious citizens if more plants are planned might be a cost that the society is unwilling to bear. How do we reconcile the dispute between two nuclear experts who, although they agree on technical matters, disagree along the following lines: one believes that the potential long-term health hazards make nuclear plants an unacceptable risk, while the other argues that the absolute necessity for nonfossil-fuel energy sources makes it unthinkable that we end the construction of new plants.

Stricktly speaking, cost-benefit analysis would attempt to provide an answer to this dispute by translating the proposed hazards, costs, and benefits into monetary units—the medical costs resulting from an accident and the economic costs of having to rely on increasingly costly fossil fuels. If we view the building of nuclear power plants as a private enterprise, a profit-making activity, then if it looks as if costs will exceed revenue, the plant will probably not be built. The point is that there is more to be considered. A decision may be made to build the plant because the social benefits (having a ready source of domestic energy) may justify building an economically inefficient project. Or, the contrary situation may occur. An economically efficient source of energy may not be developed because of its social costs.

Let us summarize the advantages and disadvantages of cost-benefit analysis. If costs and benefits can be measured in dollars, political scientists have a unit of value that can be applied in many situations. This allows them to compare policies. However, dependence on economic measures limits what can be studied—it might even create an artificial rigor, since values and power are not so easily quantified, yet they must be included in any analysis of political decision making.

ECONOMIC MODELS OF POLITICS: EXCHANGE THEORY

The second way that economics can be used to analyze politics is by applying some of the theoretical assumptions of economics to political situations. This usually entails adapting models that have helped economists understand economic phenomena. This is a methodological rather than substantive use of economics. The emphasis is not on the empirical relationships between politics and economics (emphasized in the last section) but rather on structural similarities between political and economic systems.

One of the more useful models of this sort is *exchange theory*. It conceives of politics as a process similar to economics in that both involve interacting individuals and groups who exchange goods and services in pursuit of their own interests.[7] The whole idea is that political scientists can learn something about their subject if politics operates similarly to an economic market system. In economic systems, economic goods and services are exchanged (cars, money, credit); in political systems, political goods and services are exchanged (votes, support, power, security).

Exchange theory is a micro, individualistic model that begins with an assumption of rationality. The analogy between the market system and the political system leads to the conclusion that rational, self-interested individuals will, in both politics and economics, cooperate to achieve their goals. The consensus that occurs is not the result of socialization, but it is the realization that everyone can gain from the exchange of political goods and services. Just as the classic market system of Adam Smith benefits all pro-

---

[7] The most impressive application of economic exchange theory to politics is James M. Buchanan and Gordon Tullock, *The Calculus of Consent, Logical Foundations of Constitutional Democracy* (Ann Arbor, Mich.: University of Michigan Press, 1962). Even though exchange theory is primarily an economic model, it has a closely related sociological counterpart. For a discussion of the sociological model, see Sidney R. Waldman, "Exchange Theory and Political Analysis," in Andrew Effort ed., *Perspectives in Political Sociology* (Indianapolis, Ind.: Bobbs-Merrill, 1972), pp. 101–25.

ducers and consumers, so all the participants in a political system can gain—if you vote for me, I'll vote for you. What we are really talking about is, in the language of game theory, a positive nonzero sum game. It is not the case that what I gain you lose. As the most articulate formulators of the exchange model of politics have pointed out, this notion runs counter to power models of politics (to be discussed in Chapter 14), which tend to see political decisions as resulting from the distribution of power. According to these models, there is just so much power to go around—the more you have, the less I have. Exchange theory suggests that decisions result not from grand conceptions of the public interest but from a series of decisions by individual actors exchanging political goods and services.

A COST-BENEFIT ANALYSIS OF DEMOCRATIC VOTING

One of the neatest and most influential applications of economic theory to the analysis of a particular political process is economist Anthony Downs's examination of voting in democratic political systems.[8] Downs analyzes voting as a rational process; this makes his approach different from most voting studies, which use psychological and sociological models emphasizing nonrational factors such as attitudes and opinions. Downs subjects voting to a cost-benefit analysis. The democratic electoral process is viewed as a kind of market system with voters considering what they have to gain from the expenditure of time and energy that voting requires—remember, casting a rational vote might require the acquisition of significant amounts of information. Among Downs's major conclusions is the proposition that given the costs of obtaining information about candidates and issues, it might be rational for some citizens to refrain from voting. Downs also draws conclusions about political parties and how they devise strategies to compete in the political market. One of the more obvious conclusions (confirmed by empirical research) is that the goal of parties is to win votes rather than achieve certain policy goals.

This suggests one of the most impressive aspects of Downs's model, its ability to generate testable hypotheses about the behavior of individuals and groups in the democratic political process. In this sense, it is a classic model;

---

[8] Anthony Downs, *An Economic Theory of Democracy* (New York: Harper & Row, 1957).

Downs does not claim that it is true, only that it is likely to produce some interesting generalizations. This is perhaps a good way to end the chapter. Our examination of the use of economic models should leave the impression that despite their limitations, they produce many insights into the workings of the political system; and in their assumption of rationality, they provide an important corrective to psychological and sociological models.

Role theory and small group theory

THE approaches discussed in the last two chapters are based on the assumption that the individual is the central unit of analysis in politics. In this chapter, we focus on two approaches which, while still looking at the individual, do so within a social structure. It is assumed that the individual is important only in a social context. While both role theory and small group theory accept the validity of individualistic-micro models, each argues that they don't go far enough.

ROLE THEORY[1]

To the role theorist, the reason is clear. As Heinz Eulau puts it, "Political behavior . . . is always conduct in the performance of a political role."[2] The strong implication is that political scientists will never develop sound explanations of political phenomena if they view political actors only as individ-

---

[1] For a good introduction to role theory, see Bruce Biddle and Edwin Thomas, eds., *Role Theory: Concepts and Research* (New York: John Wiley & Sons, 1966).

[2] Heinz Eulau, *The Behavioral Persuasion in Politics* (New York: Random House, 1963), p. 40.

uals, or even individual members of groups. Instead, role theory suggests that political behavior is largely the result of the demands and expectations of the role or roles that a political actor happens to be filling. Surely the personality and attitudes of the man who is President influence his decisions, but the decisions are made as he fills a role or set of roles and this fact, the role theorist argues, is of primary interest.

Most role theorists emphasize the difficulties inherent in a purely individualistic approach to politics, and therefore the advantages of role theory. John Wahlke, in the introductory essay of an application of role theory to legislative behavior, writes, "No legislature or other institution could be seen by the analyst if the human actors did not exhibit behavior in conformity, to at least some minimal extent, with the norms of behavior constituting their roles."[3] Thus, one attractive feature of role theory is its attempt to place political activity in a social context; that is, a conceptual framework is provided that views the individual as someone who depends upon and reacts to the behavior of others.

Another selling point of role theory, according to proponents, is its ability to describe institutions behaviorally. To the role theorist, a political institution is a set of behavior patterns associated with roles. Let us quote Wahlke again: "The chief utility of the role-theory model of the legislative actor is that, unlike other models, it pinpoints those aspects of legislators' behavior which make the legislature an institution."[4] An institution is a number of interrelated roles. Role theory bridges the gap between individualistic and group approaches. One can still talk about individual behavior, but now it is in terms of roles, which are the basic components of institutions.

The nature of role theory

Role theory begins with the assumption that political actors find themselves in various positions, from President to voter, with certain behavior patterns associated with them. There are certain expectations about how someone in a particular position is supposed to behave. These expectations constitute a role or roles.

---

[3] John Wahlke, Heinz Eulau, William Buchanan, and LeRoy C. Ferguson, *The Legislative System* (New York: John Wiley & Sons, 1962), p. 10.

[4] Ibid., p. 9.

There are two kinds or sources of expectation. First are those that "outsiders" have. A society has certain notions about what the President should and should not do. The "notions of society" include the expectations of private citizens, of groups, and of government officials, and they are manifested in constitutions, legislative statutes, public opinion, and deeply ingrained cultural norms. To the extent that he is aware of them, these expectations influence the behavior of anyone filling a particular role. Thus, there is a two-way psychological relationship in every role. On the one hand, there are the expectations that outsiders have. On the other hand, there are the perceptions the "insider" has of the outsiders' expectations. The President knows there are legal restrictions on his power, and if he is an astute politician, he also realizes that various publics, including other professional politicians, conceive of the President's role in terms of particular duties, responsibilities, and sanctions. The accuracy of the President's reading of these expectations is one important ingredient of presidential effectiveness. So the first kind of influence proposed in role theory stems from the relationship between the expectation of those outside the role and the perception of these expectations by those filling the role.

This suggests a second kind of influence. It is the way role occupants, insiders, interpret their roles; that is, their *own* expectations about what should and should not, can and cannot be done.[5] The President considers the expectations of outsiders, but he also comes to the office with his own ideas about the role he must play. These ideas largely reflect attitudes, ideology, and personality traits developed before his movement into the role. But, in addition, they will be conditioned by the expectations of outsiders. We have already noted that the role filler consciously considers such expectations. The outside expectations influence his own interpretation of the role. It is a case of *learning;* this is why the word "conditioned" was used. The President, to continue our example, *considers* what other politicians think he should be doing, and adjusts his behavior accordingly. But there is also a strong possibility that he will begin to adopt some of these ideas and attitudes *as his own*. He will learn, through association or reinforcement, to have a particular interpretation of the role of President. While, for purposes

---

[5] Some studies look only at internal role expectations. See James L. Gibson, "Judges' Role Orientations, Attitudes, and Decisions: An Interactive Model," *American Political Science Review* (1978), pp. 911–24.

of analysis, role theory can make the distinction between outside expectations and internal interpretations of a role, they are closely intertwined; the difference between considering outside expectations and having your own interpretations shaped by these expectations is often difficult to see. The important point to remember is that, in either case, behavior is affected by the role.

A role does not exist in isolation. Role theorists use the concept "role network" to describe the relationships among roles. Heinz Eulau provides an example:

> A legislator is "colleague" to his fellow legislators, "representative" to his constituents, "friend" (or enemy) to lobbyists, "follower" to his party leaders. . . . Whatever role is taken, simultaneously or seriatim, what emerges is a very intricate structure of relations in which one role is implicated in several other roles.[6]

Several important points are suggested by this passage. First, role theory deals with complex social situations. Any conceptual scheme or model that is developed from the approach will have to simplify the situation, in emphasizing a particular set of role relationships, and de-emphasizing others.

A second implication is that many of the most visible roles are really made up of a number of subroles. Eulau's "legislator" is a case in point. But so are "President," "politician," "citizen," and most other role concepts in widespread use. Some roles include so many subroles that they are ambiguous and nearly indeterminate; consider the roles of citizen and politician as they are commonly used. Another problem for the political scientist using role theory is the sorting out of political role networks. A legislator performs a number of political roles, but at the same time these are probably tied to roles that we would identify as social or economic. In addition to being a representative and colleague, a Senator might be a father, church member, and union member.

This leads to another important phenomenon suggested by role theory. It is the concept of *role conflict*. It is not difficult to visualize a situation where two or more of a political actor's political roles conflict, or a political role conflicts with a social or economic role. An example of the first would be the dilemma faced by a legislator who, to satisfy his constituents (who favor

---

[6] Eulau, *Behavioral Persuasion,* p. 41.

extensive federal spending in the cities), must work against the party's policy of cutting such spending, or vice versa. An example of the second would be the problem faced by the conscientous Senator-father who believes his children should be back in their home state rather than in Washington, D.C., where the Senator can be of most use to his state and his country. In both situations, the expectations attached to the several roles pull in different directions. How the role occupant resolves the dilemma is an important question for role theory.

The uses of role theory

The most obvious and, as a tool of political analysis, the most important use of role theory is as an explainer and predictor of political behavior. It is not difficult to see how role theory might accomplish these objectives. Knowledge of the expectations attached to a role by a society provides us with a basis for predicting the behavior of a particular occupant of the role. This is the starting point of an explanatory and predictive role theory of political behavior. We might say that President Ford retained most of President Nixon's White House Staff in the first months of the presidential transition because this is expected of a new President coming to power in midterm; it is part of his role.

But there is more to a role than outside expectations. Therefore, an empirical role theory must include the concepts of perception of outside expectations and internal role interpretations. The theory would be based on the three factors we discussed in the last section. If we know the societal expectations, internal perceptions of the expectations, and interpretation of the role by the role occupant, we should be able to predict and explain the behavior of the role occupant with some degree of confidence. At least this is a primary objective of role theory.

A good example of the successful use of role theory is James L. Gibson's attempt to explain judicial behavior.[7] He discovered there is, at best, a weak relationship between the attitudes and decisions of judges. But when role orientations are factored in, the level of explanation increases dramatically.

---

[7] James L. Gibson, "Judges Role Orientations, Attitudes, and Decisions: An Interactive Model," *The American Political Science Review* 72 (September 1978), pp. 911–24.

Role orientation is defined as the criteria that judges feel is proper for making their decisions—whether they should be bound by precedent; whether they should allow "nonlegal" factors (sociological, economic) to influence their decisions.

Role conflict might also be useful to the political scientist. It might explain, for instance, the seemingly erratic behavior of a particular government official. The discovery of conflict between several roles could suggest hypotheses relating role conflict and resulting behavior designed to resolve the conflict. As the number of roles increases, the likelihood of developing accurate generalizations decreases. But even in these situations, the assumptions of the approach—that political actors fill roles and that, because they often fill several roles, conflict is possible—have focused the political scientist's attention on certain kinds of potentially relevant phenomena.

The point was made in the last section that role theory provides a framework for analyzing institutions in behavioral terms. According to role theory, institutions are neither groups of individuals nor rigid structures, but systems of interrelated roles. This gives the role theorist the ability to treat an institution such as the Senate or the Democratic party as a dynamic process that has some continuity. There is some stability in roles—all modern Presidents have filled the same set of roles—and yet, because role expectations change and different individuals occupy roles, there is also a change in the nature of the role. All Presidents are chief legislators, but because of shifting outside expectations and different Presidents, the role has had several connotations throughout the history of our political system. In addition, change and development in the political system is provided for by role learning on the part of the role occupant. His interpretation upon entering the role may not be the same as the one he has when he leaves it.

Besides providing a foundation for explanations of the behavior of role occupants, role theory suggests an approach to the study of political recruitment. If a role has certain expectations attached to it, then it seems reasonable to assume that individuals meeting the requirements proposed by these expectations will be more likely to fill the role than those who don't. If a city (its political leaders) expects its mayor to be passive and subservient to the city council, then it is unlikely that an aggressive initiator will move into the position. The limits of this kind of analysis are obvious; we might predict that certain types will *not* be recruited into certain roles, but it is much more difficult to predict who the occupants will be because other factors are involved. In addition, role expectations may change, and the competitors for the position may be instrumental in changing them. This is another kind of role learning—by the outsiders. We have already mentioned its opposite—learning by the role occupant.

Our discussion of role theory would be misleading if we did not articulate the problems that every political scientist will become aware of as he uses this approach. First of all, given the complexity of most role networks, the question must always be asked: Can the roles in a particular situation be reduced to a manageable number that still describes with some accuracy the behavior involved? This leads to a second question: Are there other kinds of nonrole variables that might influence behavior and that cannot be included within a role approach? In other words, can role theory do the job by itself?

SMALL GROUP THEORY

There is another approach that begins with the same basic assumption as role theory—that the individual political actor's behavior cannot be understood outside of a social context. But while role theory tends to emphasize the impact of formal institutional positions, the topic of this section, small group theory, tends to view the social context less formally. To be perfectly fair, it should be pointed out that small group theory is not applied to every political situation. It is viewed by its supporters as applicable only to a certain type of decision-making situation—the task group.[8]

The main point is that when a group of decision makers get together, the decision they make will often be the result of the interaction among various individuals, rather than the individuals' own decisions. That is, one cannot understand political behavior in the small group simply by knowing the characteristics of those who make up the group; the group setting is the crucial factor. This is a move away from strict micro-individualism toward a middle-level macro approach.

People spend a portion of their political lives in or being influenced by groups. It is the latter case that has been studied most often by political

---

[8] The best introduction to small group theory is Dorwin Cartwright and Alvin Zander, eds., *Group Dynamics* (New York: Harper & Row, 1968); for applications to politics, see Sidney Verba, *Small Groups and Political Behavior: A Study of Leadership* (Princeton, N.J.: Princeton University Press, 1961).

scientists; as we have seen, one of the main agents of socialization is the peer group. However, this is not the kind of group that interests the small group theorist. Instead, it is the aforementioned task group, a small number of people who have come together to do something—solve a problem, make a decision, map out a strategy. It is immediately apparent how many political situations fall into this category—the Politburo, the National Security Council, the Revolutionary Council; our list has no end. Equally important, it includes special ad hoc groups called together to solve a particular problem.

According to the small group theorist, every group has two faces, one formal, the other informal. The former has to do with the structure, the official chain of command; the latter with relationships that develop among the participants outside the formal structure. While recognizing the importance of both, it is the latter that receives most of the small group theorist's attention. Research has indicated that it helps to know whether the decision-making group has an authoritarian structure (a single dominant leader), a democratic structure (one who facilitates but does not dominate), or a laissez-faire (no leader at all) structure. But, in most cases, it is more telling to examine the social and psychological relationships that develop among the participants.

There are several theoretical cornerstones for the small group approach to politics. First is *field theory,* a set of assumptions made famous by social psychologist Kurt Lewin.[9] Field theory takes a gestalt or holistic view of the group; each group has a character of its own, not reducible to its individual members. This is analogous to the holistic notion of national character; nations and small groups can react to the environment, they can change and learn. The group is something unto itself. Few contemporary small group theorists go this far in attributing holistic properties to the objects of their attention. But the spirit of field theory is there; decisions are largely the result of the group atmosphere.

Another theoretical strain is more appropriate to an understanding of the small group approach. At its core, such an approach is micro-functional; that is, the assumption is made that groups perform a number of psychological functions for their members. Most important, these functions often become more important to the group participants than the stated task of the group. The functions most often mentioned are *reality creation* (giving people a

---

[9] Kurt Lewin, *Field Theory in Social Science* (London: Tavistock, 1952).

sense of what the world is like), *affiliation* (being with other people and receiving affection) and *a sense of security* (defense against a hostile environment). People who come to a group with any or all of these psychological needs may find satisfaction in group participation. Thus, administrators who come together in the midst of a severe policy crisis to solve a particular problem may be affected more by the feeling of mutual reassurance than by the demands of the real-world problem.

To see how this set of ideas works in the analysis of political behavior, let us turn our attention to one of its more interesting applications. In his book *Victims of Groupthink,* Irving Janis argues that many well-known political decisions have been made within what he calls a "groupthink atmosphere."[10]

Groupthink describes a small group situation where the psychological functions provided by the group become more important than the stated task of the group. Janis argues that in a cohesive decision-making group, that is, one made of those with common interests, there is always the danger that the decision makers will fall into the trap of unconsciously making proposals that they think will please their colleagues. The group begins to value an atmosphere of agreement more than rational decisions resulting from a full, open, and critical discussion of the issues. Most persons in the group monitor their own words and thoughts to maintain the appropriate mood. Those who become critical in a meeting are brought back into line or isolated by self-appointed mind-guards.

The significance of his approach lies, Janis believes, in its ability to explain decisions made by groups of highly experienced and intelligent political actors which, in retrospect, had no chance of success. In Janis's words, they are "fiascos"; examples are the Bay of Pigs invasion, the escalation of the Korean War in 1950, the failure to anticipate the attack on Pearl Harbor, and the escalation of the war in Vietnam. Janis's characterizations suggest the tone of his analysis: "A Perfect Failure," "Why the Fortress Slept," "How Could It Happen?".

There is no doubt in Janis's mind that groupthink leads to defective decision making. No critical analysis is made, no outside advice is sought, and few alternatives are considered, and all because group members refuse to upset the congenial atmosphere. A cohesive group that is under pressure, an

---

[10] Irving Janis, *Victims of Groupthink* (Boston: Houghton Mifflin, 1972).

administration that has lost public confidence, both are more likely to experience groupthink. As discussion moves around the table, the participants find comfort and reassurance in their apparent agreement.

Janis's approach is a classic example of small group theory, because its central assumption is that, under certain conditions, decision makers in a group behave differently than they would as individuals outside the group. The group decision is everyone's decision, yet no one's decision.

CONCLUSION

In this chapter, we have considered several approaches to the study of politics, which bridge the gap between the micro approaches of the prior three chapters and the macro approaches of the final three. While not as imposing as some theories or as widely used as others, role theory and small group theory have proven useful as intermediate models of political behavior.

Theories of power distribution

IN a previous chapter, power was examined as a typical political concept. In this chapter, we examine several approaches that make power their central concept. Each concentrates on the question: How is power distributed? This concern is at the heart of many definitions of politics. Who gets what implies that the answer to the question must begin with who has power. If politics is the process by which values are distributed, then the main factor affecting the distribution is power. Power is not only a classic concept in political thought, but it has become a cornerstone of several important modern approaches.

While all distributive models begin with the assumption that power is at the heart of the political process, they differ in regard to how power is typically distributed within the political system. We will spend most of our time on group theory and its close relative, pluralism; they assume that power is widely distributed throughout many societies and tends to be centered in groups. To show that there is another position, we include a brief discussion of elite theory; it claims that power is always concentrated in the hands of a small minority, the elite.

From their different assumptions about how power is distributed, each approach returns to the opening contention, that if one knows who or what has power, the rest of the political system will fall into place.

THE GROUP APPROACH

Most approaches to the study of politics have been borrowed by political scientists from other disciplines. Systems theory and functional analysis are largely the products of sociology and anthropology; game theory was developed by economists and mathematicians; and psychologists are responsible for learning theory. Group theory, on the other hand, is primarily "home grown." Beginning with the groundbreaking work of Arthur Bentley in 1908, group theory has been developed and applied almost exclusively by political scientists or social scientists interested in political phenomena.[1] Thus, one question that is relevant in the analysis of many approaches—Is it applicable to politics?—is not as significant in evaluating group theory. As the authors of a recent methodological analysis of political science put it, "Emphasis on the group takes us right to the heart of the discipline."[2]

The significance of the group in the study of politics

We needn't spend much time working out a definition of "group," for there seems to be a fairly widespread consensus among political scientists about what they mean when they use the term. Most agree that a political group exists when men with shared interests organize, interact, and seek goals through the political process. The key notions are "interaction" or "relationships", "interest", and "process" or "activity." David Truman, in his modern reinterpretation of Bentley, argues that such interactions *are* the group.[3]

Assuming there is basic agreement in regard to what a group is, let us see how group theorists line up on these methodologically important questions:

---

[1] Arthur Bentley, *The Process of Government* (Chicago: University of Chicago Press, 1908).

[2] Robert T. Golembiewski, William A. Welsh, and William J. Crotty, *A Methodological Primer for Political Scientists* (Chicago: Rand McNally, 1968), p. 121.

[3] David Truman, *The Governmental Process,* 2d ed. (New York: Alfred A. Knopf, 1971), p. 24.

What is the significance of the group in the political system? How useful is group theory to the study of politics? Answers to these questions can be placed into one of two categories. On the one hand are those who say that group activity *is* politics. The founding father, Arthur Bentley, takes this position. After stressing the importance of a research concentration on groups, Bentley writes: "When the groups are adequately stated, everything is stated. When I say everything I mean everything. The complete description will mean the complete science, in the study of social phenomena, as in any other field."[4] The argument is clear. A description of group activity is a description of politics. An approach to the study of politics must be based on the concept of group; hence, the indispensability of group theory.

The second kind of group theorist is less parochial in characterizing his approach. He retains the basic assumption that group behavior is at the center of politics, but he is not ready to view a description of political groups as equivalent to a description of all politics. The following statement of David Truman is similar to Bentley's, but one senses a shift toward a more moderate position: "We have argued, in fact, that the behaviors that constitute the process of government cannot be adequately understood apart from the groups, especially the organized and potential interest groups, which are operative at any point in time."[5] This implicitly asserts that not all political behavior is group behavior, although the activities that we identify as political can ultimately be explained by facts about group behavior.

Truman, for instance, does not completely dismiss the significance of the individual in politics. "We do not wish . . . to deny that individual differences exist or that there is evidence to support the notion of individuality."[6] This, however, does not imply that the completely unaffiliated individual has much impact on political decisions. What Truman seems to say is that different individuals behave differently in the same group. Thus, the assumption is made that groups are the basic element of politics and individualistic factors are important only in a group context. "It follows that the personality of any reasonably normal individual is not wholly accounted for by any single group affiliation. This proposition not only must be accepted; it must be a central element in any satisfactory explanation of the political process in group

---

[4] Bentley, *Process of Government,* pp. 208–9.
[5] Truman, *Governmental Process,* p. 502.
[6] Ibid., p. 49.

terms.''[7] Individuals exist, and they are not described solely in terms of their membership in a group. It is more realistic to view the individual as an entity with a distinctive character moving in and out of several groups or being a member of several groups simultaneously. Thus, Truman can allow for the individual and, at the same time, develop a group theory of politics without contradiction, because while the individual is important, the basic element of politics is the group.

Bentley, however, rejects the usefulness of individualistic concepts in the study of politics. Since there is no way to get at them, attitudes, beliefs, and other psychological traits are mere ''soul stuff.''[8] We can only study political processes, and the only processes we can observe are those of groups. Again, we reach the conclusion that politics is group behavior.

Another way to look at the difference between interpretations of group theory is in terms of the individualist-holist controversy, which we have referred to in earlier chapters.[9] Truman is an individualist in that he does not view the properties of groups as emergent. A political group is made up of individuals and of relationships between individuals. This is a point that should be stressed, for it leads to the realization that one need not be a holist to advocate a group approach to politics. The philosophical position that a group is no more than the sum of its parts is compatible with the research strategy that views group behavior as the most useful unit of analysis.

Bentley, on the other hand, is closer to the holist position, and therefore represents those group theorists who view the group as the stuff of politics both philosophically (methodologically) and strategically. Few contemporary political scientists who employ the group approach make the holistic assumption. They are not necessarily conscious individualists, but they would probably react negatively to Bentley's position that ''there are no political phenomena except group phenomena.''

The major question that concerns the group theorist is: How do groups behave in the political system? He is not methodologically interested in the internal makeup or processes of groups except in how they influence the behavior of groups in the political process. Since politics is ultimately explained in terms of relationships between groups as they make claims on

---

[7] Ibid.

[8] Bentley, *Process of Government*.

[9] Ibid. See especially chapter 2.

each other and compete for the values of the society, only those characteristics of groups that are relevant to this kind of activity are studied. The resulting model of politics might be labeled "macro-atomic" or, perhaps more accurately, "molecular," for the political process is viewed as a system of bounded and somewhat compact groups attracting and repelling each other in continual competition.

While this characterization of the group approach explains its basic shape, it does not take us very far. Are we to assume, for instance, that group theorists fail to include the governmental decision-making process in their models of politics? They do talk about government; but they view the role or functions of the government (defined as the legal institutions of the state) in the political system in different ways.

There are two basic positions in regard to this question. The first, and the one that Bentley advocates, claims that government is a mere register of group pressures. "The official procedures of government are techniques through which interest groups operate rather than independent forces in the political process."[10] Thus, groups compete, pursue their interests, and government rings up the results indicating who has won and who has lost. It is obvious that the significance of government is de-emphasized in this interpretation. At best, a congress or a parliament is one group among many. Bentley admits this. He concludes that governmental institutions have interests of their own.

This realization, which Bentley feels is of no great importance, opens the door to the second interpretation of the role of government in a group model of politics. The fact that Congress or the presidency or a court is as much a group as an interest group is stressed; each is a part of the competitive political process. But this significant assumption leads to a more significant assertion about the role of government. If, say, the Senate has its own interests, then it follows that it is not merely a political cash register, an inert mechanical computer recording the interests of other groups or the balance of power among them. Government instead takes an *active* role in tipping the balance. Most group theorists today would probably argue that the governmental decision-making apparatus is the most powerful group or set of groups in the political system. The resulting model of politics is the same molecular one, but now there is a dominant central molecule, government.

---

[10] Bentley, *Process of Government.*

That David Truman views government and interest groups as significantly different is evident in the following passage: "An interest group is a shared-attitude group that makes certain claims upon other groups in the society. If and when it makes its claims through or upon any of the institutions of government it becomes a political interest group."[11]

A political group is characterized by its contact with government. This implies that not all groups are political. A labor union bargaining with industry is not political until it leaves the bargaining table and appeals to Congress, the President, or the courts. Thus, referring back to the discussion of politics in Chapter 2, we can conclude that a group theorist like Truman limits the scope of political science to group activity occurring around the official institutions of government. This is broader than it might seem, for two of the institutions that groups work through are elections and public opinion. But some group activity lies outside politics.

Governmental institutions are groups of a special kind. They are groups because they have interests and compete with other groups. Consider the struggle that occurs among the branches of government. On one side, they stand out in relation to other groups because of their position and role in the political process. Government regulates the group struggle and determines the balance of power within the system. But government also formulates the rules that somewhat determine the shape of the struggle. This all assumes that governmental decisions result from the interplay of the demands and objectives of interest groups and governmental institutions.

If politics is primarily the activity of groups as they make claims on government, then a group model of politics should be able to include or account for most political phenomena. Let us now examine some of the major concepts and relationships from which a model might be built.

The group theorist assumes that the primary objective of every political group is the successful realization of its objectives, namely, the satisfaction of its demands. This implies that a group theory must be able to identify the interests of groups if it is to account for the outcomes of the political process.

An equivalent way of saying "All groups try to achieve their objectives" is "All groups attempt to acquire power—to influence decisions in their favor." However one phrases it, this is only a beginning. Concepts must be

---

[11] Truman, *Governmental Process,* p. 37.

formulated and hypotheses generated that describe how power is sought and exercized and how, in consequence, decision are made.

THE CONCEPT OF ACCESS

The central concept is "access." As Truman argues, no interest group can influence decisions unless it gains access to decision points within the government. Thus, Truman concludes that access "becomes the facilitating intermediate objective of political interest groups. The development and improvement of such access is a common denominator of the tactics of all of them."[12] This is a commonsensical notion: If a group has nowhere in government to make its demands, it is difficult to imagine it influencing decisions. Access has a sound empirical basis. As it is used by a group theorist such as Truman, we are able to tell when and at what point an interest group has access. To achieve its objectives, an interest group will seek to influence decisions. To do this, it will have to work with, on, or through governmental decision makers. If it is successful, it has gained access, and the point of contact between the group and the decision makers is the access point.

But if access is to serve as the central concept of a model of politics, it must be more than empirically sound. It must also be useful in organizing, describing, and perhaps explaining political phenomena. There is prima facie evidence that access is useful and has *systematic import.*

Let us note some of the functions that access can perform in a group model of politics. First, it provides the all-important linkage between groups and government (realizing that governmental institutions are groups). This function must be performed in a group model because of the model's emphasis on the influence of groups on political decision making.

If the model is to generate hypotheses, access must be related to other concepts. One kind of relationship might make access the antecedent condition or independent variable in a generalization that makes power or influence the dependent variable. Thus, we might be able to explain why interest group *A* has more influence than interest group *B* by demonstrating that *A* has more access to government.

On the other hand, access is a dependent variable to be explained. We

---

[12] Ibid., p. 264.

would like to know why some groups have more access than others. Group theorists usually cite such factors as *group cohesion* (how much of its individual members' total loyalty it commands) and *organization* as important determinants of access. The more cohesive and highly organized a group is, the more access it has. Another crucial factor in group models of politics is the *status* of the group. David Truman says, "Perhaps the most basic factor affecting access is the position of the group or its spokesman in the social structure. . . . The deference accorded a high-status group not only facilitates the acceptance of its propaganda but also eases its approach to the government."[13] Other factors which might be cited are the group's *leadership*, its *wealth*, and its *geographical distribution*. As one proliferates the list of variables that might influence access, we see more of its usefulness as a central concept. Most of the important concepts used in the group approach seem to be related to access. It is truly a centralizing concept in that it is the link between independent variables, such as status, and dependent variables, such as influence and, ultimately, political decisions.

Implicit in all that we have said is the fact that "access" is a comparative concept. Remember that Truman calls it a common denominator. This means that all interest groups will at least have the seeking of access in common. This opens the door to the possibility of comparing or ranking groups according to how much access they have. If access is a central concept, then in comparing access we will also be indirectly comparing influence and effectiveness. This is the objective of the group approach.

EVALUATING THE GROUP APPROACH

While group theory seems a useful (in terms of suggestiveness) approach to the study of politics, it is not without criticism. Let us conclude our analysis of the approach by evaluating several of these criticisms. We have already mentioned one in a different context. It claims that group theory omits one important set of variables, namely, the characteristics of individuals. But as we pointed out then, the political scientist does not have to be a holist assuming the existence of emergent group properties to base a study of politics on the group. Most group theorists do not reject the importance, let

---

[13] Ibid., p. 265.

alone the existence, of individuals in politics. They only state that it is a wise strategy to stay at the group level. This criticism probably misses the mark.

There is another criticism that argues the other side of the coin. It claims that the group approach is wrong and misleading in not considering the nation, the state, or society. Instead, the argument states that group theory studies a limited range of political phenomena, never thinking about the supergroup of which they are all a part. This often leads to the related claim that group theory cannot properly handle the notion of "public" or "national interest." One reaction to this criticism is well articulated by David Truman: "In developing a group interpretation of politics . . . we do not need to account for a totally inclusive interest because one does not exist."[14] Instead, what we call the public interest is the result of the group struggle. Most group theorists would reject the idea that a public interest exists apart from or independent of the political process. Groups compete, governments make decisions, and the output can be labeled the public interest. But this is a derivative concept with no emergent status of its own. Thus, as Truman suggests, one should not be criticized for ignoring a nonexistent entity.

The assumptions of group theory go hand in hand with those of a broader model, ideology of politics. Pluralism is used both as a description of certain political systems and as a recommendation about how others ought to be structured. The theorist of pluralism argues that some political systems, like the United States, are made up of a number of competing groups, each representing a significant political, social, or economic interest. In a pluralist system, power is widely distributed and political decisions are the result of give and take.

ELITIST THEORY

Although it has had a significant impact on 20th-century political and social thought, elitist theory is probably not as methodologically rich as pluralism-group theory. It is included here to suggest how basic the question of power distribution is in the development of approaches to political analysis.

---

[14] Ibid., p. 51. For an analysis of various interpretations of "public interest," see Glendon Schubert, *The Public Interest* (New York: Free Press, 1962).

The basic contention of elitism is that every human organization is controlled by a small, cohesive minority.[15] Power is not only distributed unevenly but very unevenly. Theorists of elitism agree that the development of elites is inevitable—pluralism is a myth. Power can never be widely distributed.

The attempt to explain this "Iron Law of Oligarchy" brings out the differences between some of the elitist schools.[16] Some are micro theorists. They suggest that elites develop because of the unequal distribution of human qualities, like intelligence, courage, and will; only a few are equipped to lead, and they will rise to the top in any organization. Other elitists are macro theorists in basing the growth of elites on the notions of dominant cultural values or dominant institutions. Taking the first approach, each society has a value system that defines what and who are valuable in the society; the elite will always be drawn from this value system. Thus, in a militaristic culture, the generals rule. In a religious culture, the clergy is in charge. When a society values economic activities above all else, business leaders gain control. Some elitists focus on institutions rather than values. The results are theoretically similar: a macro approach which proposes that elites will be drawn from a society's dominant institutions.[17]

For political scientists, one of the most interesting aspects of the elite approach is its downplaying of political elites in the power system. Most elitists argue that ultimate power in most political systems is held, not by governmental leaders, but by the elites from other areas—economic, military, and religious. Most elite theories reduce public policymaking to one nonpolitical factor or another.

---

[15] The best short introduction to elitist theory is Kenneth Prewitt and Alan Stone, *The Ruling Elites* (New York: Harper & Row, 1973).

[16] This is the famous phrase of the Swiss student of elites, Robert Michels.

[17] This was the basis for the best-known modern elite theory, that of C. Wright Mills, in *The Power Elite* (New York: Oxford University Press, 1956).

Systems theory and functional analysis

TWO of the more popular methods of organizing thought in social science are *systems theory* and *functional analysis*. The latter is an offshoot of the former, and so they can be placed in the same methodological category. The basic point is that functional analysis assumes the existence of a system, and it is reasonable to begin with a brief consideration of systems theory.

SYSTEMS THEORY

Like many approaches in social science, systems theory has a commonsensical appeal. It is natural to think of phenomena as parts of wholes. For many people, it is difficult to conceive of an entity that does not fit somewhere.

This is the starting point of political systems theorists. They begin by assuming that political phenomena can best be analyzed by viewing them as parts of a systematic whole. Morton Kaplan, one of the foremost users of systems theory in the study of international politics, asserts that "a scientific politics can develop only if the materials of politics are treated in terms of systems of action.''[1] This may be a bit strong for those who are not systems theorists, but even they might admit the utility of a rudimentary notion of a system as a starting point for theory construction in political science.

The commonsensical appeal of systems models is not a phenomenon unique to contemporary social science. Plato and Aristotle viewed the polis as a political system made up of interrelated elements. More than 300 years ago, Thomas Hobbes wrote: ''By systems I understand any number of men joined in one interest or one business.''[2] While this is a primitive and perhaps unacceptable definition, at least it demonstrates the historical pervasiveness of the concept of system.

The components of systems

Systems theorists agree that every system has several components. First, it has elements that are clearly identifiable. The planets and the sun are the elements of the solar system. If we are treating the family as a system, the individual members would be its elements. The elements of a political system could be individuals, groups, or nations, depending on the scope of the system.

We don't, however, call every set of elements a system. Something else is needed. This something else is a set of relationships among the elements. A family is not a system because it is made up of identifiable elements, but because the elements interact, because they are interdependent. The characteristic of interaction prevents us from labeling every set of elements as a system. Systems theory allows us to make a methodological distinction between, let us say, all the people who happen to be in a department store at the same time and an interest group made up of a set of interacting and interdependent people.

If we are going to talk about a system, we must be able to define its

---

[1] Morton Kaplan, *System and Process in International Politics* (New York: John Wiley & Sons, 1957), p. 4. Other basic expositions of the systems approach can be found in David Easton's works: ''An Approach to the Analysis of Political Systems,'' *World Politics,* 9 (1957), pp. 383–400; *A Framework for Political Analysis* (Englewood Cliffs, N.J.: Prentice-Hall, 1956); and *A Systems Analysis of Political Life* (New York: John Wiley & Sons, 1965). For the best ''neutral'' analysis of various types of systems theories, see H. V. Wiseman, *Political Systems: Some Sociological Approaches* (New York: Praeger Publishers, 1966).

[2] Thomas Hobbes, *Leviathan,* chapter 22.

extent—where it ends and where other systems begin. Every system has boundaries that ought to be specified by the systems theorist. It makes little sense to speak of a system developing or changing or influencing other systems if its boundaries are not at least roughly described.

In general, every system has three characteristic components: identifiable elements, relationships among the elements, and boundaries. Also most systems will have subsystems. That is, the elements and relationships of a system will break down into smaller systems. For instance, the Congress is a subsystem of the U.S. political system, the Senate is a subsystem of Congress, and the Foreign Relations Committee is a subsystem of the Senate. One implication of this analysis is that systems exist at a number of levels. In addition, the indication is that every system has an environment—there are always other systems "on the outside," so to speak. The political scientist slices the conglomeration at the appropriate level, treating smaller systems as subsystems and the larger ones as possible environmental conditions.

The systems theorist who adds some substance to this rather bare frame usually does so by talking about the inputs and outputs of political systems.[3] Inputs include demands—indications from the political system's environment of what is wanted, needed, and required—and supports—the extent to which the society is willing to consider the system and/or its leaders legitimate. Legitimacy is one of the most significant concepts to flow from the systems approach. It suggests that political leaders and their government can lose authority, that is, the mass public's acceptance of their right to rule, if they are unresponsive to the demands of the people. Outputs boil down to various aspects of the policymaking process—rule making, rule interpretation, and rule enforcement. These concepts are significant because they describe how a systems model accounts for linkage between the system and its environment, or between systems. For example, we might view the decision-making apparatus of the United States (legislatures, executive branch, and courts) as a political system, and then study its inputs from the larger social system and its outputs for the social system. Or the entire set of elements—inputs, decisions, and outputs—could be viewed as a system having certain relationships (inputs and outputs) with its environment, which, in this case, would be the international society. Or one could move in

---

[3] These notions are developed in Easton, "An Approach to the Analysis of Political Systems."

the other direction, viewing, let us say, a congressional committee as a system with inputs from, decisions, and outputs for the larger political system. The point is that input-output analysis provides the conceptual basis for the notion of linkage between systems.

There is one other concept that is basic to systems theory. It is the notion of "feedback." Feedback refers to the influence of outputs on inputs and ultimately on decisions. An interest group makes demands (inputs) on Congress, asking for the passage of a particular bill. Despite these demands, Congress defeats the bill (output). There will be feedback resulting finally in a reaction of the interest group to Congress's decision. There will probably be new inputs, perhaps even the withholding of support, including civil disobedience. Congress then learns of the results of its decision through the change in inputs, and perhaps modifies its behavior.

"Feedback" is important to systems theory because it provides a kind of continuity. It builds into the approach a method for handling the two-way relationship between inputs and outputs. The behavior of systems then can be viewed as a continuous process where outputs are reactions to inputs and inputs are influenced by outputs.

The uses of systems theory

For political scientists who use it, systems theory is primarily a way of looking at phenomena—it is in many ways a state of mind. The commitment is made to concentrate on the system and its behavior, including the interaction of its elements, but not the characteristics of the elements. Systems theory is most accurately placed within the category of macro, as opposed to micro, approaches to politics. Now, as it is used by political scientists, systems theory seems to be of heuristic, not explanatory, significance. Thus, the label "theory" is a misnomer; it is much more accurate to think of the systems approach as a conceptual scheme, perhaps as a state of mind or general orientation that serves as a jumping-off place for more specialized political research.

The systems approach generates two basic sets of questions: First, how does the system handle inputs and outputs? What are the relationships between inputs and outputs? Second, how does a system cope with its environment? What kinds of system behavior lead to system survival or maintenance, what kinds lead to system deterioration or death? The second set of questions is the major concern of functional analysis, the more highly developed, and it would seem more useful, relative of systems theory.

FUNCTIONAL ANALYSIS

Ernest Nagel has said that "In the judgment of many students a comprehensive theory of social phenomena is most likely to be achieved within the framework of systematically 'functional' analyses of social phenomena."[4] While not yet the major school of thought in political science that it is in sociology and anthropology, functionalism has nevertheless come into its own as an important approach to analyzing political phenomena.[5] The label "functional analysis" is applied to a number of activities and styles of analysis. Functional analyses are used to generate hypotheses and organize existing knowledge of the political system, and at times a functional explanation is proposed to account for political phenomena. The feature which characterizes all of them is a primary focus on the functions of political systems.

Strictly speaking, the functional approach is concerned with system maintenance—how political systems survive over time. This is how functionalism ties in with the more general systems approach. However, while an assumption of system maintenance may underlie all functional analyses, practically speaking, many of them go no further than a consideration of the effects that certain variables have on a system. Thus, we should not expect every functional analysis to explain why a system is maintained. However, since this is the ultimate objective, we can legitimately criticize a proposed functional explanation if it is going in the wrong direction or no direction at all, even though it is not yet dealing directly with system maintenance.

In its simplest form, functional analysis contains the following elements: a system, variables, and arguments demonstrating the effects of the variables

---

[4] Ernest Nagel, *The Structure of Science* (New York: Harcourt Brace Jovanovich, 1961), p. 520.

[5] The main influence on functional analysis in political science has been the work of sociologist Talcott Parsons. His basic theoretical work is *The Social System* (New York: Free Press, 1951). For an application to politics see " 'Voting' and the Equilibrium of the American Political System," in Eugene Burdick and Arthur Brodbeck, eds., *American Voting Behavior* (New York: Free Press, 1959).

on the system. The fully developed system-maintaining variety has the additional feature of arguments showing how the variables contribute to the maintenance of the system by performing certain necessary functions. Thus, the analysis is called functional because of an assertion that certain conditions (functions) are necessary for the continuance of the system.

The major methodological requirements of this approach are rather simple. First, the system referred to must be explicitly defined and its boundaries clearly indicated; otherwise, it will be impossible to determine if the system is being maintained or changed. Looking at it from another standpoint, if one wants to examine the influence of a variable on a system, one has to first have the nature and extent of the system clearly in mind. This leads to a second requirement. The influencing variables must be empirically conceptualized; they must be defined in terms of testable properties of the world. Finally, in the case of system-maintenance explanations, the necessary conditions or functions that the variables are supposed to perform must be empirically defined.

Types of functional analysis

Having made these general comments about the methodological foundations of functional analysis, let us examine several of the activities that are commonly assigned this label. The first has been labeled "simple-functional" or "eclectic" by William Flanigan and Edwin Fogelman.[6] It is probably the most widespread of those activities that constitute "functional analysis." Eclectic functionalism involves the listing of activities that an institution, individual, or nation engages in. Thus, Clinton Rossiter has listed the functions of the President,[7] Herman Finer has listed the functions of the legislator,[8] and Frank J. Sorauf has listed the functions of political parties.[9]

---

[6] William Flanigan and Edwin Fogelman, "Functional Analysis," in James C. Charlesworth, ed., *Contemporary Political Analysis* (New York: Free Press, 1967), pp. 72–73.

[7] Clinton Rossiter, *The American Presidency* (New York: Harcourt Brace Jovanovich, 1960), chapter 1.

[8] Herman Finer, *The Theory and Practice of Modern Government* (New York: Holt, Rinehart & Winston, 1949), pp. 379–84.

[9] Frank J. Sorauf, *Political Parties in the American System* (Boston: Little, Brown, 1964), pp. 2–6.

"Function," is equated with "action." Ernest Nagel has characterized this activity as an attempt to "denote a more or less inclusive set of processes or operations within (or manifested by) a given entity, without indication of the various effects these activities produce either upon the entity or any other."[10] When the functional approach is used in this manner, its intention is not to explain the maintenance of a political system. Eclectic functionalism is more of a descriptive enterprise. The central concept of "function" is used to organize the behavior of political actors and institutions.

However, eclectic functionalism sometimes becomes intermingled with a more promising activity. For instance, Sorauf's listing of party functions carries the implication that they have some effect on the political system— that is, they politically educate and socialize the public. We can call this kind of functional approach "system-affecting" to distinguish it from the more basic and important "system-maintaining" variety. There is no mention of the activity or function, X, contributing to the maintenance of a system. It may be doing just that. But there is no claim that the system needs X to survive, only that X has some effect on it. It is clear that system-affecting arguments can often become system-maintaining if further analysis is carried out. Perhaps another example will clarify this point.

In his study of political party behavior in Michigan, Samuel Eldersveld makes much of the functional consequences of parties; in our language, this means the effects the parties have on the political system of Michigan.[11] Thus, Eldersveld concludes a section of his analysis with these words:

> We have seen how party effort is associated with increased voting turnout, strengthening party identifications and loyalties, and developing attitudes favorable to working for the party operation. In addition, our analysis revealed that exposure to the party results in greater interest in foreign affairs, national domestic affairs, and local public affairs.[12]

These are the findings of a study that is based upon the system-affecting functional approach. The activities of the parties have an effect on the nature of the political system. In the body of his study, Eldersveld presents statistical evidence, often in generalizations—"party exposure, combined no doubt

---

[10] Nagel, *Structure of Science*, p. 523.

[11] Samuel Eldersveld, *Political Parties: A Behavioral Analysis* (Skokie, Ill.: Rand McNally, 1964).

[12] Ibid., pp. 541–42.

with other influences and interlinked with them, seems to be related to high voting participation''—to substantiate such claims.[13] Thus, we see that the generalizations generated by the system-affecting approach are not unique. They differ from other hypotheses only in that the dependent variable is "the nature of the system" (in Eldersveld's case, a political system with high voting participation).

We said that system-affecting arguments often become, implicitly or explicitly, system-maintaining arguments. That is, the initial demonstration that element X has Y effects on system S frequently results in the claim that X contributes to S's maintenance. Thus, we find Eldersveld making such statements as this: "In strengthening the foundations for political conensus, the party effort is also functional to the system."[14] Here, we see a shift in emphasis to explaining the *maintenance* of the political system—this is clearly what "functional" means in this context. Using Eldersveld's analysis as a basis, we can succinctly summarize the nature of such an explanation: "A political system S requires for its continued existence, among other things, a certain degree of consensus among its members; political parties contribute to the realization and reinforcement of such consensus; therefore, the maintenance of the system is partially explained."[15] Political party activity is a partially sufficient condition, not a necessary one. The most general laws upon which the explanation might be based are: (1) consensus is necessary for a political system; (2) increased party activity tends to strengthen consensus. Thus, it can be seen why "increased party activity" is a partial (there may be other influencing factors at work at the same time) and sufficient (it is enough, in combination with the other factors to strengthen consensus, yet there may be other elements that could take its place) condition. While it tends to produce consensus, it is possible for other factors to do the job.

Another example of system-maintaining explanation can be found in Donald Matthews's discussion of senatorial folkways, because the maintenance or existence of the Senate is partially accounted for by the existence of the folkways.[16] Thus, "apprenticeship," "courtesy," and the like help

---

[13] Ibid., p. 467.

[14] Ibid., p. 542.

[15] Ibid. This is a compact statement of Eldersveld's argument.

[16] Donald Matthews, *U.S. Senators and Their World* (New York: Vintage Books, 1960).

keep the Senate a concern. We see the same pattern here as was manifested in Eldersveld's explanations. To operate, the Senate has to have certain functions performed. The folkways perform them, and so the Senate continues to function. In Matthews's words,

> These folkways we have suggested are highly functional to the Senate social system since they provide motivation for the performance of vital duties and essential modes of behavior which, otherwise, would go unrewarded. . . . Without these folkways, the Senate could hardly operate with its present organization and rules.[17]

The last clause implies a definition of the political system known as the "Senate." It is maintained with the help of the functions performed by the folkways.

A final example can be cited to indicate just how general this sort of analysis can be. Gabriel Almond has formulated one of the best known and most influential system-maintaining models.[18] It is a general model because he attempts to describe the main political functions of all political systems. He begins by making a list of seven functions that the political system performs for the more inclusive social system.[19] Almond argues that all political systems perform these functions; he calls this phenomena "the universality of the political functions."[20] But what is important for us is the fact that political structures, both within a society and in different societies, can perform the same functions. For instance, in modern political systems, interest groups are the primary performers of the function of "interest articulation." But, "We find in Indonesia that the few and relatively poorly organized trade unions or business associations are not the important interest-articulating structures, that we have to look at the bureaucracy, status groups, kinship and lineage groups and anomic phenomena to discover how interests are articulated."[21] Thus the same pattern appears: The social system requires that certain functions be performed for its continued existence,

---

[17] Ibid., p. 116.

[18] Gabriel Almond, "Introduction: A Functional Approach to Comparative Politics," in Gabriel Almond and James S. Coleman, *The Politics of the Developing Areas* (Princeton, N.J.: Princeton University Press, 1960), pp. 3–64.

[19] Ibid., p. 17. Almond distinguishes between input and output functions. The former include "political socialization and recruitment, interest articulation, interest aggregation, and political communication." The latter include "rule-application and rule-adjudication."

[20] Ibid., pp. 12–17.

[21] Ibid., p. 13.

and political systems perform them *in various ways*. Here is a clear manifestation of the sufficient (partially) and unnecessary nature of system-maintaining arguments. Interest groups articulate interests in the United States, but not in Indonesia.

We can conclude this section with a favorable comment about system-affecting and system-maintaining approaches. Through their use, it is possible to generate hypotheses suggesting that various political institutions can partially explain "a feature of," "the existence of," or "the maintenance of" a political or social system. This is the most important and promising activity among those that are usually classified as functional.

Equilibrium analysis

A special type of system-maintaining explanation is often thought of as a distinct approach to political analysis. This is usually called equilibrium analysis, and it seems to be most widely used in the study of international relations. We will attempt to show that equilibrium analysis is a variation on the system-maintaining approach. The main task of the political scientist seems to be an analysis of how systems retain an equilibrium. Harold D. Lasswell and Abraham Kaplan have defined political equilibrium and also have implied its relationship to system-maintaining analysis. After speaking of systems and system-maintenance, they make the following observation: "The standpoint of equilibrium analysis directs inquiry to the isolation of such systems and investigation of the conditions of their maintenance: disturbances may lead to a reestablishment of equilibrium or the disruption of the system."[22] We might say that a system is maintained as long as it is in equilibrium.

However, some political scientiss have used equilibrium in another way. They assume or attempt to demonstrate that a political system has tendencies toward a steady state. Then, political behavior is explained through the application of the resulting theory. Hans Morgenthau's famous "balance of power" theory can be interpreted as such an undertaking. Morgenthau sees a movement toward equilibrium as one of the main characteristics of all

---

[22] Harold Lasswell and Abraham Kaplan, *Power and Society* (New Haven, Conn.: Yale University Press, 1950), p. xiv.

social systems made up of autonomous units.[23] His use of the concept "balance" implies that if there were a grouping of states that did not seek such a balance, they could not be engaged in international politics among themselves.[24] This is acceptable; but one may ask if anything empirical is being said, or is the law really a tautology? Quentin Gibson has noted that, "There is of course one infallible way of preserving a higher-level law and that is to make it true by definition."[25] Furthermore, "If a procedure of this kind is persisted with, it becomes clear that the alleged empirical law is one which could not be refuted under any conceivable circumstances."[26] This, in a sense, is why Morgenthau can eventually call the present bipolar international system a "new" balance of power, even though it diverges greatly from the traditional system upon which his theory is based. The upshot of all this is that while we may better understand what Morgenthau means by "international politics," his "law" can give us no information about the world—it can neither describe nor explain—for it is analytic, not empirical.

Our criticism of Morgenthau's theory implies an important feature of any would-be explanation based on an equilibrium theory. If a political system has a tendency toward equilibrium, it has ways of maintaining itself. This is why we are discussing equilibrium in this chapter. However, if "equilibrium" is to be employed in a meaningful way, we must be able to state that to a certain degree, the system in question tends to develop characteristics that perform its necessary functions; that it tends toward an equilibrium. This is what Carl Hempel has called an "hypothesis of self-regulation." It is the basic proposition required to make an equilibrium theory nomological and potentially useful. Most equilibrium theories do not state such a law, let alone provide it with empirical referents.

However, several political scientists have attempted to give the hypothesis of self-regulation empirical content, in preparation for its use in explanations. For instance, S. Sidney Ulmer has analyzed the voting behavior of Supreme Court justices using the Shapeley Shubik power index. His objective is the testing of the hypothesis that there is "equilibrium in certain

---

[23] Hans Morgenthau, *Politics among Nations* (New York: Alfred A. Knopf, 1960), p. 167.

[24] Ibid. Morgenthau states that "the balance of power and policies aiming at its preservation are . . . inevitable . . . in a society of sovereign states."

[25] Quentin Gibson, *The Logic of Social Enquiry* (London: Routledge & Kegan Paul, 1960), p. 121.

[26] Ibid.

behavior patterns in the Court."[27] Phillips Cutwright has, in a similar vein, searched for an equilibrium law of national political development. The hypothesis he statistically tests is that if a nation is underdeveloped, it will tend to improve its position, while an overdeveloped nation will make downward adjustments to bring itself into line.[28] This first calls for the discovery of an equilibrium point where all types of development are in balance. The difficulty of such an undertaking is obvious; but the *attempt* is what is important for our analysis, because it indicates that some political scientists realize that equilibrium theory requires an *empirical* law of self-regulation. We have seen the shortcomings of a theory that is not given empirical content.

One of the most interesting uses of equilibrium theory is in the explanation of revolutionary change. In this type of analysis, the emphasis is placed not on how political systems keep themselves in a state of balance, but on what causes them to lose their equilibrium and undergo revolutionary change. The most thorough development of this idea has been carried out by Chalmers Johnson.[29] His central hypothesis is that revolutions are largely the result of a "disequilibrated social system—a society which is changing and which is in need of further change if it is to continue to exist."[30] Disequilibrium is usually the result of a growing discrepancy between a society's value system and the other institutions of the society. Johnson argues that the source of change can be the value system or the social structure, and it can come from outside the system or start inside. To cite one example, the introduction of a new religion from a foreign culture might cause a rapid shift in mass attitudes. If the social structure doesn't adjust to the new set of values, the basis for greater turmoil is established. Within a disequilibrated social system, the factor that more often than not stimulates the revolution is "power deflation—the fact that during a period of change the integration of a system depends increasingly upon the maintenance and deployment of force by the occupants of the formal authority statuses."[31]

---

[27] S. Sidney Ulmer, "Homeostatic Tendencies in the United States Supreme Court," in S. Sidney Ulmer, ed., *Introductory Readings in Political Behavior* (Skokie, Ill.: Rand McNally, 1961), pp. 167–88.

[28] Phillips Cutwright, "National Political Development: Its Measurement and Social Correlates," in Nelson W. Polsby, Robert A. Dentler, and Paul A. Smith, eds., *Politics and Social Life* (Boston: Houghton Mifflin, 1963), pp. 569–82.

[29] Chalmers Johnson, *Revolutionary Change* (Boston: Little Brown, 1966).

[30] Ibid., p. 91.

[31] Ibid.

Functional-teleological analysis

Political scientists sometimes argue that a particular behavior pattern or institution is explained if they can demonstrate that it performs a necessary function for the political system. For instance, the origin and present nature of the interest group would be explained by showing that it performs the functions of interest articulation and integration, functions that have to be performed in every political system. If this kind of analysis helps the researcher sort out structures that might perform important functions, then it is of heuristic value. But as an explanation it is unsound.

Let us examine its methodological weak points. First of all, it is difficult enough to demonstrate that a certain function—interest articulation, for instance—is necessary for the maintenance of a system. But it is empirically conceivable. However, it is another thing to demonstrate that a particular political institution or activity is the only one that can perform the function. For it is always possible that another institution might perform the same function. We have already pointed out that, in assuming that different structures can perform the same function, the functional approach provides a foundation for meaningful comparative analysis. If it is true that a function is performed by different structures in different political systems, why is it not possible that the function is or could be performed by several *structures* within a political system?

An example might help clarify our argument. We will use Donald Matthews's study of the folkways of the Senate as a *point of departure*.[32] This usage of Matthews's analysis should be emphasized, for we are not claiming that he attempts the unsound kind of functional argument we are criticizing here. We will fit a part of the discussion folkways into a schema provided by philosopher of science Carl Hempel.[33] It is as follows:

1. At time *T, S* (the Senate) functions adequately in setting of kind *C* (under certain conditions).
2. *S* functions adequately in a setting of kind *C* only if a certain necessary condition *N* (adequate assignment of work loads) is satisfied.
3. If trait *i* (apprenticeship) were present in *S*, then, as an effect, condi-

---

[32] Matthews, *U.S. Senators.*

[33] Carl G. Hempel, "The Logic of Functional Analysis," in L. Gross, ed., *Symposium on Sociological Theory* (Evanston, Ill.: Row, Peterson, 1959), p. 301.

tion *N* would be satisfied.

4.   Therefore, at *T*, trait *i* is present in *S*.

In this way, the folkway of apprenticeship seems to be accounted for. However, it is not explained by showing that it contributes to the maintenance of the Senate. Now, apprenticeship may perform such a function. If such an argument were made, then we would be giving an explanation of the system, using the folkways as causal factors. Thus, the folkways help explain why the Senate continues to function. This is a sound system-maintenance explanation. However, we need only observe that the apprenticeship cannot be explained in the above manner because there might be other ways of assigning work loads. These would be, like apprenticeship, sufficient conditions for carrying out the requisite function. There is no way to demonstrate why apprenticeship has a preferred status. It is the possible existence of these "functional equivalents" that deprives the argument of explanatory power. Thus, we see why it is fair to say that the folkways can help explain the maintenance or nature of the Senate, while they cannot be explained on the grounds that they contribute system-maintenance. Perhaps it is now clear why this functional approach is sometimes labeled *teleological*. The present existence or nature of a political phenomenon is being explained by its end. It exists to perform function *X*. The influence of biology and physiology can be discerned in such social-scientific arguments. In other words, the same approach—the heart is explained on the basis of its blood-circulation function—has long been taken in these fields, and some political scientists have no doubt been impressed.

A tempting way out of this methodological bind is to make the folkways part of the definition of the Senate. This can be done if the Senate and its conditions *(C)* are not clearly described. Then, any functional alternative that is discovered can be dismissed as insignificant as the same system is no longer being referred to. The shortcoming of this tactic is that analytic statements tell us nothing about the world. Making the statement "the Senate has the structure apprenticeship" analytic removes it from the class of useful empirical generalizations. These difficulties have led some philosophers to the position articulated by Ernest Nagel: "The cognitive worth of functional explanations modeled on teleological explanations in physiology is therefore and in the main very dubious."[34]

---

[34] Nagel, *Structure of Science,* pp. 534–35.

There is another way to interpret some apparent teleological arguments so as to give them a sound logical structure. These are the arguments that refer to human purposes. A behavioral pattern is explained by demonstrating that an agent believes that something is functional either for himself or for a valued system, and then employing a law that describes what a person with such a belief and such an intention tends to do. Thus, we know why he performs or seeks it. For instance, referring again to Donald Matthews's study of Senate folkways, we might argue that they are desired by Senators. That is, the Senators believe that to function efficiently, the Senate cannot allow the public venting of personal animosities. Thus, they have intentionally adopted the folkway, "courtesy." The Senators consider the folkways functional for the Senate—they are a means to a desired end. This kind of argument falls within both the functional and intentional approaches. But the important point is that it is not teleological.

Communications theory

I T has been suggested that an important ingredient of the political process, communications, has been largely ignored in the theoretical literature of political science. Several political scientists have set out to correct this gap by developing models of politics based on this "missing ingredient." Karl Deutsch, the leading proponent of a communications approach to the study of politics, has pointed out that cybernetics, the science of communications and control, "represents a shift in the center of interest from drives to steering."[1] When applied to politics, this means an emphasis on *decisions, control,* and *communications,* rather than power, which has without a doubt been the primary, and at times exclusive, interest of political scientists.[2]

The communications theorist does not claim that communication is the only topic that should interest political scientists. However, quoting Deutsch once again, "It is communication, that is, the ability to transmit

---

[1] Karl Deutsch, *The Nerves of Government* (New York: Free Press, 1963), p. 76.

[2] Chapter 5 of this book discussed the concept of power.

messages and to react to them, that makes organizations,"[3] any thorough analysis of political organizations and systems must at least include a consideration of the role of communication.

The ultimate significance of a communications approach does not, however, lie in its concentration on communications but rather on the ability to describe and explain the behavior of political systems that follows from such concentration. More specifically, "communications is viewed as vital in implementing man's control of his environment."[4] This is the key point and the main contribution of the communications approach to the study of politics. Recall the stress in systems theory on inputs and outputs, and in functional analysis of the maintenance of systems. According to the approach now under consideration, it is through communications that inputs are received and acted upon, and outputs are generated by a system; in short, the effectiveness of a system—how well it handles the demands of its environment—can be measured in terms of its ability to accurately analyze messages from the environment and effectively transmit messages that express reactions.

It is through communications that a political system relates to and copes with its environment. A system is constantly bombarded with messages. It must be able to read them and react to them. This is the way a system achieves its goals, including self-maintenance. A quote from political scientist Robert C. North should clarify the communications theorist's conception of the political process: "Politics could not exist without communication, nor could wars be fought. In these terms a modern nation-state may be viewed essentially as a decision and control system which relies upon the exchange of messages in both its domestic affairs and its foreign relations."[5]

This conception of politics and its emphasis on communications is not surprising when one realizes that its major impetus comes from the already mentioned science of cybernetics. As conceived by its major developer, mathematician Norbert Wiener, cybernetics is the study of communication and control in all types of organizations, from machines to large-scale orga-

---

[3] Deutsch, *Nerves of Government,* p. 77.

[4] S. Sidney Ulmer, *Introductory Readings in Political Behavior* (Skokie, Ill.: Rand McNally, 1962), p. 397.

[5] Robert C. North, "The Analytical Prospects of Communications Theory," in James C. Charlesworth, ed., *Contemporary Political Analysis* (New York: Free Press, 1967), p. 301.

nizations.[6] The first significant advances were made in the development and study of the former. Cybernetics can be viewed as the attempt to apply knowledge gained of the workings of such self-monitoring devices as antiaircraft guns, thermostats, and electronic computers to analogous social systems. Communications theory in political science can be viewed as the application of the general approach of cybernetics to political situations.

THE CONCEPTS OF COMMUNICATIONS THEORY

The communications approach to the study of politics assumes that the behavior and survival of political systems can best be analyzed in terms of communication. It attempts to accomplish this with a small set of explicitly defined concepts. Knowledge of the meaning and interrelationships of these concepts provides a basic understanding of the uses and limitations of communications theory.[7]

The first concept is *information,* and the first assumption of a formal theory of communications is that communication transfers information. Information is usually viewed as "patterened relationship between events."[8] This becomes the basic unit of analysis—information is what flows through the channels of communication, is received, analyzed, and reacted to.

A political system receives information about how its environment is changing relative to the system's goals. In other words, the environment places stress on the system. This is labeled *load.* Communications theory suggests several hypotheses at this point. For instance, other things being equal, the greater the load, let us say demands for political equality, the more difficult it is for the system to adjust and meet the load.

It is at this point that we reach the heart of communications theory, for now the system must cope with the load of its environment. The system receives the information, translates and interprets it, and then decides how to react. The time between the reception of the information (the realization of the load) and the reaction to it is called *lag.* Again, hypotheses are sug-

---

[6] Wiener's basic treatment of cybernetics in *Cybernetics,* 2d ed. (New York: John Wiley & Sons, 1961). A more readable version is *The Human Use of Human Beings* (Boston: Houghton Mifflin, 1950).

[7] For a thorough discussion of these concepts, see Deutsch, *Nerves of Government,* part 3.

[8] Ibid., p. 82.

gested: The greater the lag, the less efficient a system is—the less able it is to cope with its environment. The fact that a political system takes years to process information about basic demands from its environment might be indicative of its inability to maintain itself. On the other hand, some systems might overreact, make a decision too rapidly and before sufficient information is received. Thus, insufficient lag can be just as dangerous as too much lag. Lag has a number of determinants, including the clearness of the meaning of the load and the ability of the system to process load information quickly and accurately.

This suggests another important concept of communications theory, *distortion*. Norbert Wiener notes that "in control and communications we are always fighting nature's tendency to degrade the organized and to destroy the meaningful." More specifically, the concept of distortion refers to the changes that occur in information between the time it is received and the time it is reacted to. If a system allows or produces much distortion, it is in trouble, for it is not reacting to the actual situation, but to a distorted impression of it. One measure of a capable system is the amount of distortion produced in the reception and transmission of information.

The reaction of a system to load is summarized by the concept *gain*. Gain can be defined as the amount of change a system makes as a result of load. If the information is soundly processed, then the gain will be enough to meet the stress or demands of the environment. If the change is insufficient, then the gain has been too small; if the change is more than needed, the gain has been too large. Both under- and overreactions are possible.

At this point, the political system will begin to receive information about how successful its reaction has been; in other words, whether the gain was sufficient. This kind of information is called *feedback*. If the system is at all self-monitoring or self-adjusting, it will make adjustments in its behavior when it next reacts to the stress. This is what a thermostat does when it adjusts a furnace to maintain a particular temperature, what an antiaircraft gun does when it corrects its aim to the speed and the flight pattern of its target, and what a President does after he observes the consequences of a particular executive order.

In addition to correcting its reaction to the immediate load, the system will file away information about the success or failure of its reaction; in other words, it will *learn*. The information will be stored and used when a similar situation arises. For example, consider what goes on in the mind of a football quarterback who throws a long pass to a new end, only to find that the pass is underthrown because the end is much faster than expected. The quarterback notes that next time he will lead the end more—throw the ball farther ahead of him. So we can say that in any situation in which a political system is responding to its environment, there will be two kinds of relevant information: first, the new information (which might be considered as initial conditions), and second, a storehouse of learned information (which might take the form of generalizations) indicating what the probable outcomes will be if a number of alternative reactions are made. Thus communications theory includes a notion of learning. As a matter of fact, it is this notion that allows us to talk about a political system keeping up with the changes in its environment.

In a simplified environment, a system might be able to react to stress as it occurs, making satisfactory adjustments as it goes, so to speak. Thus, the thermostat on a furnace is able to keep the temperature at the desired level through this simple receive-react pattern of behavior. But a social organization, such as a political system, faces more complex kinds of stress. If it reacts only to the present load, the environment will probably always be at least one step ahead. It will become increasingly difficult for the system to catch up. This suggests another concept, called *lead* by the communications theorist. It refers to the ability of an organization to predict future states of the environment so as to, in effect, make or anticipate the necessary adjustments in advance. Obviously, a system that can generate this kind of prediction, let us say about potential urban disturbances, is in the long run going to be more effective in realizing goals, including survival, than one that "plays it by ear." Returning to our football example, the most successful passer is one who anticipates his receiver's moves and so throws the ball where the receiver will be, not where he is. This calls for knowledge of the pattern being run and the characteristics of the receiver. Similarly, the decision makers of a political system must attempt to make decisions that take into consideration predicted changes in the system and the environment.

For leading communication theorists like Karl Deutsch, the most important feature of a political system is its capacity to keep up with a changing environment through innovation. One can already see from our discussion of "learning" and "lead" that the communications theorist does not visualize a static environment. Thus, a static system has no chance of surviving. Consequently, some of the most suggestive hypotheses generated by the model deal with change and innovation. For instance, Deutsch argues that too many models of politics have emphasized the concept of "power," which he equates with not having to learn or change. Communications theory, on the other hand, emphasizes the other side of the coin. No system can maintain itself through the use of power alone. More important is its ability to learn and even change its basic behavior patterns and institutions.

THE USES OF COMMUNICATIONS THEORY

Communications theory perceives the political system as an organization (more obviously, a set of organizations) depending upon information about its environment for the making of decisions, and then adjusting its decisions according to the feedback information it receives about the consequences of its decisions. It is not difficult to place this approach within the more general context of systems theory, for, clearly, communication is one aspect of the political system and the political process. As a matter of fact, communications theorists are often less imperialistic than the advocates of other approaches, for they readily admit that their model emphasizes only one aspect of the political system. Other concepts—power, for instance—are still recognized as being important in their own right.

But an emphasis on communications is still promising because of the pervasiveness of control and steering in all social organizations, and the possibility of describing such behavior in terms of communication. Thus, it comes down to the ability to systematically and meaningfully measure communications. While an analysis of this topic would take us too far afield, let us simply note that political scientists like Deutsch are grappling with the problem of developing units of measure that can catch the significance of information flow in political systems and allow the development of useful hypotheses relating communications variables to variables referring to other aspects of the political system.[9]

---

[9] For an early attempt at empirical application of the approach, see Karl W. Deutsch, *Nationalism and Social Communication* (New York: John Wiley & Sons, 1953). For more recent applications, plus timely analyses of the relationship between communication and political integration and cohesion, see "Communication Theory and Political Integration" and "Transaction Flows as Indicators of Political Cohesion," both in Philip E. Jacob and James V. Toscano, eds., *The Integration of Political Communities* (Philadelphia: J. B. Lippincott, 1964), pp. 46–74 and pp. 75–97. The most thorough and readable summary of the empirical implications of communications theory is Richard R. Fagen, *Politics and Communications* (Boston: Little, Brown, 1966).

glossary

agents of socialization Those people and institutions that teach the individual social and political values. Included are the family, schools, peer groups, secondary groups, and the mass media.

aggregate personality A group personality concept, such as national character.

analytic statement A statement that deals with the analysis of definitions or logical relationships.

approach The set of assumptions that structures the research of any political scientist.

behavioralism A contemporary school, perhaps the dominant one in political science, which argues that political analysis should begin with the behavior of political actors.

behaviorism The psychological school, concentrating on overt behavior, which influenced behavioralism in political science.

causal relationship A relationship between two concepts which asserts that one factor, the cause, is responsible for another, the effect.

classificatory concept A concept that is used to sort a number of items into two (dichotomous) or more (multiple) categories.

cluster sample A survey sample that selects from certain predetermined areas or levels (regions, states, cities, counties, etc.).

cognitive dissonance theory A theory of attitude formation and change which assumes that individuals adjust their value systems to make them consistent.

cognitivist One who believes that normative statements can be tested and found to be true or false.

communications theory An approach to social and political analysis which emphasizes the communications process, and asserts that the most crucial aspect of any political system is how information is received and processed.

comparative concept A concept that describes the members of a population by ranking them; also called an ordinal concept.

concept A universal descriptive word. A concept is a characteristic that refers to a class, not an individual.

contextual definition A concept that can be defined only in specific situations or contexts. Similar to cluster concepts.

cost-benefit analysis An approach to political decision making that emphasizes the rational calculation of the benefits and costs of each proposed policy.

cross-sectional relationship A noncausal relationship that asserts only that two concepts occur together, not that they are causally related.

deductive explanation An explanation in which universal generalizations are used. The relationship between the generalizations and the phenomenon being explained is deductive.

dependent variable The variable or concept in a generalization that is being explained.

descriptive word A word in any scientific language that refers to or names something observable. A particular descriptive word refers to something specific; a universal, to a class of things. The latter is also called a concept.

determinism The assumption, basic to any science, that all events are caused.

discovery The process of generating scientific concepts and hypotheses.

dispositional approach An approach to politics that emphasizes dispositions, such as attitudes, personality traits, and opinions, in explaining political behavior.

empirical import A requirement of scientific concepts which asserts that a concept must be defined, directly or indirectly, in terms of something observable.

empirical statement A statement about and based upon evidence referring to the world of experience and observation.

equilibrium analysis An approach to society and politics which assumes that social and political systems operate according to a balancing principle—they constantly attempt to keep their various parts in a state of balance.

exchange theory A theory that concentrates on how individuals and groups exchange goods and services in pursuit of their self-interest.

explanandum That which is explained by a scientific explanation.

explanans That part of a scientific explanation which explains.

explanation Showing why an event, situation, or relationship exists or happens.

explanation sketch An argument which has the form of an explanation but is not complete.

feedback In systems theory, the process that sends information about the outputs of the political system back to the society.

functional analysis An approach which assumes that political and social phenomena can best be understood in terms of the functions they perform for the society.

game theory An approach to social and political analysis which assumes that behavior is rational and uses the common game as a model of politics.

genetic explanation An explanation which explains a phenomenon by showing how it developed through several stages.

generalization A statement that states a relationship between two or more concepts.

heuristic Anything which suggests new concepts and hypotheses is said to be of heuristic value.

holism The philosophical position that there are *emergent* group properties; that is, properties that groups have which are not reducible to their individual members.

hypothesis A generalization that has not yet been tested—an educated guess about the relationship between two or more concepts.

ideal type A concept that is made intentionally unrealistic for heuristic purposes.

ideology The broadest type of disposition—a set of related attitudes.

independent variable The variable or concept in a generalization which, it is assumed, is influencing the dependent variable, the one that is being explained.

individualism The position that all group properties can be reduced to individual properties.

induction The basic logical process of going from a set of individual observations to a generalization. It is the basic method for testing hypotheses.

initial conditions Specific facts that are used, along with generalizations, to explain political phenomena.

input In systems theory, the demands and supports that are sent from the society to the political system.

intersubjective A requirement of science which recognizes that while all scientists are to some extent subjective (they have values), science can move beyond subjectivity if research is openly discussed; this allows scientific knowledge to develop from a continual process of scientific criticism and give and take.

interval scale A type of quantification concept that establishes equal intervals between categories, but no zero point.

intuitive definition The initial definition that one has of a concept. In order to make it useful in scientific analysis, the intuitive definition must be translated into an operational definition.

intuitionism A cognitive position which claims that people have an inner moral sense which tells them what is right and wrong.

instrumental statement A statement which indicates that something is good because it helps achieve an ultimate good.

"is" statement An empirical statement.

is-ought distinction A distinction, accepted by many philosophers and political scientists, which claims that empirical and normative statements are logically distinct because only the former are testable.

ismorphism A similarity between one thing and another (its model). There must be a one-to-one correspondence between certain characteristics of each.

law A generalization that has been tested and confirmed—there is evidence to support it.

learning theory A theory of human action which assumes that behavior is the result of conditioning. There are two varieties: association theory and reinforcement theory.

logical word   A word in any scientific language that is used to structure and relate descriptive words.

macro approach   An approach to politics that concentrates on the largest unit of analysis, the system.

measure   A factor that is used to operationalize a variable. The score on a questionnaire might be the measure of the variable, "liberalism."

micro approach   An approach to politics that concentrates on the smallest unit of analysis, the individual.

micro-functionalism   Any approach to social or political behavior which asserts that the group or social setting performs psychological functions for the individual.

model   Something that is a simplified representation of something else. Thus a model airplane represents the real thing, and the theory of games is a model of politics.

naturalistic   Any cognitive moral philosophy that defines the "good" in terms of an observable property, such as happiness.

necessary condition   A causal factor which, it is thought, always occurs before another factor. The second concept will not occur without the former.

nominal definition   Assigning a meaning to a concept; rejects the notion of real definitions.

nomological   Any argument that contains generalizations.

noncognitivist   One who believes that normative statements are neither true nor false.

nonzero game   A game situation in which the gains and losses do not cancel each other.

normative statement   A statement that asserts a value position.

objective   Decision making based on facts and logic, not values; often equated with science.

operational definition   The basic requirement of scientific concept formation, which asserts that all concepts must be defined in terms of observable properties.

ought statement   A normative statement; a value judgment.

output   In systems theory, the decisions of the political system.

paradigm   The dominant approach in any science that structures research in the science.

personality theory   The approach to politics which concentrates on the political actor's personality—that set of deep-seated dispositions which are supposedly the main cause of human behavior.

post-behavioralism   A school of political science, developed in the mid-1960s, which, while accepting the methodological progress achieved by the behavioralists, argues that they have, in trying to be scientific, too often overlooked the important questions of politics.

prediction   Explaining into the future; showing why something will or is likely to occur.

psychobiography   A personality approach which examines a single political decision maker in great depth, with an emphasis on psychological factors.

quantitative concept   A concept that is defined in such a way that certain mathematical operations can be performed; ultimately to be able to determine how much of a characteristic something has.

random sample   A requirement of any good survey which makes the survey representative. It ensures that every member of the population has an equal chance of being selected.

ratio scale   The most highly developed quantitative concept—it allows for all mathematical operations because it has a zero point.

rational approach   An approach that focuses on the conscious, goal-seeking elements of political decision making.

reactive methods   Methods for testing hypotheses that require the reaction of political actors. The most common example is the attitude survey.

real definition   A definition that states what is the one and only true definition of a concept; rejected by most political scientists of today.

reliability   A requirement of scientific concepts which asserts that the concepts should produce similar results in similar situations, that is, that they be consistent.

role theory   An approach to social and political analysis which assumes that political actors are greatly influenced by the positions they fill.

simulation   A research strategy in which a real-world political situation is replicated or fabricated in a laboratory or classroom. It can be a major source of hypotheses.

small group approach   An approach to social and political behavior which assumes that in decision-making situations, the decision is often the result of the group atmosphere rather than the individual charcteristics of decision makers.

social experiment   An attempt by policymakers to bring about changes in social, political, or economic systems in certain predictable ways, and then to evaluate the success or failure of their policies.

socialization theory   The application of learning theory to social and political situations. It attempts to explain the learning of social and political values.

spurious association   An association between two concepts which appears to be causal, but is really the result of a third factor.

statistical explanation   An explanation in which statistical laws are employed. Such an explanation shows that the phenomenon being explained is highly probable.

statistical generalization   A generalization which claims that only a portion of the items in a certain category has a particular characteristic. "Most politicians are rich."

stratified sample   A survey sample that selects from certain predetermined demographic categories (sex, race, occupation, etc.).

subjective   Decision making that is influenced by one's values; the opposite of objective.

sufficient condition   A causal factor which by itself is enough to bring about another; but it is not a necessary condition.

survey   A type of reactive method that is designed to describe and analyze a population by asking them questions.

systematic import   A requirement of scientific concepts which asserts that they must be potentially related to other concepts to be considered useful.

systems theory   Any approach to political and social analysis which operates on the macro level and assumes that political decisions can be understood only if the entire system is examined.

theoretical concept   A concept that has meaning only within a particular theory.

theory   A set of generalizations that are related. A theory is used to describe and explain an area of political science.

traditional political science   Those orientations in political science which predate the modern behavioral approach. They include the historical, legalistic, and institutional approaches.

universal generalization   A generalization which claims that all of the items in a certain category have a particular characteristic. "All politicians are rich."

validity   A requirement of scientific concepts which asserts that they measure what it is they are supposed to measure.

variable   A characteristic that things have in varying degrees.

verstehen   A technique for generating hypotheses in which the political scientist attempts to gain empathic understanding of a political actor—to put oneself into the actor's shoes, so to speak.

zero-sum   A game situation in which the gains and losses cancel each other. A political situation of total conflict.

index

A

Abel, Elie, 35
Abramson, Paul, 201
Absolute zero, 88
Access, 269 ff.
Adorno, T., 216
Agents of socialization, 209 ff.
Aldrich, John, 201
Allison, Graham, 35, 151
Almond, Gabriel, 281
Analytic political philosophy, 6, 13
Analytic proposition, 6
Antibehavioralist, 43
Applied value judgment, 5
Approach, 185 ff.
Aristotle, 11, 274
Arithmetical representation, 171
Arrow, Kenneth, 180
Association learning theory, 204
Asymmetricaı power relations, 98
Attitude, 39, 79, 146 ff., 196 ff., 213
Authoritarianism, 224
Authoritative allocation of values, 21 ff.
Authority, 19, 99, 100
Autonomous socialization, 211

B

Bachrach, Peter, 99
Barber, James D., 220 ff.
Behavioralism, 38 ff.
Behaviorism, 39
Belief, 198
Bennett, Stephen E., 213
Bentham, Jeremy, 5, 10
Bentley, Arthur, 264 ff.
Bergmann, Gustav, 72, 125
Binkley, Wilfred E., 157
Blalock, Hubert, 128
Bluhm, William T., 20, 235
Boundries of political science, 21
  between the social sciences, 42
Braybrooke, David, 110
Brecht, Arnold, 29, 30, 104, 165

Bridgman, B. W., 137
Brodbeck, May, 40, 146, 173, 174
Brown, Robert, 137, 149, 226
Bruck, H. W., 226
Buchanan, James M., 250
Building blocks of science, 71

C

Campbell, Augus, 154, 157, 200 ff.
Case study, 35
Causal relationship, 124
Causality, 29, 124 ff.
Chance, 113
Christie, Richard, 216
Classification, 83–84
Cluster sample, 120
Cobban, Alfred, 7
Coexistence, laws of, 125
Cognitive dissonance theory, 211 ff.
Columbia University, 36
Combinations of explanations, 158 ff.
Common sense, 29
Commonsense knowledge, 16, 65 ff.
Communication, 289 ff.
Comparison, 85 ff.
Complete explanation, 143
Completeness of explanations, 142 ff.
Complexity of political phenomena, 52 ff.
Concept, 31, 71 ff.
Conceptual scheme, 172, 186
Conditional nature of generalizations,
  105 ff.
Conflict, 19, 238
Connolly, William E., 6, 60
Conspiracy theory, 229
Constant conjunction, 124 ff.
Contextual definition, 78–79
Corwin, Edward S., 36
Cost-benefit analysis, 247 ff.
Covering law model of explanation, 133 ff.
Crick, Bernard, 43
Cross-sectional generalization, 125–26
Cutwright, Phillips, 284
Cybernetics, 290–91

This book has been set Linotron 202 in 10 and 9 point Times Roman leaded 2 points. Part titles are 24 point Times Roman and chapter titles are 14 point Helvetica Black. The size of the type page is 28 by 46 picas.